Managing National Park System Resources

The Conservation Foundation is a nonprofit research and communications organization dedicated to encouraging human conduct to sustain and enrich life on earth. Since its founding in 1948, it has attempted to provide intellectual leadership in the cause of wise management of the earth's resources. The Conservation Foundation is affiliated with World Wildlife Fund.

Managing National Park System Resources

A Handbook on Legal Duties, Opportunities, and Tools

Edited by
  Michael A. Mantell

with Contributions from
  Don Barry
  Frank Buono
  Richard Dawson
  Christopher J. Duerksen
  Jacob Hoogland
  Michael A. Mantell
  Carol McCoy
  Dwight Merriam
  Philip C. Metzger
  C. Luther Propst
  Molly N. Ross
  William E. Shands
  Barbara West

The Conservation Foundation
Washington, D.C.

Managing National Park System Resources;
A Handbook on Legal Duties, Opportunities, and Tools

Typography by Rings-Leighton, Ltd., Washington, D.C.
Printed by Thomson-Shore, Inc., Dexter, Michigan.
Second printing, January 1991.

Book orders should be directed to The Conservation Foundation, P.O. Box 4866, Hampden Post Office, Baltimore, Maryland 21211. Telephone: (301) 338-6951.

Library of Congress Cataloging-in-Publication Data
Managing National Park System resources: a handbook on legal
    duties, opportunities and tools / edited by Michael A. Mantell ;
    with contributions from Don Barry . . . [et al.].
            p.   cm.
        Includes bibliographical references.
        ISBN 0-89164-114-9
        1. National parks and reserves—Law and legislation—United
    States. 2. Environmental law—United States. 3. Conservation
    of natural resources—Law and legislation—United States.
    I. Mantell, Michael A.
    KF5635.M36   1990
346.7304 '69516—dc20
[347.306469516]   89-20993
                                                                      CIP

 Text printed on recycled paper.

Contents

Preface

The National Park System contains resources of unsurpassed significance. The parks celebrate the nation, both the wonders of nature and the achievements of people. At the heart of the national park idea is a vision of distinctive places protected from impairment yet democratically accessible to all who wish to visit them.

Yet preserving the resources within America's "crown jewels" is becoming more and more difficult in times marked by ever increasing population growth, development pressures, and urbanization. The national parks are indeed America's "crown jewels," and they require and deserve steadfast stewardship to ensure their continued grandeur and special identity in this country as well as throughout the world. *Managing National Park System Resources: A Handbook on Legal Duties, Opportunities, and Tools* is intended to assist in efforts to maintain the integrity of the parks' natural and cultural resources.

This handbook grows out of materials presented at three different week-long courses to National Park Service Natural Resource Management Trainees. Additional funds were generously provided by the Richard King Mellon Foundation and the project was overseen by the park service's Cooperative Park Studies Unit and the Department of Parks, Recreation, and Tourism Management at Clemson University. This book is intended to serve as a reference source for those concerned—both the citizen and park professional alike—with the management of National Park System resources.

The book is divided into four parts. The first part examines the legal context for the park system, including how laws and courts operate in general and how the specific law governing parks and the National Park Service has been refined and interpreted in recent years. Part II examines key federal laws as they relate to park resources. Part III looks at the nonfederal setting in which parks operate and what opportunities states, localities, and the private sector provide for assist-ing in the management of park resources. The final section focuses on the challenges ahead, including what is involved in preparing for court battles over park resource decisions—largely from the perspective of a park natural resource specialist called to testify as an expert witness—and on some select issues that likely will play a major role in influencing the future condition of park resources. The material throughout is applicable to both natural and cultural resources, although natural systems are emphasized.

The handbook begins with the premise that the legal system imposes certain requirements that must be satisfied in managing park resources. Its principal thrust, however, is that laws also provide opportunities to further the purposes of the parks. Laws and legal processes are not simply bureaucratic requirements to dread; they can be useful tools that enable the astute park professional and advocate to assert park resource needs and values more effectively.

This handbook is filled with material that demonstrates the power to protect park resources aggressively that many laws (and interpre-tations of laws) have given to the National Park Service. These laws provide flexibility in selecting the means to manage resources and adapt to the needs of changing conditions. As the material in this book shows, the park service is given a great deal of deference by the courts when it bases its resource management actions on well-articulated policies and plans, scientifically acceptable studies, and consultation with interested members of the public.

Because of the broad scope of the powers given to the park service, some of the most significant obstacles to managing park resources effectively are neither legal doctrines nor court rulings. Major con-straints are more often imposed by politics and economics. In fact, the material in this book shows that laws and legal doctrines provide the park service with many of the necessary tools to help leave the National Park System "unimpaired for the enjoyment of future gener-ations," as mandated in the law governing the parks.

Many people have contributed a great deal of time and effort to this project. Its genesis resulted from the dedication and fine work of Carol Aten, current chief of the Office of Policy, and Dr. Richard Briceland, former associate director for natural resources, within the National Park Service. Carol, in particular, has continued to provide valuable oversight and guidance throughout the many iterations of this material. Dr. Brian Mihalik has served as an able colleague and project director at Clemson University, as has Dr. Dominic Dottavio from within the park service both at Clemson and at the Southeast Regional Office. Dr. Bill Walker, who oversees the natural resources management trainee program, and the trainees themselves also provided helpful comments throughout the development of these materials.

Aside from them, the greatest credit goes to the authors of the various chapters. They are among the country's leading legal and practical thinkers about National Park System issues from both inside and outside the park service. Their material, of course, reflects their individual judgments and not necessarily those of the institutions with which they are affiliated. The handbook has benefited as well from the writings and insights of Professor Joseph P. Sax and Robert B. Keiter and from the helpful review of various materials and statistics by several individuals including Lawrence Aten, Warren Brown, Tracy Fortmann, Jim Loach, Barry Mackintosh, and Karen Simpson.

At The Conservation Foundation, Jack Noble provided his usual high degree of wisdom and conceptual guidance. Brad Rymph efficiently supervised editing and production of the volume, while Rosemary O'Neill ably oversaw typing, cite checking, and a variety of last-minute research-related tasks. Among those who assisted them were Jean B. Bernard, Bonita Franklin, and Sharon Jonas.

With the growth in size and popularity of the National Park System comes the inevitable clash between competing interests in our society and park resources. Efforts to protect park resources raise cries from users who seek uncontrolled access in a variety of forms. Increasing development outside park boundaries conflicts with the need to preserve park resources.

Now, more than ever, there is a need to ensure that the country's laws concerning park system resources are understood, implemented, and enforced and that policies and legal institutions keep pace with the changing needs of these areas and the great expectations Americans—and people from around the world—have for them. This handbook will, we hope, play a valuable supporting role in accomplishing that goal.

Michael A. Mantell
November 1989

Part I

The Legal Framework

Two broad areas provide an essential context for understanding the legal duties, tools, and opportunities pertaining to the management of National Park System resources. The first entails a basic understanding of how laws are made, implemented, challenged, and interpreted. The legal world has its own distinct vocabulary and way of operating; having a casual familarity with this special world can help improve the way actions are taken to protect and manage park system resources. Lawsuits are typically the end product of a long process involving several decisions and attempts at negotiating some sort of settlement. What role do lawsuits play? Who can bring them against the National Park Service in the context of managing park system resources? For what reasons? How do courts decide cases?

A second area that provides the basic legal framework for managing park resources is the guiding law of the National Park Service and System—the so-called Organic Act. Every legal action and all legal duties, opportunities, and tools concerning the protection and management of park resources originate with and come back to the 1916 Organic Act. Understanding its meaning and evolution over time is key to operating effectively within the legal structure surrounding the National Park System.

Chapter 1

Lawsuits and Courts

by Michael A. Mantell

As the United States enters the 1990s, its national parks are increasingly being confronted with legal issues that affect the parks' resources. It is crucial that these issues be better understood by the American people—and especially by park professionals. This means that some of the special aura that surrounds the legal system must be demystified and some basic principles about how the legal process operates must be understood.

Gaining a better sense of the basic legal framework under which parks operate depends on several factors. One is understanding the terminology. Common legal terms—such as *statute, executive order, common law,* and *regulation*—are defined in the box, "Glossary of Some Basic Legal Sources and Authorities."

A second part is understanding the role of lawsuits (or litigation) and how laws are interpreted. As has often been stated, "Law is an art, not a science." That is to say, there are few absolute truths in the legal world: laws and interpretations of them are continually refined by Congress, attorneys, and judges as new situations arise and societal values change. More often than not, more than one interpretation of a law's meaning in a particular context is possible.

The interpretation of a law's meaning is an incremental process. As specific cases arise, a law is interpreted as it relates to particular sets of facts or issues. Thus, its meaning is gradually refined over time. Lawyers and judges will cite earlier interpretations of a law to support a particular interpretation in the case before them. The interpretation given to a law, therefore, may change to reflect the different circumstances in individual cases and the societal values that exist at the time.

Lawsuits should be avoided. They are expensive and enormously time-consuming. They typically involve high stakes. But if lawsuits do arise, and they almost surely will at least be threatened sometime during the career of an active National Park Service manager, they are not to be avoided at all costs, especially at the expense of protecting park resources. Lawsuits are not the only way disputes over park resources are resolved, of course. In fact, they are probably the least used avenue for conflict resolution. Negotiation among the parties is more common and sometimes is the most effective approach. If desired, a neutral, third party—called a facilitator or mediator—can be used as part of negotiations!

Glossary of Some Basic Legal Sources and Authorities*

Constitutional: The Constitution is "the organic fundamental law of the nation . . . the absolute rule of action and decision for all departments and officers of the government." It is the supreme law of the land and thus takes precedence over all others. An act that is constitutionally authorized is one that is expressly or implicitly authorized in the written constitution. An example in the national parks context is the "Property Clause," which appears in Article 1, Section 8 of the U.S. Constitution: "The Congress shall have power . . . to make rules for the government and regulation of the land . . . ."

Statute: A statute is an "act of the legislature declaring, commanding or prohibiting something; a particular law enacted and established by the will of the legislative department of government." The word statute "is used to designate legislatively created laws [as distinguished] from common

*Many of the definitions in this glossary quote from Henry Campbell Black, *Black's Law Dictionary* (St. Paul, Minn.: West Publishing Co. 1968.).

law, i.e., court-decided or unwritten laws." A key park service statute is the 1916 Organic Act: "The National Park Service shall promote and regulate the use of national parks . . . by such means and measures as conform to the fundamental purpose of the said parks . . . which purpose is to conserve the scenery and the natural and historic objects and the wild life therein and to provide for the enjoyment of the same in such manner and by such means as will leave them unimpaired for the enjoyment of future generations."

Common Law: The common law comprises the body of those principals and rules of action that derive their authority from usage, custom, or from prior court decisions as opposed to legislative enactment. An example in the parks context is the concept of nuisance, which is a judicially created doctrine.

The term 'nuisance' is incapable of an exhaustive definition which will fit all cases—it is very comprehensive—it includes everything that endangers life or health,

A third step in understanding the legal process is having some familiarity with how courts function in making decisions. Answers to three issues are of primary importance in understanding courts and the judicial system and how the National Park Service operates in it:

- What can the park service be sued for in a resources management context?
- Who can sue the park service for action it takes or does not take with regard to resources?
- How do courts decide cases?

SUITS AGAINST THE SERVICE

In general, the National Park Service can be sued for actions or inactions that someone considers to be inconsistent with the mandates of the laws governing the park system. When the park service is sued

---

gives offense to the senses, violates the laws of decency, or obstructs the reasonable and comfortable use of property.[1]

Executive Order: "An order or regulation issued by the President or some administrative authority under his direction for the purpose of interpreting, implementing, or giving administrative effect to a provision of the Constitution or of some law or treaty. To have the effect of law, such orders must be published in the Federal Register." A key executive order (E.O.) concerning the parks involves off-road-vehicles (ORVs): "E.O. 11644 directs that specific ORV zones be established on applicable federal lands."[2]

Regulation: "Regulations are issued by various governmental departments to carry out the intent of the law. Agencies issue regulations to guide the activity of those regulated by the agency and of their own employees to ensure uniform application of the law." The National Park Service has established many regulations to guide the management of park resources. One example

is the following concerning setting public use limits:

Consistent with applicable legislation and Federal administrative policies, and based upon a determination that such action is necessary for the maintenance of public health and safety, protection of environmental or scenic values, protection of natural or cultural resources, aid to scientific research, implementation of management responsibilities, equitable allocation of management responsibilities, equitable allocation and use of facilities, or the avoidance of conflict among visitor use activities, the superintendent may:

(1) Establish, for all or a portion of a park area, a reasonable schedule of visiting hours, impose public use limits, or close all or a portion of a park area to all public use or to a specific use or activity. . . .[3]

in the natural resources area, the complaint can be that park service action goes further than the law permits in protecting resources at the expense of a plaintiff's particular interest—be it hunting, commercial fishing, off-road vehicle use, or property rights. In other cases, the complaint can be that park service action does not go far enough in fulfilling the requirements of a particular law. For example, lawsuits have asserted that the service failed to prepare an environmental impact statement or that the service did not take adequate action to protect redwoods in Redwood National Park. The service also has been sued by parties who contend that maintaining the status quo—simply doing nothing—is a failure to perform duties imposed by law.

STANDING

Who can sue the National Park Service over resource decisions or, as lawyers say, who has "standing" to challenge a park service action? In most cases, standing typically has not been a barrier in getting into the judicial process to take issue with the service over park resources. The U.S. Constitution generally has been interpreted to require that the individual bringing the suit show:

- some actual or threatened injury as a result of the agency's allegedly illegal conduct;
- that the injury is fairly traceable to the challenged action; and
- that a favorable decision by the court will provide the redress sought.[2]

In other words, a concrete controversy must exist; it must be a controversy related to the actions of the park service and the interests of the person bringing the suit; and the controversy must be one that courts can do something about. (There are a few other rules involved in standing, but generally they do not prevent someone from challenging actions involving the National Park Service and park natural resources.)

An organization representing its members generally can sue when:

(a) its members would otherwise have standing to sue in their own right; (b) the interests it seeks to protect are relevant to the organization's purpose; and (c) neither the claim asserted nor the relief requested requires the participation of individual members in the lawsuit.[3]

TOOLS FOR DECIDING CASES

Courts have a clear hierarchy of things they look at when it is claimed that the park service has violated a statute—for example, violating its statutory charge to preserve the parks and provide for visitor enjoyment. Courts consult various rules of statutory construction. They first look to the "plain language" of the statute. In doing so, they generally presume that where some items are specified in the law, those items not specified were deliberately excluded. For example, a few park enabling statutes expressly permit hunting and trapping of wildlife. Most enabling laws, however, make no mention of these activities, speaking only about the natural, cultural, and scenic values of an area. In a recent case, a court used this presumption in ruling that the service could ban hunting and trapping in those parks where it was not specifically authorized in the enabling legislation.[4]

When a statute is unclear, courts will examine the intent of the legislators who enacted it—the legislative history. To learn the legislative intent, they will look to congressional committee reports that reflect how issues contained in the bill were resolved or addressed and to remarks made by senators and representatives when voting on it.

Next, courts look to see how the law has been interpreted by the agency administering it. They will focus on present and past interpretations and the degree of technical expertise required to implement and interpret it. The higher the degree of agency technical expertise required, the more likely courts are to defer to the agency's interpretation of the law.

In addition to considering the language of the statute, its legislative history, and agency interpretations, a court examines decisions it and other courts have made previously regarding the same law. Courts rely heavily on prior, analogous decisions—called precedents—in an attempt to build a consistent, somewhat predictable interpretation of the law. Hence, the incremental, case-by-case nature of the legal process. Within the federal court system, decisions by the U.S. Supreme Court carry the most weight, followed by decisions of the U.S. courts of appeal (or circuit courts), and then by rulings of U.S. district courts.

Finally, courts look at commentaries and analyses of laws and cases contained in legal books and law review articles for insights and support.

STANDARD OF REVIEW

A key issue when the park service is challenged involves the standards courts use to determine whether it has complied with the law. How closely does a court scrutinize agency action? What standards do courts hold the service to?

When reviewing a specific park service action that is being challenged—for example, a ban on commercial fishing in a park or a systemwide prohibition on hunting—court review is "highly deferential." As the court in *Organized Fishermen* v. *Watt* stated:

> The courts should neither substitute their judgment for that of the agency nor rewrite an agency's regulations by reading requirements into statutes which are not clearly there. Furthermore, there is a presumption of administrative regularity.[5]

The presumption that an agency acted in accordance with the law is quite strong. It is made even stronger when the action is consistent with objectives and strategies articulated in policy and planning documents, when research has been conducted, and when internal records (or the administrative record) demonstrate a thorough consideration of the issue.

Courts use different terms to describe the standards they are using to determine whether the agency has acted properly. Generally, however, they lead to the same level of review or scrutiny. One, used by the court in *NRA* v. *Potter*, is "whether the [park service action] was based on a consideration of the relevant factors and whether there has been a clear error of judgment." Another is whether the action is "arbitrary or capricious." The court in *Organized Fishermen* v. *Watt* applied this standard and explained it by quoting from a U.S. Supreme Court decision:

> The agency must examine the relevant data and articulate a satisfactory explanation for its action including a "rational connection between the facts found and the choice made." . . . In reviewing that explanation, we must "consider whether the decision was based on a consideration of the relevant factors and whether there has been a clear error of judgment." . . . Normally, an agency rule would be arbitrary and capricious *if the agency has relied on factors which Congress has not intended it to consider, entirely failed to consider an important aspect of the problem, offered an explanation for its decision that runs counter to the evidence before the agency, or is so implausible that it could not be ascribed to a difference in view or the product of agency expertise.*[6] [emphasis in original.]

As will be seen in the discussion of several recent cases involving challenges to park service action, courts do show a great deal of deference to well-thought-through, carefully articulated park service actions, especially when based on data and established policies and plans. Laws affecting the park service, however, impose some strong duties to protect park resources. Thus, despite the deference given, the park service has been forced at times, through challenges in court, to comply more thoroughly with those duties.

REFERENCES

1. See Gail Bingham, *Resolving Environmental Disputes: A Decade of Experience* (Washington, D.C.: The Conservation Foundation, 1986).

2. *National Rifle Association* v. *Potter*, 628 F. Supp. 903 (D.D.C. 1986).

3. Ibid.

4. Ibid.

5. 590 F. Supp. 805 (S.D. Fla. 1984); *affirmed* 775 F.2d 1544 (11th Cir. 1985).

6. 590 F. Supp. 805, 811.

Glossary of Some Basic Legal Sources and Authorities

1. *United States* v. *County Board of Arlington County*, 487 F. Supp. 137, 143 (E.D. Va. 1979).

2. *Conservation Law Foundation* v. *Clark*, 590 F. Supp. 1467 (D. Mass. 1984).

3. 36 C.F.R. 1.5 (1984).

Chapter 2

The Organic Act and the Stewardship of Resources within Park Boundaries

by Michael A. Mantell and Philip C. Metzger

Although the National Park Service has been recognized for decades as preserver of some of the nation's most precious places, the methods it uses to implement its basic mission are continually being refined in response to changing needs and increasing scientific awareness. Like the park system itself, which expands and evolves to reflect societal changes and values, the service and its mission continue to evolve as well.

Today, the system and the service grapple both with new issues and with old ones that appear in a new context of changed societal values and fiscal constraints. For many years, the physical isolation of the parks was their greatest defense against internal overuse as well as external pressures on park resources. Both internal resource problems and external pressures, however, have been mounting on the parks in recent years. The expansion of the park system in the 1960s and 1970s to incorporate urban areas and places of mixed land ownership has further heightened the pressures placed on park resources and the opportunities for addressing them.

At such a time, when the responsibilities and burdens of maintaining America's crown jewels are more diverse than ever before, it is crucial to understand the origins and characteristics of the park service's legal obligations and authorities and how these have been interpreted in various actions to manage park natural resources. Moreover, the changing conditions of park management have produced an evolution in both the interpretation and the very wording of these authorities and obligations, requiring an examination of their meanings today in light of the charge to leave the parks "unimpaired for the enjoyment of future generations."

This chapter discusses the basic laws under which the National Park Service operates and how they have been interpreted over the years in terms of managing park resources within authorized boundaries. How has the park service interpreted its legislative authority? What powers does this authority give and what constraints, if any, does it impose? What have court decisions held?

When examined together, these laws and court rulings reveal that, when the park service's decisions are consistent with authorizing statutes and based on well-articulated resource needs, plans, and studies, the service has significant authority to take actions to protect resources within the authorized boundaries of park units, regardless of who actually owns the property affected.

THE ORGANIC ACT: STARTING POINT AND DRIVING FORCE

The National Park Service Organic Act remains after some 70 years the core of park service authority and the definitive statement of the purposes of the parks and of the National Park Service's mission. That mission is to:

> promote and regulate the use of the federal areas known as national parks, monuments, and reservations hereinafter specified, . . . by such means and measures as conform to the[ir] fundamental purpose . . . to conserve the scenery and the natural and historic objects and the wildlife therein and to provide for the enjoyment of the same in such a manner and by such means as will leave them unimpaired for the enjoyment of future generations!

The Organic Act warrants frequent rereading. Several issues are raised by its eloquent charge:

- It says that actions by the park service must conform to the "fundamental purpose," not purposes, of the parks. What is the "fundamental purpose"?
- What does "conserve" mean in the context of a 1916 statute? Is it the same as "preserve" today?
- Does "unimpairment" mean absolutely no alteration or is some unspecified, minimal level of degradation contemplated?
- Is there a built-in conflict or ambiguity between conserving these areas "unimpaired" and providing for their "enjoyment?"

These are some of the issues with which lawyers, judges, and park service managers have grappled for decades. The statute has been interpreted to support various kinds of decisions, such as enabling a particular facility to be built in a park or banning certain activities in an area because of their effects on fragile resources. There are, at times, genuine differences of opinion over how much impairment is permitted by the statutory mandate.

Yet there is consensus on the overall resource protection focus of the Organic Act. The language regarding "conservation" and "unimpairment" is very strong. The conservation orientation has repeatedly been the basis for park service management policies and actions as well as court rulings that favor and support strong resource protection initiatives. Moreover, as a practical effect, if the obligation to "leave" park resources "unimpaired" is neglected, both conservation and enjoyment will ultimately become difficult, if not impossible, to achieve.

While the individual and site-specific decisions by park managers and policy makers give meaning to the statutory language, the relatively simple and eloquent Organic Act statement of purpose itself has been amplified and elaborated on over the years by the agency, the courts, and the Congress.

Park System Diversity and the Organic Act

As the National Park System grew, it became more diverse. The original "parks" and "monuments" were followed by military parks, rivers, recreation areas, preserves, historic or cultural parks, seashores, and so on in confusing variety—more than 20 different designations by one count. The authorizing laws for many of these park system units included special provisions regarding acquisition powers, permitted uses such as trapping, management procedures, and boundary delineation. Added to the confusion of terminology was uncertainty over management authority and mission, when in 1964 the park service divided its units into natural, historical, and recreational categories and specified management practices for each category according to distinct policies.

By 1970, Congress responded by amending the Organic Act to state:

> that the national park system, which began with establishment of Yellowstone National Park in 1872, has since grown to include superlative natural, historic, and recreation areas in every major region of the United States . . . ; that *these*

areas, though distinct in character, are united through their inter-related purposes and resources into one national park system *as cumulative expressions of a single national heritage; . . . and that it is the purpose of this Act to include all such areas in the System* and to clarify the authorities applicable to the system. [emphasis added.][2]

Each park system unit, the 1970 Act continued, was to be administered not only under the terms of its own authorizing law but also under a unified standard—all other systemwide laws, "including but not limited to the" Organic Act.

These legislative additions to the Organic Act were an affirmation that, unless Congress specified otherwise for a particular unit, all units were to be governed under the same mission and were subject to the same management obligations as set forth in the Organic Act. Moreover, they reinforced the idea that units of the National Park System were all to be viewed as special places, "expressions of a single national heritage."[3]

The Organic Act Amended, Again

Litigation concerning Redwood National Park in the mid-1970s raised congressional interest in clarifying the importance of park resources systemwide. When Redwood was enlarged in 1978 to include some of the watershed lands omitted 10 years earlier and to address the resource problems that were the basis of a series of suits brought by the Sierra Club (see discussion below), a provision amending the basic Organic Act was also included:

The authorization of activities shall be construed and the protection, management, and administration of these areas shall be conducted in light of the high public value and integrity of the National Park System and shall not be exercised in derogation of the values and purposes for which these various areas have been established, except as may have been or shall be directly and specifically provided for by Congress.[4]

The language in this amendment is not particularly easy to follow. It talks about activities construed and conducted "in light of the high public value" of the park system. It uses the phrase "protection" for the first time in the legislative context of the parks and the Organic Act. A key phrase is that activities "shall not be exercised in derogation of the values and purposes for which these areas have been established." Finally, it is applicable unless Congress has "directly and specifically provided" otherwise.

Such language raises some important questions:

- What is this amendment intended to do? What was in the law-makers' minds when they enacted it? What was going on in the parks and outside them that gave rise to its passage?
- What is its effect on the Organic Act language?
- What are the "values and purposes" of the units of the system?
- Is the clause that exempts it from being applied where Congress has specifically provided otherwise to be read narrowly—only in those situations where Congress explicitly authorizes an activity that threatens park resources—or more broadly to include, for example, the general authorization of multiple-use management on neighboring federal lands that can affect park resources?

When the 1978 amendment was put into law, it was part of the legislative package to expand Redwood National Park. Congress was concerned over the threats to resources in Redwood from outside its boundaries as well as the apparent lack of authority Redwood and other parks had to deal with such threats. Congress wanted to strengthen the ability of the U.S. secretary of the interior to protect park resources. It has been read in this context, with the intent of clarifying the Organic Act and as elaborating on both that act and the "single system" amendment of 1970.

Part of the legislative record that existed when it was enacted states:

The Secretary has an absolute duty, which is not to be compromised, to fulfill the mandate of the 1916 Act to take whatever actions and seek whatever relief as will safeguard the units of the National Park System.[5]

Another part of the legislative history of this amendment also states that:

The protection of the units of the system is to be carried out in accordance with the maintenance of the integrity of the system, and management of these areas shall not compromise these resource values except as Congress may have specifically provided.[6]

The clause limiting the exceptions to those "directly and specifically provided for by Congress" has been the subject of much debate as to whether it is to be interpreted broadly to cover all kinds of activities generally authorized by Congress or limited to only those cases where Congress has expressly permitted the threatening activity. Several legal scholars and commentators contend that it is to be construed narrowly to apply only to those situations where Congress has explicitly authorized a threatening activity. Court decisions have not addressed this issue directly.

ENABLING LEGISLATION

One of the key ways Congress explicitly authorizes the type of activity that can derogate park values and purposes as contemplated by the 1978 Organic Act Amendment is through the legislation creating individual parks—so-called enabling legislation. Specific enabling legislation for a park unit, for example, may provide for the continuation of preexisting uses of an area (such as hunting, grazing, or mining) following park establishment. In these cases, Congress has "directly and specifically" provided for an activity, even if it is "exercised in derogation of the value and purposes for which" an area has been established, to use the language of the 1978 statute.

Every park unit is created by congressional legislation or presidential proclamation through an executive order. Such enabling legislation (including executive orders) generally sets forth the boundary of the unit, the reasons for creating it—be they significant natural, historical, and/or recreational resources—and any other specific conditions that apply to the area. Provisions in enabling legislation are thus very relevant to managing that unit. Moreover, those that permit hunting or other preexisting uses of the area to continue set forth a key rationale for the area's designation or specifically reference some other factor about a unit that can act to restrict, expand, or refine in some way the interpretation of the Organic Act as it is applied to that particular unit. Therefore, it is important to be familiar with individual park enabling legislation and to read it in light of and as part of the Organic Act charge to manage park resources.

OVERLAY STATUTES

Several acts of Congress add additional policies to and requirements for managing park natural resources beyond those embodied in the Organic Act, specific enabling legislation for each unit, and more general federal environmental laws. These laws—wilderness, wild and scenic rivers, and scenic and historic trails—designate certain areas within parks for specific additional values and management purposes. While their legal authority to require the park service to take concrete action has not been tested and remains questionable, these laws do give the service added means and rationales for increasing protection of particular natural resources.

Wilderness Areas

Passage of the Wilderness Act (P.L. 88-577) in 1964 gave Congress the authority to designate public lands as part of the National Wilderness Preservation System. Lands designated as wilderness are managed by one of four agencies: Forest Service, National Park Service, Fish and Wildlife Service, and Bureau of Land Management. Of the 89.1 million acres in the federal wilderness system as of 1986, 36.8 million are in the National Park System units.

Certain criteria are mandatory in order to include land within the wilderness system. A wilderness area must provide opportunity for primitive and unconfined types of recreation, be largely untouched by human activities, be of sufficient size to be preserved in an unimpaired state, and possess features of scientific interest. Restrictions on activities allowed in wilderness areas (subject to valid existing rights) protect them from drilling, logging, mechanized forms of transportation, and permanent development, including roads. Principal recreational activities in designated wilderness areas are hiking, primitive camping, cross-country skiing, nonmotorized boating, and horseback riding.

The passage of the Alaska Native Interest Lands Conservation Act (ANILCA) in 1980 made a significant contribution to wilderness acreage, especially for national parks and national wildlife refuges.[7] A total of 56.4 million acres were added, including 5.4 million acres in national forests, 32.4 million acres in National Parks and 18.6 million acres in national wildlife refuges. The act also required the review of an additional 80 million acres of public lands in Alaska for possible inclusion as wilderness.

Wild and Scenic Rivers

The Wild and Scenic Rivers Act (P.L. 90-542) was enacted in 1968, establishing a system to protect rivers with outstanding scenic, recreational, geologic, wildlife, historical, cultural, or similar values in a free-flowing condition. Eight river systems were designated by this legislation. The Wild and Scenic Rivers System includes three categories of rivers based on the level of disturbance to the river and its surrounding habitat: wild, scenic, and recreational. Of the nearly 3.6 million miles of rivers in the United States, there are 72 rivers or river segments, totaling 7,365 miles, protected in the system.

The Wild and Scenic Rivers Act established a federal-state system of river conservation. The main protection tool is planning, although a designated river also can be protected through federal land acquisition of surrounding land and prohibition of federal dam building. Designations are made by an act of Congress or by a state request and the approval of the secretary of the interior. A river may continue to be overseen by state and local governments and, where appropriate, be managed in partnership with the federal government. Rivers designated for protection by Congress are managed under plans approved by the secretary of the interior or secretary of agriculture. No federal agency can then permit or financially assist the construction of water-resource projects that might adversely affect a designated river segment.

Section 11 of the Wild and Scenic Rivers Act authorizes the National Park Service to assist local, state, and federal government agencies; private groups; and landowners interested in developing river conservation plans. Regional offices of the park service provide this assistance on request, subject to the availability of congressional funding.[8]

National Scenic and Historic Trails

The National Trail System was created by Congress in 1968 (P.L. 90-543) to promote the development of a national network of scenic trails. (It was amended later to include historic trails.) The National Trail System Act immediately designated the Appalachian Trail (AT) and the Pacific Crest Trail (PCT) and named 14 others for study. The act consolidated management of these two trails, giving the park service primary responsibility for the AT (it is now a unit in the park system) and the Forest Service the lead for the PCT. By their very nature, designated trails are devoted primarily to hiking and primitive camping.

The National Trail System Act encourages federal, state, and local agencies to work together to establish scenic trails, preserve their natural setting and protect them from incompatible development. As with wild and scenic rivers, federal ownership is not mandated. The Appalachian Trail, for example, is protected by a variety of means including the acquisition of land and easements by federal and state governments and private land trusts and trail clubs. As of 1986, 8 national scenic trails (about 14,500 miles) and 6 national historic trails (about 10,500 miles) had been designated.[9]

REGULATIONS GOVERNING THE PARK SYSTEM

The basic laws governing the park system are, for the most part, relatively silent about how the service is to implement the statutory mandate contained in them and its overall statutory mission. Thus, another element in resource management beyond a statute that authorizes action or control is a regulation issued by the service specifying how that action is to take place or that control is to be carried out.

Park service authority to regulate activities within park areas comes from a provision enacted as part of the original Organic Act in 1916:

> The Secretary of the Interior shall make and publish such rules and regulations as he may deem necessary or proper for the use and management of the parks, monuments, and reservations under the jurisdiction of the National Park Service.[10]

The park service has issued numerous regulations flowing from this authority; most of them appear in volume 36 of the Code of Federal Regulations (CFR). Properly issued regulations have the force of law. If a statute, such as the Organic Act, is sufficiently clear about the powers available to or obligations imposed on the agency, and the regulation is clearly related to furthering those objectives, courts are generally satisfied and the agency is free to act accordingly.

As might be expected, regulations and their relationship to parent statutes differ in terms of specificity. In several park system units, Congress has provided enabling legislation that contains provisions explicitly governing certain aspects of park use; many of the regulations concerning these areas slightly enlarge on or simply reiterate the statute. The regulation on scientific study at Mesa Verde National Park (36 C.F.R.7.39[a]), for example, closely reflects a provision in that park's enabling act (16 U.S.C. 113).

Sometimes, a regulation will take a simple approach in implementing congressional intent. The enabling statute for Voyageurs National Park (16 U.S.C. 160g[a]), for example, authorizes the interior secretary to regulate fishing in Voyageurs in accordance with applicable state and federal law, and, in consultation with the state, to designate no-fishing zones where resource management and visitor interests warrant. The applicable regulation (36 C.F.R. 7.33[a]) simply reads, in full: "Unless otherwise designated, fishing in a manner authorized under applicable State law is allowed."

In contrast, regulations governing off-road vehicle use typically go into extensive technical detail for one or more full pages. See, for instance (in 36 C.F.R.), 7.20(a), Fire Island National Seashore; 7.65(b), Assateague Island National Seashore; and 7.67(a), Cape Cod National Seashore.

The Organic Act, especially in the absence of specific enabling legislation, gives authority and imposes a duty on the park service that is broad and sweeping without being specific. While management regulations can be and have been drafted based on such a broad mandate, they may be either fairly narrow in focus and straightforward or not very helpful in resolving difficult resource-management problems. One example of the former is alcoholic beverage regulations. In contrast, off-road vehicle regulations are among those that give little help in resolving the real management problems, noting only that "[t]he designation of [off-road vehicle] routes shall be in accord with the procedures and criteria" (36 C.F.R. 4.19[b]) given elsewhere in the regulations and in the applicable executive order. That order, in turn, states that designation "shall be based upon the protection of . . . resources, . . . the promotion of . . . safety, . . . and the minimization of conflicts among the various uses" (E.O. 11644, 3[a])—a directive that adds little, if anything, to the Organic Act mandate.

As the examples illustrate, there is rarely a magic legal formula that can instantly resolve use conflicts and fulfill the obligation to prevent impairment of park resources. In light of this, the bases on which the park service may act need to be understood more clearly, so as to appreciate better the opportunities for and the constraints on effective resource management.

COURT INTERPRETATIONS

Specific resource managment actions in the parks serve to give meaning to, refine, and reconcile the eloquent language and uncertainties inherent in the Organic Act, as amended; the various pieces of enabling and overlay legislation; and relevant park service regulations. Courts act as the ultimate interpreters of these laws and rules when specific actions or nonactions by the park service are challenged. Key questions include:

- What has the Organic Act, with its amendments, come to mean when specific decisions made by the service regarding park resources are reviewed by the courts?
- How have enabling legislation provisions been factored into court decisions concerning the Organic Act?

- What types of authority do these laws give the park service to manage activities within park boundaries on federally owned land?
- What types of authority do these laws give the service to manage activities within park boundaries on privately or state owned lands?

The Courts and Activities on Parklands

Court decisions involving five different areas and actions by the park service illustrate how the questions above have been addressed. They also give meaning to the Organic Act, as amended, define its relationship to specific park enabling legislation, and reinforce the role of regulations in implementing various laws. These cases involve commercial fishing in Everglades, hunting and trapping systemwide, the damaging effects on park resources of logging activities outside Redwood, off-road-vehicle use in Cape Cod, and a prohibition on camping in sections of the National Capital Parks.

Commercial Fishing in Everglades

In *Organized Fishermen* v. *Watt*, the park service was challenged by commercial fishermen for prohibiting commercial fishing in Everglades National Park.[11] Also challenged were regulations to establish sanctuaries for endangered and threatened species within the park by closing off areas to public entry and restricting recreational shellfish harvest.

Issues. Two key issues were presented in this case, one factual and one legal:

- Did the park service have sufficient evidence of harm and resource degradation to ban commercial fishing and significantly restrict recreational uses of certain areas of the park?
- Did the park service have sufficient legal authority under the enabling legislation and the Organic Act to take such actions?

Ruling. The court found the park service action to be factually and legally supportable. The court methodically reviewed the steps taken by the park service that led to the regulations banning commercial fishing:

- the receipt of 5,000-name petitions expressing concern over the diminishing sport fish population and requesting that bag limits be set on certain species;

- a management study of options to address the problem that included a projection of catch rates and a socioeconomic analysis of various actions;
- extensive public workshops, comments, and consultation with various federal and state agencies;
- a review of management alternatives indicating the preferred use and a decision not to do an environmental impact statement under the National Environmental Policy Act (NEPA);
- proposed rule making and extensive public hearings and comments; and
- publication of the final regulations.

The court observed that while there seemed to be general agreement from all interested parties—park service, commercial fishermen, state of Florida, environmentalists, and so forth—"that the fish resources needed protection, there was substantial disagreement on the extent of the problem and its cause." Despite this disagreement, the court found that the careful process followed in making the decision warranted strong deference to the actions of the service, noting that:

> The task of weighing the competing uses of federal property has been delegated by Congress to the Secretary of the Interior. As such, the Secretary has "broad discretion in determining what actions are best calculated to protect park or public land resources."

In examining the governing legal authorities, namely, the Organic Act and its amendments plus the enabling act creating Everglades, the court ruled that actions taken by the park service were consistent with the purposes of these laws:

> Commercial exploitation of the natural resources is not one of the purposes for which Congress established the Park. The Secretary, as a matter of policy, can implement measures such as those challenged herein, which, in effect, eliminate one predator from the park and enhance the use of the park by recreational users.

Interestingly, the court went on to indicate that the relevant laws would have permitted the secretary of the interior, through the park service, to go further to restrict fishing activities, if he had found such action necessary. Because the secretary had taken significant action, though, the court did not want to "second guess" his decision since "Congress has entrusted [to him] the authority to make these judgements."

Hunting and Trapping throughout the System

In *National Rifle Association* v. *Potter*, the park service was similarly challenged for being over-protective.[12] The National Rifle Assocation challenged park service regulations that banned hunting and trapping in all units of the park system, unless such activity was clearly provided for in a park's enabling legislation.

Issue. Since the facts concerning the ban and its implications were not disputed by the parties, only one issue—a legal one—was presented by this case:

- Is the 1983 Park Service regulation that prohibits hunting and trapping throughout the National Park System, except where such activities are specifically authorized by Congress, valid under the Organic Act as amended?

Ruling. The court found the regulations to be valid and supported by the Organic Act. It upheld the park service interpretation of the law to require preservation of wildlife except where Congress expressly provided for the consumption of such resources.

As in the Everglades case, the court reviewed the legislative authorities governing the system and particular parks, as well as the reason for the change in park service policy. In this case, the change in policy came about because of the emphasis Congress placed on a unified system and resource protection in the 1970 and 1978 amendments to the Organic Act, respectively.

The court concluded that nowhere in the legislative history of the Organic Act did Congress contemplate "consumptive" uses of the park system. More important, the court specifically equated the charge to conserve in the Organic Act with preservation, declaring that:

> the paramount objective of the Park System with respect to indigenous wildlife, and the philosophy which came to pervade the new Park Service to whom it was entrusted, was, from the beginning, one of protectionism.

In very strong language, the court ruled that the park service was correct in concluding that its "primary management function with respect to Park wildlife is its preservation unless Congress has declared otherwise."

Like the court in the Everglades case, the court in *NRA* v. *Potter* was highly respectful of the park service decision to change policy and become more protective of park resources. It found ample authority in the relevant statutory authorities for the service to do so, and concluded that a sufficient relationship existed between the purpose of the parks and the specific action taken. The court made clear, however, that where the enabling legislation for various parks expressly provided for hunting or trapping, these activities were to continue in those specific units.

Logging outside Redwood

The third case involved a series of suits brought over resource damage at Redwood National Park. The boundaries of most park system units are not based primarily on ecological principles.[13] Political and economic concerns often predominate. Perhaps the archetypal example of such boundaries is Redwood National Park, where part of the Redwood Creek watershed was originally excluded from the park in a compromise between concerns for preservation and for timber harvest.

In awareness of this compromise, Congress also ordered the park service, within the specific statute creating Redwood, to "afford as full protection as is reasonably possible" to resources within the park. To do this, Section 3(e) of the Redwood Park Act authorized the interior secretary to acquire easements from and conclude management agreements with the timber companies that owned the adjoining lands in the watershed (16 U.S.C. 79c[e]). But the park service took no effective action under this provision, and damage to the park resulted from lumbering practices outside the boundaries.

A series of lawsuits followed, brought by the Sierra Club against the interior secretary. Three decisions resulted, all of which were significant for illuminating the scope of the park service's duty to protect park resources.

Redwood I Issues. The first suit, decided in 1974, was in a real sense the most significant of the three cases.[14] Two issues were presented in this initial litigation over Redwood:

- Could an environmental group sue the park service (through the secretary of the interior) for not taking—what it claimed— appropriate action under the law to protect park resources?
- Was there a legal responsibility on the part of the park service to take action against activities outside the park that were threatening park resources?

Ruling. The court decided that a suit by an outside organization to challenge the interior secretary's management decisions was permissible. The court also determined that the secretary's responsibility to protect the parks, imposed under the Organic Act and the 1968 Redwood Enabling Act, turned an authorization to take out-of-park actions at Redwood, under Section 3(e), into a "paramount legal duty . . . to utilize the specific powers given to him whenever reasonably necessary to protect the park."

The court found that, in this context, the Organic Act and the enabling act imposed "a general trust duty" to maintain park resources unimpaired. While the enabling act Section 3(e) itself defined the terms of the duty in the case and made it clear that the duty extended to lands beyond the park's borders, the Organic Act directive to "leave" park resources "unimpaired" gave 3(e) the special force needed to make an action that the park service could initiate on its own into a duty that it could be compelled to undertake by the courts.

Redwood II Issue. Having won the right to sue on the issue, and having established a park service duty to protect resources, the Sierra Club returned to court to challenge the substance of the interior secretary's actions at Redwood. There was principally one issue involved in the second Redwood suit:

- Had the park service (or interior secretary) taken the appropriate actions to protect the park?

Ruling. This challenge was also successful, as the court found that the secretary had not taken in good faith any of the actions authorized in Section 3(e) or recommended by a park service task force on the issue.[15] That is, the secretary had not adequately sought modification of the park boundary in light of damages occurring to park resources or agreements with applicable landowners to prevent future damages.

The decision is important not only for the specific terms of the interior secretary's duty or even for that duty's application beyond park borders, for both were spelled out in Section 3(e). It is also important because it demonstrated that in certain cases the Organic Act's obligations, combined with the language in a park's enabling statute, can be real and enforceable and that the park service, at times, must take affirmative action to maintain park resources "unimpaired" in the face of a clear threat to them.

Redwood III Issue. In the third of these suits, the court determined that the specific elements of the paramount duty to act—the authorities spelled out in Section 3(e) to seek modifications of the boundary and agreements with neighboring landowners—were also the limits to that duty, as an obligation.[16] In essence, the issue in this third case concerned the outer limits of park service authority:

- What additional steps, if any, could the park service be compelled to take, under the law, to protect park resources?

Ruling. The court concluded that the park service could be required to take only those steps specifically authorized by the statute. Additional ones could not be compelled.

By the time this suit was decided by the court, the park service had taken the good faith steps required by the second decision, and that having been done, the court decided it could not direct the service to do more. In effect, once the interior secretary had asked Congress for help, he was held to have complied with the court's ruling and to have fulfilled his statutory duties, notwithstanding a lack of congressional response. (The court, however, did not address the issue of whether the park service had the authority to do more had it so chosen to take action on its own.)

Thus, the Redwood suits stand for three important principles:

- The park service has, under the Organic Act (and any other directives relevant to the specific unit), "a paramount legal duty" to protect the resources of its parks from fundamental impairment.
- The actions necessary to carry out that duty may be specified by the courts. Courts will do so where Congress has written a provision enumerating the acts or standards, as in Redwood, and those actions may be given the force of a requirement by the dictates of the Organic Act. The extent to which this principle may, in practice, be applicable to other park units depends in some part on the legislation authorizing that unit. For example, in authorizing legislation for a park, Congress may have articulated what amounts to park-specific resource protection standards when it states the rationale for creating the new unit and the resources to be protected in it. Often, however, enabling legislation may be fairly general, leaving it unclear as to whether a court would find a park service obligation to prevent impairment inside park boundaries.
- Good faith efforts and relevant statutory provisions define the limits of how far a court will require the park service to go to carry out its paramount duty to prevent fundamental impairment of the parks. The extension of this obligation outside the park in the Redwood cases was defined by and limited to Section 3(e) of the Redwood Enabling Act.

ORVs in Cape Cod

Regulations concerning the use and resource impacts of off-the-road vehicles (ORVs) at Cape Cod National Seashore and other units have long been controversial. The case concerning Cape Cod in a sense summarizes the ones discussed above, as it illustrates both the extent of park service discretion and the significance of language in enabling legislation as a limit to the exercise of that discretion. Here, three New England environmental organizations challenged a management plan adopted by the park service to regulate ORV use, contending that their use was too disruptive to be allowed to continue, even under the limited conditions specified in the plan.

Issues. The case presented two key issues:

- Was the interior secretary's management plan for Cape Cod National Seashore compatible, as a factual matter, with the preservation of the seashore's ecological and physiographic condition as required by the law, embodied in the Organic Act, the enabling legislation, and various presidential executive orders on ORV use?
- Was ORV use of the seashore an "appropriate public use" under the seashore's enabling act and the executive orders on ORVs?

Ruling. On the factual question on the impact of ORVs, the court found that the ORV management plan adequately protected the ecology of the seashore. The court, however, returned the case to the park service for it to determine whether ORV use, both generally and as regulated under the plan, was an "appropriate use" of the unit.[17]

The court concluded that the plan, the process and studies that went into designing it, and the subsequent monitoring of environmental effects during its implementation met the needs of resource protection. The case is noteworthy, in part, because the court placed great emphasis on the process used by the park service to support continued ORV use on the seashore, while noting the strong philosophy of protection that it found articulated in the Cape Cod enabling statute, along with the Organic Act.

The court noted that the act creating Cape Cod "gives primacy to preservation of the Seashore as it existed in 1961." It went on to conclude that, like the Seashore enabling act, the Organic Act:

> emphasizes the preservation of park lands in their natural, scenic, and historic condition. . . . Both statutes allow for a balancing of preservation and development only to the extent that such development does not derogate from the overriding preservation mandate.

Considering this strong preservation mandate and the well-recognized effects of ORV use on dune areas, the court generally upheld the park service's actions allowing ORV use in certain areas and under certain conditions based on resource management grounds. What mattered most to the court was that park service decisions were the result of carefully designed, scientifically based studies and continuing monitoring efforts. The court found a "rational basis" for the service's actions and a more thorough factual basis than the evidence presented by the outside groups challenging the service.

The court, however, faulted the park service for not considering whether continued ORV use was an "appropriate use" of the park and returned the case to the agency to examine the issue from this perspective. The court held that the appropriateness of ORV use in Cape Cod was called into question by both the National Seashore's own enabling act and the Organic Act. The Seashore's enabling act stated that:

> . . . no development or plan for the convenience of visitors shall be undertaken therein which would be incompatible with the preservation of the unique flora and fauna or the physiographic conditions now prevailing and that the Secretary may develop for appropriate public uses such portions of the seashore as he deems especially adaptable for camping, swimming, boating, sailing, hunting, fishing, the appreciation of historic sites and structures and natural features of Cape Cod, and other activities of similar nature.[18]

The court contested the seashore superintendent's decision that ORVs, as a "traditional" use of the area, were necessarily "of similar nature" to the other, nonmechanized activities listed and therefore an appropriate park use: "the mere fact of traditional use should not weigh heavily in a present day determination of appropriateness." Under this case, the "paramount duty" to "leave" park resources "unimpaired"—first enunciated in the Redwood cases—is given substance, under the amended Organic Act, by the specific language of each park's authorization. This applies not only in terms of park resources, but also in terms of park use.[19]

Camping in a Park

The park service was challenged all the way to the U.S. Supreme Court over its regulations that restrict camping to designated areas only. It had granted a permit to homelessness activist Mitch Snyder's Community for Creative Non-Violence (CCNV) to demonstrate in

Washington, D.C., in Lafayette Park across from the White House and on the Mall to call attention to the needs of the homeless. Yet relying on its camping regulations, the park service denied CCNV's request that demonstrators be allowed to sleep in these areas in symbolic tents. CCNV sued the park service, largely on grounds that the action violated its First Amendment rights to freedom of expression.

Issue. Since the actions of the demonstrators previously had been held to constitute expression, the case presented a constitutional question within the context of the park service's overall authority to take action:

- Did a park service regulation prohibiting camping, except in carefully designated areas, violate the First Amendment when it was applied to prevent "Reaganville" demonstrators from sleeping in noncamping areas in connection with a demonstration intended to call attention to the plight of the homeless?

Ruling. The court decided that the regulation limiting camping is valid and that such camping can be prohibited in this case and others, showing striking deference to the park service's judgment on "how much protection of park lands is wise and how that level of conservation is to be attained."[20]

The case is noteworthy because the U.S. Supreme Court strongly endorsed park service action to protect and manage resources, even in the face of potentially restricting long-recognized constitutional rights. The court's decision largely revolved around weighing the infringement of constitutional rights—to free speech in this case—against the authority of the park service to manage and protect valuable public resources adequately.

Even with a constitutional question presented, the park service action (a regulation, in this case) is presumed to be authorized by statute and otherwise valid. The court found that the regulation legitimately and narrowly focused on the park service's strong interest in maintaining parks in an attractive condition. "To permit camping," the court said, "would be totally inimical to these purposes, as would be readily understood by those who have frequented the National Parks across the country and observed the unfortunate consequences of the activities of those who refuse to confine their camping to designated areas." It went on to say that:

All those who would resort to the parks must abide by otherwise valid rules for their use, just as they must observe the traffic laws, sanitation regulations, and laws to preserve the public peace.

The Courts and Activities on Private Property within Park Boundaries

What happens to park service authority under the Organic Act when it attempts to protect resources from activities on private lands within park boundaries? Have the courts permitted the park service to regulate activities on these lands when necessary to protect park resources?

Recent court interpretations have clarified park service authority to control activities on nonfederal property within park boundaries in the course of managing and protecting park resources. As a result, the service can also exercise sovereign or governmental authority over nonfederal property within its borders separate from the management decisions it makes concerning federal land. This authority over lands within park boundaries derives from two principal sources, the Cession and Property clauses of the U.S. Constitution.

Cession

One source of park service authority over nonfederal lands within park boundaries is cession—that is, the ceding (giving up) of state police power to the federal government (the park service) within park boundaries.[21] Under our federal system of government, the states traditionally have held and exercised police power over the day-to-day, private activities of most individuals' lives. (Police power is the authority to protect and promote public health, safety, and general welfare.)

The 20th century, however, has seen the federal government increasingly involved in police-power-related areas such as labor, safety, and environmental laws.[22] Once federal power is exercised (by a statutory grant of authority to a federal agency from Congress), the Supremacy Clause of the Constitution then acts to preempt any conflicting or competing exercise of state power when constitutional, federal laws conflict with state or local ones. In essence, federal laws override state and local ones when a conflict arises.

Nevertheless, as a matter of deference to states' traditional role, the park service has typically sought cessions of state police power within the boundaries of park system units after their establishment. Where such cessions are "exclusive," with the state giving up total authority within the unit's borders, the park service may exercise all powers of a sovereign state government. These powers can include zoning or any constitutionally acceptable form of land-use controls as well as more mundane regulation of motor vehicles, alcoholic beverages, and the like. As of 1988, approximately 35 of the units then in the National Park System had received a cession of exclusive jurisdiction from states.

As this number suggests, states more often choose to cede something less than exclusive jurisdiction. As a consequence, many parks operate under what is known as partial or concurrent jurisdiction, with both the park service and the applicable state-government body having specified authority over selected issues or activities.

The courts have held that states must explicitly withhold specific authorities in their cession statutes enacted for each park, if they wish to continue to exercise them. Thus, for example, in *Collins* v. *Yosemite Park and Curry Co.*, California was found to have given up the power to regulate liquor use or licensing but to have retained power to extract excise taxes for liquor sales.[23] More broadly, and more important, courts have decided that states' cession statutes must clearly withhold jurisdiction over private land in a park if the state does not want to cede all general legislative authority over such lands to the United States.[24]

Thus, if there is either a cession of exclusive jurisdiction or a cession that fails to specify explicitly the authority retained by a state, the park service's authority over lands within park boundaries (the subject of the cession) is complete.

The Property Clause

Even if a cession is explicitly less than exclusive (that is, "partial" or "concurrent"), the park service may not be prohibited from acting with regard to privately owned land within park boundaries. In addition to having authority to act on its own, the park service may be able to supersede state law as a result of the Property Clause of the U.S. Constitution. This clause provides the clearest source of authority for the management and protection of all federal lands:

> The Congress shall have the power to make all needful rules and regulations respecting the Territory or other property belonging to the United States.[25]

This seemingly simple sentence enabled Congress to create many national parks in the first place and to provide for their management by a National Park Service under the Organic Act. While the park service has thus been delegated the effective power to manage the park system on a continuing basis, Congress retains the authority to make, at any time, more specific provision for the particulars of park administration in a given unit or systemwide.

Not only did the Property Clause provide the constitutional basis for enactment of the Organic Act; it also is the key to interpreting the broad mandates of this act by outlining the scope of the powers available to the park service in implementing it. Though the powers granted by the Property Clause have been clearly defined in some respects, its limits, combined with the purposes of the Organic Act, are still very much untested.

One of the earliest major cases, and still to some degree the leading case in defining the powers granted to the federal government by the property clause, is *Camfield* v. *U.S.*, decided by the U.S. Supreme Court in 1897.[26] A western landowner, whose tracts were checkerboarded with public lands, enclosed the entire area—public lands and private—with a fence located only on his own lands. In upholding the enforcement of a federal law prohibiting enclosure of the public lands, the Court decided that the Property Clause vested the federal government with power to protect the management and uses of its own lands. While the Court held that the offender's action amounted to a common law "nuisance"—interference with the use and enjoyment of one's property of the sort that an ordinary landowner would have grounds for suit—it also clearly upheld the right of Congress to pass its own laws to protect federal property, even if state law was to the contrary: "A different rule would place the public domain of the United States completely at the mercy of state legislation." A more recent case involving wild roaming burros also affirmed federal authority to regulate activities on private lands in pursuit of legitimate management purposes on public lands, even where no direct damage from those private activities was alleged.[27]

Thus, from an early stage, and recently reaffirmed by the U.S. Supreme Court, the law has been clear that "the power granted by the property clause is broad enough to reach beyond territorial limits."[28] Other questions have not been answered definitively, however. For example: How far beyond such territorial limits may that power reach? What subjects may it encompass? For what protective purposes? (Such issues are explored in chapter 14.) But for regulation of actions on private (or any nonfederal) land within a unit of the park system, the leading Property Clause cases and subsequent park service management actions seem at this point to leave little doubt that park service authority is complete.

This authority was clarified in *United States* v. *Brown*, when the

Federal Court of Appeals for the 8th Circuit sustained a conviction for hunting in Voyageurs National Park.[29] The defendant had claimed that, being on a lake within the park at the time, he was on state-owned waters (a fact the park service admitted) which federal regulations could not reach. The court, however, had no hesitation in affirming the basic point that the park service's prohibition on hunting even on nonfederal property within the park was "a constitutional exercise of congressional power under the property clause" and, as such, a power delegated to the park service by the Organic Act. It also expressly adopted the rationale articulated in *Kleppe* that such regulation could be valid not only if needed to protect the park's resources (a point established by *Camfield* 80 years earlier) but simply if the regulation was deemed useful "to promote the purposes" of the park.

This finding is especially important. If, to fulfill the requirements of any legitimate management purpose under the Organic Act, non-federal land within a park must be regulated, *Kleppe* and *Brown* clearly state that the Constitution poses no obstacle. This was articulated further in the context of a case involving a Forest Service wilderness area, in which a court ruled that a federal ban on motorized craft on lands and water under state jurisdiction was permissible. In that decision, the court stated:

> under this authority [the property clause to protect public land] Congress' power must extend to regulation on or off the public land that would threaten the designated purpose of federal lands.[30]

Thus, in legal concept if not practical effect, the presence or absence of state cession may no longer be a relevant concern in exercising park service management authority within park borders. In practice, of course, the refusal of a state to cede police power might suggest caution, and a due awareness of political and economic concerns, in pursuing regulation of private land in a park. But it certainly should not bar such regulation where resource management needs require that it be done.[31]

If there were any lingering doubts about the legal ability of the park service to impose all needful regulations within park boundaries, they were effectively put to rest by the decision in *Free Enterprise Canoe Renters Association of Missouri v. Watt*.[32] A group of private canoe liveries challenged the park service's power to require them to obtain concessioner's permits, arguing that their only presence within the Ozark National Scenic Riverway was to retrieve canoes using nonfederal (state and private) access roads and lands. Rejecting that argument, the appellate court gave sweeping approval to park service regulation of *"everything* within the outer boundaries" (emphasis added) of the unit, expressly including "state and county roads." Indeed, the park service's authority to regulate nonfederal lands in a park must be taken as settled, at this point. This was the conclusion reached by the appeals court in the *Free Enterprise Canoe* case, which did not even see a need to cite other cases in support of the "recognized federal power to regulate nonfederal land."

CONCLUSION

The park service has been challenged during the last decade in various cases, both by those who would like greater protection of park resources and by those who view a particular decision as going too far in protecting resources. Generally courts have interpreted the Organic Act to authorize and require the protection of park natural resources.

Courts have been uniformly supportive of measures to ensure greater protection of park natural resources. In particular, courts:

- find adequate authority in the Organic Act, as amended, and various enabling laws to enable the park service to take strong actions to protect park natural resources;
- show strong deference to park service actions to protect natural resources within park boundaries, regardless of who owns the land;
- give even greater support to park service actions when they are based on well-articulated plans and studies; and
- have compelled the park service to take specific actions to protect natural resources, consistent with the mandates of enabling legislation for a particular unit.

The courts, however, have not completely defined the extent to which the Organic Act can require the park service to take action to protect natural resources, beyond that specified in relevant enabling legislation. In other words, it is not clear whether the Organic Act alone—without such park-specific legislative directives as in the case of Redwood—can be used to compel the park service to take actions to prevent impairment.[33] In the *Organized Fisherman of Florida* case, for example, the authority of the Organic Act alone was found to provide sufficient support for park-service-initiated action to protect Everglades fish populations by prohibiting commercial fishing in park waters. It may be that, if the park service failed to act in such a case, similar factual findings would support a legal challenge to that inaction. But the findings would have to be clear and strong to outweigh the deference normally given by courts to agency discretion.

Beyond these basic messages, court decisions—like the natural resource management actions of the park service itself—will continually define the meaning and outer limits of the Organic Act and other related laws. For the manner in which agency management discretion is exercised is, like the pressures on park resources, subject to evolutionary change over time. Because demands on park resources evolve in response to changes in society, the reconciliations made by one generation must always be reconsidered by the next.

In all likelihood, some earlier reconciliations of conflicting demands will seem surprising—or clearly inappropriate—to later observers. People today may cringe, for example, on hearing that park service staff once entertained visitors by feeding grizzly bears in sight of the dining room in Yellowstone, knowing now that these practices endangered visitors and led to difficult management choices that have come to threaten the very survival of the bears in the park. The flagstone-rimmed road that entirely surrounds Crater Lake contrasts starkly with the more sensitive recent treatment of the world's tallest redwood, where the visitor drives part of the way but approaches the tree on foot.

By the same token, some of today's responses to changing demands would have been unacceptable only a few years ago. Visits to the back country in some popular wilderness areas are limited and available by advance reservation, and visitors are prohibited from using some coastal dune areas due to severe erosion problems. Similarly, controls that might not be politically acceptable today because neither the uses to be controlled nor the effects on park resources have emerged may become commonplace in the future.

During the 1960s, a consensus arising from the lessons of ecology began to alleviate the resource disruption that had previously resulted from some well-intentioned but inadequately informed interventions by park managers. Responding to increasingly sophisticated understanding and the pressures of resource scientists and conservationists, park service policy began to recognize that preservation of resources requires more respect for natural processes. Though often controversial in application, this standard represents another fundamental step in the evolution of the park ideal.

Clearly, the setting for management in the national parks has changed dramatically in the last 25 years. Not only has the National Park System expanded to include new units in more populous, growth-prone areas, but development itself has moved to the very brink of formerly isolated parks. In response, both legal and administrative interpretations of the park service's Organic Act mandate have of necessity endorsed a more active stance than had previously been either acceptable or required.

The ability of the courts to support such action without major new legislation is testimony to the virtues of the Organic Act, its underlying foundation in the Property Clause, and language in specific park enabling legislation. The Organic Act is, like the Constitution, general enough to adapt to changing conditions without being vague or meaningless, and yet it is still clear enough to enunciate a lasting statement of the system's fundamental values. These qualities are essential if the park system is to survive, for they contain the promise of future adaptation to changing needs and values. Regardless of management demands, it is clear that the Organic Act will support active park service responses to protect park resources.

Key to this support will be decisions based on studies, sound research, and well-articulated policies and plans. The need for technical study and documentation is not new, but it has become much more urgent with the proliferation of pressures on park natural resources and the need for management decisions in response to such threats. Whether the park service decides to act in a particular situation and however it decides to act, the service must have both clear technical analyses assessing any relevant resource problem and an equally clear and complete record of its decision on how to address the problem. Courts repeatedly have given broad discretion to the park service in deference to its administrative expertise, but there must be evidence of that expertise in action. The ban on commercial fishing in Everglades is a primary example of well-reasoned park service decisions that courts have had little trouble supporting.

To the need for clear technical thinking must be added a responsiveness to specific statutory duties to safeguard park resources. Congress' two amendments to the Organic Act in the 1970s were an explicit directive to the park service that its "management . . . shall not compromise these resource values," that "unimpaired" was not a rhetorical flourish but a "paramount duty." The Organic Act thus not only empowers but also inspires the National Park Service to be a steadfast and active guardian of park resources.

REFERENCES

1. 16 U.S.C. §1 *et seq.*, (1988).
2. General Authorities Act, 16 U.S.C. §1a-1 (1988).
3. 16 U.S.C. §1c. (1988).
4. Redwood National Park Expansion Act Sec. 101(b), P.L. 95-250, 16 U.S.C. §1a-1.
5. *Sierra Club* v. *Andrus*, 487 F. Supp. 443 (D. D.C. 1986), quoting S. Rep. No. 95-528, 95 Cong. 1st Sess. 9 (Oct. 21, 1977).
6. H. Rep. No. 95-581, p. 21.
7. The Conservation Foundation, *State of the Environment: A View toward the Nineties* (Washington, D.C.: The Conservation Foundation, 1987), p. 286.
8. See Rolf Diamant, J. Glen Eugster, and Christopher J. Duerksen, *A Citizen's Guide to River Conservation* (Washington, D.C.: The Conservation Foundation, 1984).
9. The Conservation Foundation, *State of the Environment: A View toward the Nineties*, p. 286.
10. 16 U.S.C. §3.
11. 590 F. Supp. 805 (S.D. Fla. 1984); *affirmed*, 775 F. 2d 1544 (11th Cir. 1985).
12. 628 F. Supp. 903 (D.D.C. 1986).
13. See, for example, Alfred Runte, *National Parks: The American Experience* (Lincoln, Neb.: University of Nebraska Press, 1979); and Joseph L. Sax, "Buying Scenery: Land Acquisition for the National Parks" *Duke Law Journal* (1980):709, 712.
14. 376 F. Supp. 90 (N.D. Calif. 1974).
15. 398 F. Supp. 284 (N.D. Calif. 1975).
16. 424 F. Supp. 172 (N.D. Calif. 1976).
17. *Conservation Law Foundation* v. *Clark*, 590 F. Supp. 1467 (D. Mass. 1984).
18. 16 U.S.C. §459b-6(b)(1) (1984).
19. The issue of appropriate use of parks is more fully addressed in chapter 14.
20. 468 U.S. 288 (1984).
21. Article I, Section 8, Clause 17.
22. Federal authority to act has come largely from the Commerce Clause of the U.S. Constitution, with promoting the flow of interstate commerce as the primary rational for such legislation.
23. 304 U.S. 518 (1938).
24. See Joseph L. Sax, "Helpless Giants: The National Parks and the Regulation of Private Lands," *Michigan Law Review* 75 (1976):246, N. 43.
25. Article IV, Section 3, Clause 2.
26. 167 U.S. 518 (1897).
27. *Kleppe* v. *New Mexico*, 426 U.S. 529 (1976)
28. Ibid.
29. 552 F.2d 817 (8th Cir. 1977).
30. *State of Minnesota by Alexander* v. *Block*, 660 F.2d 1240, 1249 (8th Cir. 1981).
31. See, *U.S.* v. *Moore*, 640 F. Supp. 164 (S.D. W.Va., 1986), where a federal court ruled that the Property Clause required the state of West Virginia to get a park service permit to spray pesticide within the New River Gorge National River, irrespective of the cession agreement and the fact that the service did not own the land within the authorized boundary of the area.

32. 711 F.2d 852 (8th Cir. 1983).

33. The most recent case on this issue involved a challenge by the National Wildlife Federation to the park services' decision to keep the Fishing Bridge campground in Yellowstone open, pending completion of an environmental impact statement. The court ruled that the Organic Act, absent specific enabling act language in this case, gave the park service discretion to decide what was in the best interest of the park and refused to compel the service to close the campground. *National Wildlife Federation v. National Park Service*, 669 F. Supp. 384 (D. Wyo. 1987).

Part II
Key Federal Environmental Laws

Besides the Organic Act and enabling legislation for individual units, several other federal laws affect the management of National Park System natural resources. Statutes such as the Clean Air Act, the National Environmental Policy Act (NEPA), and the Endangered Species Act are among the country's most well-known and powerful environmental legal tools. They can also have dramatic implications for the parks.

Many of these laws provide not only requirements that the park service must follow in managing resources but also opportunities for the park service to influence the outcome of decisions made by others concerning activities outside park boundaries that may affect those resources. Generally, these laws seek the improvement of the nation's environment. Since they are consistent with the overarching mission of the park service and the service may choose to use one or all of them to urge a neighboring landowner to take a specific action to protect a valuable park resource, its own compliance with these laws as they affect the internal management of park resources is especially important. In essence, the park service will have a difficult time asking a sister federal agency or private individuals to take a specific action on lands they manage under a certain federal environmental law, if the service itself has been remiss in complying with the law as it applies to an activity within a park.

The chapters in this section look at a few of the most important federal laws that apply both to the National Park Service in its management of park units and to others as they engage in certain activities on neighboring lands that may affect parks' natural resources.

Chapter 3

The National Environmental Policy Act

by Jacob Hoogland

The National Environmental Policy Act of 1969[1] (NEPA) serves as "our basic national charter for protection of the environment."[2] Its passage ushered in the environmental decade and became the foundation for environmental law as it is known today.

The policies and directions of NEPA are far-reaching and include a statement of policy that the federal government will:

> use all practicable means and measures, including financial and technical assistance, in a manner calculated to foster and promote the general welfare, to create and maintain conditions under which man and nature can exist in productive harmony, and fulfill the social, economic, and other requirements of present and future generations of Americans.[3]

Specifically, the act directs that all agencies of the federal government shall "Utilize a systematic, interdisciplinary approach which will insure the integrated use of the natural and social sciences and the environmental design arts in planning and in decisionmaking which may have an impact on man's environment."[4] The act further establishes the Council on Environmental Quality (CEQ), charged with the implementation and oversight of NEPA.[5] To carry out its mandates, NEPA requires every federal agency to prepare a detailed statement on the environmental impact of agency actions.[6]

Because NEPA has become so institutionalized, it is difficult to realize how thoroughly it has revolutionized federal agency decision making. To an unprecedented degree, it has both opened up agency decision making to the public and required agencies to factor environmental considerations into their decisions. Initially, some proponents of NEPA hoped that its provisions would also result in the development of substantive "environmental rights." However, through agency actions and judicial interpretations, the act has been held to impose duties that are "essentially procedural."[7] These procedural requirements are the primary "action forcing" mechanisms of the act and require agencies to take a hard look at the environmental consequences of proposals.

NEPA applies to all federal activities, with most of its requirements directed to major federal actions significantly affecting the quality of the human environment. This includes those actions funded, permitted, or licensed by a federal agency. Over the years the emphasis has become directed not on whether an action is "major" in funding or scale but on whether an action "significantly affects" the quality of the environment. Thus, a seemingly minor action can have significant effects triggering the full application of NEPA.

At its most elemental level, the NEPA process is environmental planning that evaluates and documents several key elements: existing environmental conditions; problems and needs to be addressed by an action; alternative solutions; the impacts of the alternatives on the human environment; and what the decision is.

NEPA is the principal means by which the National Park Service can evaluate the actions it is proposing to take on parkland and determine ways to mitigate potential harmful effects. Review of NEPA documents prepared by other agencies on actions that may effect parks is also a vital but often overlooked link in the protection of park resources.

NEPA is unique in that it provides one of the few opportunities for an integrated look at a proposal and its impacts. This results from the fact that the NEPA process is carried out, to the fullest extent possible, in concert with duties under other environmental review statutes such as the Endangered Species Act and the National Historic Preservation Act.[8]

In the National Park Service, compliance with NEPA most commonly is associated with planning efforts, such as general management plans and similar documents. However, environmental assessments for site- or project-specific activities—construction activities, natural or cultural resources management projects, and actions on proposals such as mining plans of operation—constitute the vast majority of NEPA documents prepared by the park service.

Implementation of the NEPA process in the park service is guided by the regulations of the CEQ,[9] the NEPA guidance of the *Department of the Interior Manual*,[10] the National Park Service appendix to the *Departmental Manual*,[11] and NPS-12, the "NEPA Compliance Guideline" that describes the internal procedures for the park service's implementation of NEPA.

All activities undertaken or authorized by the park service are subject to NEPA compliance. However, different activities demand differing levels of NEPA documentation. The three levels of documentation under NEPA are: (1) categorical exclusions (CE); (2) environmental assessments (EA); and (3) environmental impact statements (EIS). In evaluating any activity, the first step is to characterize the action and then determine what level of documentation is most appropriate.

CATEGORICAL EXCLUSIONS

An initial determination must be made as to whether an activity is categorically excluded from the NEPA process. Categorical exclusions are those types of actions that do not individually or cumulatively have a significant effect on the human environment. As a result of this lack of impact on the environment, neither an environmental assessment nor an environmental impact statement need be prepared for such an activity. Examples of park service categorical exclusions include: commercial use licenses involving no construction; installation of signs, displays, kiosks, etc.; and upgrading or adding new overhead utility facilities to existing poles, or replacement poles that do not change existing pole line configurations.[12]

If an action falls within a categorical exclusion, it must be reviewed to see if it is a departmental exception to categorical exclusions. At minimum, environmental assessments must be prepared on those activities that are exceptions to categorical exclusions.

Actions are exceptions to categorical exclusions if they:
- have significant adverse effects on public health or safety;
- adversely affect such unique geographic characteristics as historic or cultural resources, park, recreation, or refuge land, wilderness areas, wild or scenic rivers, sole or principal drinking water aquifers, prime farmlands, wetlands, floodplains, or ecologically significant or critical areas, including those listed on the department's National Register of Natural Landmarks;

- have highly controversial environmental effects;
- have highly uncertain environmental effects or involve unique or unknown environmental risks;
- establish a precedent for future action or represent a decision in principle about a future consideration with significant environmental effects;
- are related to other actions with individually insignificant but cumulatively significant environmental effects;
- adversely affect properties listed or eligible for listing in the National Register of Historic Places;
- affect a species listed or proposed to be listed on the list of endangered or threatened species; or
- threaten to violate a federal, state, local, or tribal law or requirements imposed for the protection of the environment or which require compliance with Executive Order 11988 (Floodplain Management), Executive Order 11990 (Protection of Wetlands), or the Fish and Wildlife Coordination Act.[13]

Once it has been determined that an action is a categorical exclusion, documentation should be prepared for the park files to that effect. This documentation need not be burdensome but can consist of a memo to the files signed by the superintendent showing that the activity falls within a specific park service categorical exclusion and is not a departmental exception to the categorical exclusion process.[14]

ENVIRONMENTAL ASSESSMENTS

The next level of NEPA compliance is the environmental assessment (EA). An EA is a concise public document that describes the natural, cultural, and socioeconomic impacts of a proposed undertaking and its reasonable alternatives. An EA serves to: (1) briefly provide sufficient evidence and analysis for determining whether to prepare an environmental impact statement or a finding of no significant impact (FONSI); (2) aid in an agency's compliance with NEPA when no EIS is necessary; and (3) facilitate preparation of an EIS when one is necessary.[15]

An EA must contain an explanation of the need for the proposal, alternatives to the proposal, environmental impacts of the alternatives, and a listing of persons and agencies consulted.[16] At minimum, public notice of the availability of the assessment must be provided. While a 30-day period of formal public review is customary, longer or shorter review periods may be provided for, depending on the anticipated level of interest or controversy.

Based on the information obtained or developed during the public review period and the analysis contained in the assessment, an evaluation is then made as to whether a FONSI can be issued. A FONSI is a brief document that presents reasons why an action does not have a significant effect on the human environment and provides the rationale for not preparing an environmental impact statement.[17] A FONSI is signed and recommended for approval by the park superintendent and then forwarded to the regional office for final signature and approval by the regional director.

If the impacts associated with an undertaking cannot support the issuance of a FONSI, then a notice of intent (NOI) to prepare an EIS is developed. A notice of intent, published in the *Federal Register*, indicates that a complete environmental impact statement will be issued.[18]

ENVIRONMENTAL IMPACT STATEMENTS

In contrast with EAs, environmental impact statements (EIS) have more detailed format and public-review requirements. In addition, the scoping process, which is optional for use with an EA, is a required and necessary step for developing environmental impact statements.

The scoping process is intended to determine the issues and concerns of both the public and agencies that need to be addressed in the EIS. This process of scoping does not necessarily require public meetings or hearings. Any method can be used that will assist in developing public comment on the issues needed to be addressed in the EIS. When the scoping process is completed, the alternatives to be considered in the draft EIS can be better defined and the issues to be addressed can be more clearly established.[19]

The suggested format for an EIS consists of several items, including: a cover sheet; summary of the document; table of contents; purpose and need for the action; alternatives, including the proposal; a description of the affected environment; the environmental consequences of the proposal and alternatives; a list of preparers; a list of agencies, organizations, and persons to whom the statement is sent; and an index and appendices.[20]

When a draft EIS has been circulated for 60 days, written comments from federal, state, and local agencies and Indian tribes are then printed in full in the final document. These comments, along with substantive comments from the public, are answered in the final document, and any necessary changes resulting from the public review process are made.[21] The final document is circulated subsequently to agencies and members of the public who have made substantive comments. No action can be taken until 30 days have elapsed from the release of the final EIS.

At the conclusion of the process, a "record of decision" (ROD) is issued that states what decision has been made and identifies all the alternatives considered by the agency in reaching a decision. This record of decision also identifies which alternative was environmentally preferable and the factors involved in the final selection. The ROD also discusses any mitigation measures required by the project to lessen any unavoidable impacts. With the issuance of the record of decision, the NEPA process is completed and the action may be implemented, unless otherwise challenged in court.[22]

NEPA IN ACTION

Aside from the fact that NEPA is a federal law that applies to the park service, what benefits does it afford the agency? In addition to the opportunity it provides for looking at the so-called big picture, NEPA can enable agencies to integrate compliance with other legal mandates such as the Endangered Species Act, floodplain and wetland requirements, and Section 106 of the National Historic Preservation Act.

NEPA also provides a structured format for public involvement and for the agency to evaluate more fully and take into account the analyses and conclusions of outsiders who may be affected by the decision. This structure is especially helpful in dealing with controversial proposals. The NEPA public review process is governed by regulations of the CEQ as well as a substantial body of case law regarding public review periods, response to public comment, and initiation of agency action. Through this public review process, the park service has an ability to use the established procedures of NEPA rather than relying on the free-form public review processes commonly used outside of the NEPA process. Public review processes not subject to NEPA's regulation may be more likely influenced by political considerations and can be prolonged indefinitely to suit the circumstances while not assuring meaningful public participation, comment, and response.

The use of the NEPA process also enables the park service to "build a record" in defense of park resources and policies. Substantive public and agency comments must be responded to in final environmental impact statements. This enables the park service in its own forum to clear up confusion concerning its policies or laws applicable to its areas and establish a baseline for its management activities. Recent park service responses to agency and public comment on environmental statements, for example, have provided opportunities for the service to restate law and policy on the closure of its areas to new mining claims and the use of off-road vehicles in fragile ecosystems.

PARTICIPATING IN OTHER AGENCY ACTIONS UNDER NEPA

With increasing frequency, the park service is involved at the park, region, and Washington headquarters levels in the development and review of other agency NEPA documents. This review can be a product of federal proposals on lands adjacent to park service areas (such as national forests) or a result of park service review responsibilities as an agency with "jurisdiction" or expertise in recreation, land management, and historic preservation. Participation in other agency NEPA processes ranges from involvement in scoping and issue identification to serving as a cooperating agency in the development of an EIS.

Unfortunately, the park service has been hesitant in many cases to exercise the authorities available under NEPA and other legislation to comment on other agency activities having an impact on park resources. A recent case study conducted by professors Joseph Sax and Robert Keiter noted that park service officials "exhibited a kind of amnesia in matters where the law has been the key to controlling development across their borders."[23]

As a participant in the scoping process, or other early involvement activities such as preliminary permit approvals, agencies under NEPA have an opportunity to develop information that will compel another agency to identify potential areas of conflict with resources under the jurisdiction of the park service. Too often, park service comments consist of vague and general expressions of concern over potential harm or ill-defined impacts to wildlife or sensitive resources. Park service personnel who comment on other agency proposals must remember that, even at the earliest stage, an administrative record is being established that the other agency or project sponsor must consider and to which the public will have access. This is especially true in the development of NEPA documents for land-use plans on nearby public lands. In such cases, identification of competing and conflicting land uses that may have an impact on the management of park service lands must be made. As an example, the park service should note at the scoping level those adjacent lands containing resource values such as critical habitats for wildlife, migration routes, or wetlands and those activities which may adversely affect water quality, vegetation, or cultural resources under its jurisdiction. By documenting and identifying such issues to the other agency, that agency then will be required either to address or dismiss with justification the potential for resources damage.

Another, and generally underused, opportunity for park service participation in other agency NEPA procedures exists through potential park service status as a cooperating agency. A cooperating agency is an agency "with jurisdiction by law or special expertise with respect to any environmental impact involved in a proposal (or a reasonable alternative). . . ."[24] The "lead" agency may request the participation of the park service, or the service itself can request participation. Once participation as a cooperating agency is allowed, the cooperating agency has a responsibility to participate in the scoping process and in the environmental analysis and to provide or develop information. The cooperating agency may also prepare environmental analyses that include portions of an EIS with which the cooperating agency has special expertise.[25]

In dealing with potential threats to park service resources, cooperating status enables it to provide information and analysis on the impacts of a proposal during the development of the environmental document using park service skills and standards. Early participation in the study process allows the park service to act positively rather than to react to existing faulty analysis contained in draft documents. Comments on other agency documents and participation as a cooperating agency must be coordinated through the National Park Service Washington Environmental Compliance Division and regional environmental coordinators.[26]

CONCLUSION

The passage of NEPA changed and broadened the way decisions are made in the National Park Service and all federal agencies. The implementation of the act in the park service has provided for valuable interaction of the public, managers, and resource specialists in the decision-making process and has helped to ensure that park resources are protected to the maximum extent in the park service's own development processes. Perhaps equally important, NEPA is also a tool that can enable the service to participate in the evaluation of impacts and decisions made by other agencies when those actions may result in impacts to its resources. The challenge, however, remains to use NEPA fully, to integrate it across all of the divisions within the service (whether maintenance, planning, resource management, or interpretation), and to participate actively in review and preparation of other agency NEPA documents. Through this integration and participation, the NEPA process becomes more than a paper exercise and can result in excellent action.[27] In practice, the full use of NEPA can help to achieve the direction of the National Park Service Organic Act to preserve the unique resources of the National Park System for future generations.

REFERENCES

1. P.L. 91-190, 42 U.S.C. §4321 *et seq.* (1982).
2. 40 C.F.R. 1600.1(a) (1988).
3. 42 U.S.C. §4331(a) (1982).
4. 42 U.S.C. §4332(A) (1982).
5. 42 U.S.C. §3242 (1982).
6. 42 U.S.C. §4332(C) (1982).
7. *Vermont Yankee Nuclear Power Corp. v. NRDC*, 435 U.S. 519, 558 (1978).
8. 40 C.F.R. 1502.25(a) (1988).
9. 40 C.F.R. 1500 *et seq.* (1988).
10. 516 Departmental Manual.
11. 516 Departmental Manual 6, appendix 7.
12. A complete listing of NPS categorical exclusions is contained in 516 Departmental Manual 6, appendix 7, and is reprinted in NPS-12.
13. These exclusions can be found in 516 Department Manual 2, appendix 2.
14. Some regional offices require categorical exclusions to be documented. Proposed revisions of NPS-12 would require such documentation for all actions.
15. 40 C.F.R. 1508.9 (1988).
16. 40 C.F.R. 1508.9(b) (1988).
17. 40 C.F.R. 1508.13 (1988).
18. 40 C.F.R. 1508.22 (1988).
19. The scoping process is outlined briefly in NPS-12 and detailed further in appendix 3 of NPS-12.

20. 40 C.F.R. 1502.10 to 1502.18 (1988).

21. 40 C.F.R. 1503.1 to 1503.4 (1988).

22. 40 C.F.R. 1505.2 (1988).

23. Joseph L. Sax and Robert B. Keiter, "Glacier National Park and Its Neighbors: A Study of Federal Inter-Agency Relations," *Ecology Law Quarterly* 14, no. 2 (1987):207-49.

24. 40 C.F.R. 1508.5 (1988).

25. 40 C.F.R. 1501.6 (1988).

26. A complete description of the comment process is contained in NPS-12.

27. 40 C.F.R. 1500.1(c) (1988).

Chapter 4

The Clean Air Act

by Molly N. Ross

Air pollution can damage the very resources and values that the units of the National Park System were created to preserve. Research and monitoring already reveal that manmade air pollution affects all parks to some degree. For example, fine pollutant particles, especially sulfates, impair natural visibility in all parks. Higher than natural ozone concentrations injure sensitive vegetation in many parks. Acidic deposition alters the chemistry and biota in certain park aquatic systems. Acidic deposition and sulfur pollutants accelerate the decay of many park cultural resources.

The air pollution that affects parks can come from large, individual sources or, cumulatively, from many small or regional sources. It can originate from nearby or far-distant sources or anywhere in between. The one common ingredient is that the air pollution affecting parks originates largely outside parks and, therefore, beyond the National Park Service's management jurisdiction.

The Clean Air Act (CAA) provides some tools and many opportunities to protect park resources. In certain cases, the CAA gives the federal land manager a special role in regulatory decisions directly affecting park resources. In most other cases, the CAA provides opportunities to participate in the decision making that determines the quality of the air affecting parks. The CAA augments the fundamental resource-protection responsibilities of the National Park Service Organic Act with respect to air quality and related values in park areas. Together, these authorities form the basis for the park service's general

51

policy of promoting and pursuing measures to safeguard park resources and values from the adverse impacts of air pollution.

THE STRUCTURE OF THE CLEAN AIR ACT

The central goal of the CAA for the entire nation is safe and acceptable ambient air quality through the attainment and maintenance of "national ambient air quality standards." The "primary" standards are to protect the public health "with an adequate margin of safety," and the "secondary" standards are to protect the national "welfare" from all "known or anticipated adverse effects." The CAA defines the term "welfare" broadly to include virtually all the kinds of resources and values associated with park areas.

The primary and secondary standards are air pollutant concentrations set at protective levels on the basis of scientific "criteria documents." The Environmental Protection Agency (EPA) has set national ambient air quality standards for six widespread pollutants; that is, sulfur dioxide, particulate matter, carbon monoxide, ozone, nitrogen dioxide, and lead. The CAA requires the EPA to review and, if appropriate, revise these standards no less often than every five years. State and local governments may set additional, and more stringent, standards.

At any time, a particular area may be "cleaner" or "dirtier" than the national standards for these pollutants. The CAA supplements its nationwide goal of attaining and maintaining these standards with specific goals for these "clean" and "dirty" areas. For the clean areas of the country, the CAA seeks to "prevent the significant deterioration" (PSD) of the air quality, particularly in areas of special natural, recreational, scenic, or historic value. It also seeks to protect the special visibility values of certain clean air areas, for example, the scenic qualities of many parks. For the "dirty" or "nonattainment" areas of the country, the CAA demands that "reasonable further progress" be made toward the attainment and maintenance of the primary and secondary standards, including attainment of the primary health standards by specified deadlines and attainment of the secondary welfare standards "as expeditiously as possible."

Measures

Typically, the measures used by the CAA to pursue its several goals are various performance and emission restrictions on individual sources. In other words, the CAA generally attempts to control overall pollution levels by limiting the amount of pollution emitted into the air by specific sources. These requirements are sometimes technology-forcing, in that they encourage both the general growth of the pollution technology industry and specific applications of advanced technology to individual sources. Examples of the CAA's performance and emissions restrictions read like an alphabet soup of regulatory jargon: NSPS (new source performance standards), NESHAPS (national emission standards for hazardous air pollutants), BACT (best available control technology), BART (best available retrofit technology), RACT (reasonably available control technology), LAER (lowest achievable emission rate), and FMVCP (federal motor vehicle control program).

Means

The CAA uses the State Implementation Plan (SIP) process as the principal means for implementing and enforcing its goals and its source restrictions. In brief, the SIP is a plan devised by the state and approved by EPA with source-specific measures for carrying out the CAA. For example, these plans can include specific emission limitations, transportation controls, and economic incentives for reducing pollution. Through the SIP, the state can allocate its air resource. States may always include measures more stringent than the federal requirements.

PARKS AND THE ACT

Throughout each aspect of the CAA's structure—its goals, measures, and means—are numerous *opportunities* to influence a regulatory agency's action to protect the air quality and related values of parks. Examples of regulatory actions that can affect park air quality protection significantly are the determination of national ambient air quality standards, control technology requirements, state implementation measures, and individual source permits. All of the CAA's regulatory actions involve notice to the public of proposed actions and opportunity for comment. Many provisions require consultation with affected federal land managers, and certain provisions give additional influence to the federal land manager's opinion. Generally, the better the National Park Service's scientific information on the sources and effects of air pollution affecting parks, the more influential the service can be on proposed regulatory actions. By taking advantage of these opportunities, the park service can ensure that EPA and applicable state agencies consider the special benefits and costs of their regulatory decisions with respect to park air quality and related values.

Preventing Significant Deterioration

The prevention of significant deterioration (PSD) title of the CAA is an important authority for protecting the resources of parks. One of its express purposes is "to preserve, protect, and enhance the air quality in national parks, national wilderness areas, national monuments, national seashores, and other areas of special national or regional natural, recreational, scenic, or historic value."[2] PSD addresses resource protection through the establishment of ceilings on additional amounts of air pollution over base-line levels in "clean" air areas, the protection of the air quality-related values of certain special areas, and additional protection for the visibility values of certain special areas. The PSD title reserves an important resource protection role to the federal land manager, which the CAA defines as the secretary of the department with authority over the affected lands. For parklands, the secretary of the interior has delegated his authority as federal land manager to the assistant secretary for fish and wildlife and parks.

More specifically, the PSD title reflects Congress' judgment that, among the "clean" air regions of the country, certain areas—the "Class I" areas—deserve the highest level of air-quality protection. Congress designated 158 areas as Class I areas, including national parks larger than 6,000 acres and national wilderness areas larger than 5,000 acres, in existence on August 7, 1977. These "mandatory" Class I areas may not be redesignated to a less protective classification. Forty-eight areas within the National Park System are designated Class I. (Large national parks and wilderness areas established since 1977, such as most park areas in Alaska, have not been designated subsequently as Class I.)

The PSD title also contains measures that can protect the remaining "clean" areas—the Class II areas. Furthermore, states and Indian governing bodies may redesignate Class II (and Class III) areas to Class I.

Preconstruction Permit

The principal mechanism of the CAA for implementing the special protection for clean air areas is the PSD preconstruction permit program. To obtain a permit, major new and modified sources proposing to locate in "clean" air areas must:

- install "best available control technology";
- analyze all impacts of the proposed source's emissions, together with emissions from "secondary growth" associated with the source, as well as emissions from already existing and permitted sources;
- not violate a national ambient air-quality standard;
- in most cases, not violate an "increment," as described below;
- not have an "adverse impact" on a Class I area; and
- generally have to conduct preconstruction and possibly post-construction monitoring of air quality and, in some cases, additional resources.

In addition, all major new and modified sources with the potential to affect the visibility of a "mandatory Class I" area must obtain a new source permit that assures no adverse impact on the Class I area's visibility, regardless of whether the source proposes to locate in a "clean" or "dirty" air area.

Since 1978, the National Park Service has reviewed many PSD permit applications. Often, the service's involvement has resulted in changes in the proposed permit, such as adoption of more efficient control technology, downsizing of the operation, selection of a new location, commitment for monitoring and study of park resources, and other changes that have helped to protect the potentially affected parks.

A closer examination of the park service's procedure for reviewing a proposed permit for a new source illustrates the importance of combining credible factual information with knowledge of the law. The service's procedure requires:

- the monitoring expert to examine park service data or extrapolate from other data in order to determine existing pollutant levels in potentially affected park areas;
- the modeling expert to determine which park areas would be potentially affected by the source's emissions and to estimate the contribution of these emissions to the park's ambient air;
- the vegetation-effects expert to conduct field surveys of existing air pollution symptomology, perform literature checks of research on the condition of relevant park species at the predicted ambient pollutant concentrations, oversee laboratory and field fumigations to supplement available research, and suggest additional research on and monitoring of park vegetation resources for

recommendation as a condition of the permit;
- the wildlife-effects expert to perform a similar review with respect to park wildlife species;
- the visibility specialist to determine the type and degree of visibility impairment that could result from the predicted pollutant concentrations, and to evaluate the effect of any impairment on the park visitor's experience;

- the control technology expert to examine the proposed engineering process and review the literature in order to determine the "best available control technology" for the source in light of its potential impact on park areas;
- the regulatory expert to examine the proposed permit for compliance with the formidable federal and state legal requirements for new source review, particularly requirements relevant to protection of park resources, and to interact with the appropriate federal and state regulatory officials; and
- the policy expert to help prepare testimony for public hearings consistent with departmental and servicewide policies and to ensure that the applicable federal and state implementation measures include proper involvement of the Service and proper consideration of air pollution impacts on units of the National Park System.

Class I Areas and the Adverse Impact Test

In Class I areas, once baseline is triggered by submission of the first PSD preconstruction permit application from a major new or modified source, the PSD provisions allow only the smallest increment of certain pollutants—initially, only sulfur dioxide and particulate matter—to be added to the air. Actually, the CAA requires EPA to promulgate increments or equivalent protective measures for all pollutants that have national ambient air quality standards. As a result of litigation based on this requirement, EPA promulgated nitrogen oxide increments in 1988.

Of special importance to many parks, the PSD title also establishes a site-specific resource test, known as the adverse impact test, to determine whether emissions from major new and modified sources will cause an "adverse impact" on the "air quality related values" of the class I area. "Air quality related values" include all values of an area dependent upon and affected by air quality, such as scenic, cultural, biological, and recreational resources, including visibility itself. In the case of a major new or modified source, the adverse impact test works as follows:

- If the federal land manager determines, and convinces the permitting authority, that the source will adversely affect the Class I area's resources—even though the source's emissions will not contribute to an increment violation—a "PSD permit" shall not be issued.
- If the federal land manager certifies that the source will not adversely affect the Class I area's resources—even though the source's emissions will contribute to an increment violation—the permitting authority may issue a "PSD permit."

The adverse impact test imposes an "affirmative responsibility" on the federal land manager "to protect the air quality related values (including visibility)" of Class I areas, and, as the Senate committee wrote, "[i]n the case of doubt, . . . [to] err on the side of protecting the air quality related values for future generations."

The National Park Service's current working definition of adverse impact under the CAA is any impact that:

- diminishes the area's national significance; and/or
- impairs the structure and functioning of ecosystems; and/or
- impairs the quality of the visitor experience.

EPA has further defined adverse impact on visibility to mean perceptible visibility changes that "interfere with the management, protection, preservation, or enjoyment of the visitor's visual experience."

Class I and Visibility Protection

In addition to increment ceilings and the adverse impact test, Congress enacted one more resource protection measure for Class I areas, namely, "visibility protection" for the 156 (of 158) statutory Class I areas where visibility is an "important value." In the PSD title of the CAA, "Congress declares as a national goal the prevention of any future, and the remedying of any existing, impairment of visibility in mandatory Class I federal areas which impairment results from manmade air pollution." In this provision, Congress expressed the national desire to preserve the ability to see long distances, entire panoramas, and specific features associated with the statutory Class I areas.

EPA is still developing the regulatory program to assure "reasonable progress" toward the national visibility goal. Prodded by lawsuits,

EPA has issued so-called "Phase I" visibility regulations that address "plume blight" and other visibility impairment "reasonably attributable" to a specific source or sources. EPA has not yet proposed "Phase II" regulations to address visibility impairment from "regional haze."

The current visibility regulations attempt to protect visibility in mandatory Class I areas in several ways. Through "new source review," major new and modified sources may not receive an air quality permit if they will have an adverse impact on visibility within the Class I area. States must establish a monitoring strategy for evaluating visibility conditions, baselines, and trends and develop a long-term (10 to 15 years) strategy for making "reasonable progress" toward eliminating all manmade visibility impairment from mandatory Class I areas. Existing sources found to impair Class I visibility may have to retrofit pollution controls as a result of an analysis to determine best available retrofit technology (BART).

EPA's visibility regulations also allowed the federal land managers until December 31, 1985, to identify "integral vistas," but the secretary of the interior declined to do so. "Integral vistas" are views from inside a mandatory Class I area looking outward to specific important panoramas or landmarks beyond the Class I area's boundaries, which views have scenic, scientific, or cultural importance to the Class I area. The National Park Service issued a preliminary list of integral vistas for its Class I areas on January 15, 1981. Had these vistas been promulgated as final regulations, they would have become mandatory factors for the states to consider in the review of development activities that might impair the vistas. States would not have had to protect these vistas, but would have had to consider vista protection along with energy, economic, and other factors in the decision-making process. As a policy matter, the Department of the Interior has nevertheless encouraged the park service to seek protection of these park-related resources on a case-by-case basis in individual permit and SIP proceedings.

As the above indicates, the CAA creates several opportunities and tools for protecting the resources and values of Class I areas. New pollution after the establishment of baseline in Class I areas is generally limited to the small Class I increment; the federal land manager must determine whether major new and modified sources will affect the areas adversely, and measures must be developed to protect the visibility of Class I areas from manmade pollution impairment. States must develop their PSD plans in consultation with federal land managers and following a public hearing. Major new sources must undergo an equally public permit review involving air quality monitoring; analysis of resource impacts; application of "best available control technology"; and effective emission ceilings based on the Class I increment, national ambient standards, adverse impact threshold, or possibly visibility impairment threshold. Existing sources may be regulated to protect visibility or to remedy a violation of an increment, national ambient standard, or even Class I resource protection.

Class II Areas

The Clean Air Act's concern for resource protection is not limited to Class I areas. Congress designated all other "clean" air regions of the country "Class II." In fact, most of the units of the National Park System are "Class II." Congress prohibited redesignation not only of statutory Class I areas to any other classification, but also of certain Class II areas to the dirtier Class III classification. These so-called Class II floor areas include the following areas when greater than 10,000 acres: national monuments, national primitive areas, national preserves, national recreation areas, national wild and scenic rivers, national wildlife refuges, national lakeshores and seashores, in existence on August 7, 1977, as well as national parks and wilderness areas established since August 7, 1977.

In Class II areas, the Class II increment ceilings on additional pollution over base-line concentrations allow for moderate development. Class II increments constitute an absolute ceiling on additional pollution in these areas, however, because Congress did not qualify the Class II increment with a variance procedure similar to the adverse impact test for Class I areas.

As part of the PSD permit application, major new and modified sources with the potential to affect a park service Class II area must analyze their impacts on the area's ambient air quality, climate and meteorology, terrain, soils and vegetation, and visibility. The Department of the Interior also has encouraged the park service to seek protection of "integral vistas" associated with Class II areas in individual permit and plan proceedings.

Although the act does not create as many resource protection tools for Class II areas as for Class I areas, it nevertheless creates opportunities. The park service can participate in State Implementation Plan proceedings, new source reviews, and other federal, state, and local activities that potentially affect the air quality of these areas. For example, the service can oppose sources that threaten park resources and values, seek more stringent control technology for sources of concern, and recommend special preconstruction and postconstruction monitoring if more information is needed. In proceedings concerning units of the National Park System, the land manager can invoke the strong language of the park system's Organic Act for protection of park purposes and values from adverse air pollution impacts, in addition to the clear mandate of the CAA. Furthermore, as appropriate, the land manager can undertake or encourage efforts to redesignate the area to Class I. (See discussion below on redesignation.)

Class III Areas

At this time, there are no Class III areas. States or Indian governing bodies have the authority to redesignate to Class III any clean air area except a statutory Class I or Class II "floor" area. Class III designation could allow for substantial air pollution increases over base-line concentrations, subject—as with all increments—to the ceiling imposed by the national ambient air quality standards. The redesignation process itself, as well as subsequent new source reviews and implementation proceedings, provide opportunities to seek protection of park values.

Redesignation

By following the CAA's procedural requirements, a state (or Indian governing body, where appropriate) may redesignate any area within its jurisdiction, with the following two exceptions:
- mandatory Class I areas may not be redesignated; and
- Class II "floor" areas may not be redesignated to Class III.

Prior to proposing a redesignation, the redesignating authority must describe and analyze the health, environmental, economic, social, and energy effects of the redesignation. In addition, if the redesignation is to include federal lands, the redesignating authority must provide notice to and opportunity for a conference with the federal land manager. If the federal land manager responds with written comments, the state must explain any inconsistency between those comments and the state's redesignation decision. The CAA establishes additional procedural obstacles for redesignation of "clean" air areas to Class III. For example, such a redesignation requires the legislated concurrence of local governments representing a majority of the residents in the area proposed for redesignation.

The legislative history of the 1977 CAA amendments reveals much controversy over the initial classification of areas. For example, the primary House bill (H.R. 6161) would have designated as mandatory Class I areas all existing national parks and wilderness areas over 25,000 acres in size, and national monuments, primitive areas, and recreation areas over 100,000 acres. It also would have designated as discretionary Class I areas—that is, areas subject to redesignation to Class II—all national parks and wilderness areas between 1,000 and 25,000 acres; international parks over 1,000 acres; and national monuments, primitive areas, recreation areas, and preserves in excess of 10,000 acres. The Senate considered an amendment that would have designated as Class I all national monuments in excess of 10,000 acres that are managed as natural areas. The classification scheme ultimately enacted in the 1977 amendments was necessarily a compromise that included, in addition to the already-described Class I and Class II designations, the following provision:

> The federal land manager shall review all national monuments, primitive areas, and national preserves, and shall recommend any appropriate areas for redesignation as Class I where air quality related values are important attributes of the area.

In compliance with this provision, the federal land manager published the so-called Section 164(d) Report in 1980, finding that 44 of the 95 areas under review possess air quality related values as important attributes based on the areas' enabling legislation, planning documents, and management.

Kerr-McGee Chemical Corporation challenged the Section 164(d) report as it applied to Death Valley National Monument, one of the 44 areas found to merit consideration by the states of California and Nevada for redesignation to Class I. The appellate court rejected the challenge, holding that Kerr-McGee had failed to demonstrate any "legally cognizable injury" as a result of the federal land manager's recommendation. Thus, without a "case or controversy" before it, the court ordered dismissal of the lawsuit. In its opinion, the court said that the federal land manager's recommendation serves neither as a "prerequisite" nor a "trigger" to state redesignation; rather, the federal land manager's recommendation is "purely advisory," and the state may "act independently of and inconsistently with the recommendation" under the scheme of the CAA.[3]

Nonattainment Areas

For parks that are in, or affected by, the "dirty regions" of the country where the national ambient air quality standards have not yet been met, the PSD provisions do not apply. Instead, the "nonattainment" requirements apply.

As with Class II and III areas, the CAA does not generally establish an explicit role (other than consultation) for the federal land manager. One limited exception provides for federal land manager review of a major new or modified source proposing to locate in a nonattainment area in one of the 36 states covered by EPA's visibility regulations, if the source might affect the visibility of a mandatory Class I area.

Nevertheless, the nonattainment title of the CAA provides opportunities to seek park protection in various public proceedings. For example, the state must hold a public hearing prior to promulgating a nonattainment implementation plan, which is a plan for attaining all national ambient air quality standards "as expeditiously as practicable," most primary standards by 1982, and primary standards for ozone and carbon monoxide by 1988. (Since many areas have not yet attained the ozone and carbon monoxide standards, Congress may amend the CAA to extend this deadline and possibly to revise other aspects of the act.)

The nonattainment plan must:

- demonstrate "reasonable further progress" toward the national ambient standards in the interim;
- provide for reasonable available control technology on sources in the area;
- analyze effects on air quality, welfare, health, society, and economics; and
- require a public hearing prior to issuing a permit for a new source.

To obtain a permit, new sources in urban areas must secure from other facilities "emission offsets" greater than the new source's proposed emissions unless the applicable implementation plan otherwise "accommodates" the source. In addition, a new source's control technology must comply with the "lowest achievable emission rate" (LAER) for such a source.

CONCLUSION

Directly or indirectly, CAA provisions can address many air quality and related development concerns affecting parks. However, the

CAA—at least as currently interpreted or implemented—does not address all such resource protection concerns. For example, the CAA often does not deal effectively with the following problems:

- the individual and cumulative air quality impacts of sources not subject to PSD permit requirements, such as "minor" sources, sources located in nonattainment areas, existing sources, sources of "fugitive emissions" (for example, surface coal mines) that require an EPA rule making to make them subject to new source review, and sources located in foreign countries;
- regional loadings of air pollutants, characteristic of regional haze, ozone, and acid deposition;
- long-range transport of air pollutants, also characteristic of regional haze, ozone, and acid deposition; and
- adverse impacts of air pollution on non-Class I units of the National Park System.

For these problems not effectively addressed by the CAA, what remedies for park protection remain? Certain laws contain limited park protection potential, such as Section 522(e) of the Surface Mining Control and Reclamation Act, or common law actions in trespass and nuisance. The use of these remedies to protect parks from the adverse effects of air pollution, however, might be challenged simply because there is a Clean Air Act. In other words, some might argue that Congress addressed the entire subject of air pollution in the CAA and thereby preempted the use of other legal remedies. Others might refute this argument with strong legal and policy reasons for allowing other remedies in situations where the CAA does not protect park property and purposes.

At best, the availability of remedies other than the CAA to address air pollution concerns is uncertain. The CAA, even with its limitations, remains the strongest legal tool to protect park air quality and related values. As discussed in this chapter, the CAA provides several effective approaches to park resource protection. Essential to making the existing statutory authority work for the protection of the resources, however, is the gathering and development of the relevant scientific and technical information on which the legal system depends and effective participation by park managers in decisions affecting park air quality.

SELECTED BIBLIOGRAPHY

Statute and Regulations

Clean Air Act, as amended, 42 U.S.C. §7401 *et seq.*
Legislative History:
S. Rep. No. 127, 95th Cong., 1st Sess. (1977)
H.R. Rep. No. 294, 95th Cong., 1st Sess. (1977)
Environmental Protection Agency Regulations:
Prevention of Significant Deterioration, 40 C.F.R. 51.166, 52.21.
Visibility Protection, 40 C.F.R. 51.300 *et seq.*, 52.26 *et seq.*, 81.400 *et seq.*
Intergovernmental Consultation, 40 C.F.R. 240.

Cases

Prevention of Significant Deterioration:
Alabama Power v. *Costle*, 636 F.2d 323 (D.C. Cir. 1979).
Kerr-McGee Chemical Corp. v. *Dept. of the Interior*, 19 ERC 1372 (9th Cir. 1983).
Sierra Club v. *Thomas*, 658 F. Supp. 165 (N.D. Cal. 1987).
Visibility Protection:
Friends of the Earth, Inc. v. *Costle*, No. 79-2311 (D.C. Cir., filed Nov. 5, 1979).
Mountain States Legal Foundation v. *Costle*, No. 80-2454 (D.C. Cir., filed Dec. 1980).
Environmental Defense Fund v. *Gorsuch*, No. 82-6850, (N.D. Cal., filed Dec. 20, 1982; settled April 19, 1984; settlement amended Sept. 9, 1986; August 26, 1988; and July 6, 1989 (*sub nom. Environmental Defense Fund* v. *Reilly*)).
Maine v. *Environmental Protection Agency*, 29 ERC 1833 (May 18, 1989).
Vermont v. *Thomas*, 850 F.2d 99 (2d Cir. 1988).
Nuisance/Trespass:
United States v. *Atlantic Richfield*, 478 F. Supp 115 (D. Mont. 1979).

Articles and Miscellaneous

Fayad, Elizabeth A., "The Clean Air Act: New Horizons for the National Parks," and Squillace, Mark, "Common Law Protection for Our National Parks," in D. Simon, ed., *Our Common Lands: Defending the National Parks*, (Washington, D.C.: Island Press, 1988).

Impacts of Air Pollution on National Park Units: Hearings before the Subcommittee on National Parks and Recreation of the House Committee on Interior and Insular Affairs, 99th Cong., 1st Sess. (1986).

National Park Service, *Air Quality in the National Parks: Natural Resources Report 88-1* (1988).

Oren, Craig A., "The Protection of Parklands from Air Pollution: A Look at Current Policy," *Harvard Environmental Law Review* 13 (1989):313.

REFERENCES

1. 42 U.S.C. §7401 *et. seq.* (1963).
2. 42 U.S.C. §7470 (2) (1983).
3. *Kerr-McGee Chemical Corp. v. Department of the Interior*, 19 ERC 1372 (9th Cir. 1983).

Chapter 5

The Clean Water Act and Other Tools for Managing Water Resources

by Barbara West

Clean water is an important attribute of virtually every unit of the National Park System whether it provides extensive water-based recreation, serves as the focal point of a significant scenic view, or functions in ways that add valuable dimensions to a historical scene. Water in parks may be a source of drinking water for visitors or integral to the existence and functioning of ecosystems.

Appropriate management of National Park System areas is not limited to the management of water as a single component; the National Park Service seeks to preserve and protect entire ecosystems by maintaining their integrity and by finding ways to avoid interferences with the natural ecosystem processes that perpetuate them. Those natural systems and resources depend on the existing quantity and quality of water to function properly. Ensuring the physical and legal availability of the quantity of water necessary to sustain the continued unimpaired existence and functioning of habitats and ecosystems that form parks is also an important function.

"Single resource" statutes, such as the Clean Water Act with its antidegradation provisions, offer opportunities for park service managers to move toward the goal of preserving and protecting water quality for natural systems. Water quality standards that implement antidegradation and other provisions of the Clean Water Act can be successful in maintaining and enhancing water quality in parks by protecting the water from new discharges in parks and in limiting changes to the quality of water that flows into parks as well.

THE CLEAN WATER ACT AND REGULATING WATER QUALITY

The Clean Water Act, passed in 1972 as amendments to the Federal Water Pollution Control Act, and significantly amended in 1977 and 1987, was designed to restore and maintain the integrity of the nation's water.[1] The law set ambitious goals for the nation's waters: swimmable and fishable waters by 1983 and no further discharge of pollutants into the nation's waterways by 1985. The two strategies incorporated into the act to achieve these goals were a major grant program to assist in the construction of sewage treatment facilities and a program of "effluent limitations" to limit the amount of pollutants that could be discharged. Effluent limitations are the basis for permits issued for all point source dischargers, known as National Pollutant Discharge Elimination System (NPDES) permits. The Environmental Protection Agency (EPA) has set limits for pollutants that may be released based on available technology and cost of treatment for various industrial categories.

Also as part of the act, Congress recognized the primary role of the states in managing and regulating the nation's water quality, within the general framework developed by Congress. Part of that framework, namely Section 313, requires that all federal agencies, including the National Park Service, comply with the requirements of state law for water quality management regardless of other jurisdictional status or land ownership. The act states:

> Each department, agency, or instrumentality of the executive, legislative, and judicial branches of the Federal Government (1) having jurisdiction over any property or facility, or (2) engaged in any activity resulting, or which may result, in the discharge or runoff of pollutants, and each officer, agent, or employee thereof in the performance of his official duties, shall be subject to, and comply with, all Federal, State, interstate, and local requirements, administrative authority, and process and sanctions respecting the control and abatement of water pollution in the same manner and to the same extent as any non-government entity including the payment of reasonable service charges. The preceding sentence shall apply (A) to any requirement whether substantive or procedural (including any recordkeeping or reporting requirement, any requirement respecting permits and any other requirement, whatsoever), (B) to the exercise of any Federal, State, or local administrative authority, and (C) to any process and sanction, whether enforced in Federal, State, or local courts or in any other manner. This subsection shall apply notwithstanding any immunity of such agencies, officers, agents, or employees under any law or rule of law.[2]

The technology-based program of the 1972 act has been largely successful in controlling point source discharges from industrial facilities; substantial progress also has been made with municipal discharges. The program has been less successful in preventing degradation of lakes, rivers near large populations, and marine estuaries. Because of these factors, the continuing existence of toxic pollutants (even where dischargers have installed required pollution control technologies) and persistent non-point source pollution (such things as runoff from streets, construction activities, and farmland), Congress enacted the Water Quality Act of 1987, which amends the 1972 act.[3] This act takes a more water quality-based approach to clean water restoration. The act aims to identify water bodies that have continuing pollution problems and to devise ways of dealing with the problems identified.

Of particular relevance to park service managers, section 319 of the Water Quality Act of 1987 requires that federal development projects, which include most construction projects in parks, be reviewed for their potential effect on water quality and that such projects be "consistent" with the state's nonpoint source pollution management program. The service has worked with states recently to develop memoranda of agreement and other cooperative processes for coordinating state and park service efforts in controlling sources and effects of nonpoint source pollution.

Water Quality Standards

The method by which the states implement the protection of water quality is through water quality standards. Standards are composed of the use or uses made of a water body or segment, the water quality criteria necessary to protect that use or uses, and an antidegradation provision to protect the existing water quality. Criteria are descriptions of maximum or minimum physical, chemical, or biological characteristics of water that reflect tolerances and requirements for human health, aquatic biota, and aesthetics that will protect the defined uses. Uses generally are expressed as such categories as drinking water, fish and wildlife propagation, body contact recreation, or industrial uses. The standards also serve as the basis for water quality-based treatment and establish the water quality goals for the specific stream segment or water body. Every three years, EPA conducts a review of the state's water quality regulatory program, called the triennial review, to determine whether the program is in conformance with EPA policy.

Antidegradation

A state's antidegradation policy represents a three-tiered approach to maintaining and protecting various levels of water quality and uses. At its base, the existing uses of a water segment and the quality level necessary to protect the uses must be maintained. This establishes the absolute floor for water quality.

The second level provides protection of existing water quality in segments where quality exceeds levels necessary to support propagation of fish, shellfish, and wildlife, and recreation in and on the water (that is, those segments meeting the "fishable/swimmable" goals of the Clean Water Act). In such segments, limited water quality degradation can be allowed only after it has been shown through a demonstration process which includes public participation, that the quality will continue to support the "fishable/swimmable" uses.

The third tier provides special protection for waters for which ordinary use classifications may not suffice and which are classified as Outstanding National Resource Waters (ONRW). The purpose of this special protection is to safeguard the state's highest quality waters and also to maintain the quality of waters that have ecological importance. EPA's guidance in the *Water Quality Standards Handbook* states:

> Where high quality waters constitute an outstanding National resource, such as waters of National and state parks and wildlife refuges and waters of exceptional recreational or ecological significance, that water quality shall be maintained and protected.[4]

For waters designated as ONRW, water quality must be maintained and protected and only temporary and short-term changes may be permitted. The specific nature of the protection provided by ONRW designation differs by state, but it often means that no new point source discharges are permitted.

Ordinarily, this category would be thought to protect only the highest quality waters, and indeed, the need to maintain and protect high quality waters is the policy's primary intent. However, the ONRW category also offers a means to protect waters of "ecological significance." These are water bodies that are important, unique, or sensitive ecologically, but whose water quality as measured by traditional parameters (dissolved oxygen, pH, etc.) may not be particularly "high" or whose character cannot be described adequately by these parameters. Such unique waters might include swamps or hot springs.

ONRW as a Resource Management Tool

ONRW designations, either within park system units or for waters outside such units that influence or affect park resources, offer significant potential benefits to the park service.

First, ONRW designations can help ensure protection of water that flows into a park. Although the National Park Service may have responsibility for management of the area within the park's boundaries, water resource-related laws and programs are administered by other agencies. In some cases, it may be possible to develop cooperative working arrangements or agreements that can result in management that, by and large, meets park service management standards. In most cases, however, given differing state goals and objectives for water resources management, it may be difficult to develop agreements that will result in comprehensive resource protection based on a recognition of the interconnected web of natural systems that constitute a unit of the park system. That recognition should also include acknowledgment of the fact that the interconnected web is related to systems outside the park's boundaries. Designation of waters as ONRW can provide protection that closely approximates park service management standards.

Second, developers may be less likely to propose activities for a given area if a designated ONRW would be affected. From an environmental permitting perspective, developers seek areas where they are free from the constraints to development posed by more stringent water quality standards—like those associated with ONRW. If fewer development proposals are made, park staffs will be able to spend their time and energies on park management rather than trying to modify proposed developments that may adversely affect park resources.

Third, ONRW designation can help the Park Service politically. The park service can be perceived negatively by other agencies and some individuals because it is often in the position of opposing developments or activities that have the potential to affect park resources adversely. The nature of park service resources management frequently results in managers seeking to protect the status quo. When a federal land manager appears at a hearing, he or she is rarely perceived as just another landowner. To many, the specter of a federal bully is seen from participation in such processes. ONRW designation for park waters may result in fewer permit applications and, thus, fewer hearings and permit reviews. In such cases, the status quo is protected with no further action required of the park service manager.

Fourth, ONRW shifts the burden of proof onto development proposals. It is often difficult to demonstrate a clear and unequivocal connection between changes to water quality and resource damage. Comprehensive data to prove unequivocally that resource damage will occur are rarely available, and defining what discharges cause "degradation" is a difficult task. In many cases, the effects of discharges on park service resources may be subtle and long term. Because changes would not occur in the short term, it is possible that park service concerns may be discounted or ignored by permitting authorities. However, if there is an ONRW designation, there is less need to prove damage because the designation, in and of itself, allows no degradation. The burden of proof is thus on the proponent to demonstrate there will be no degradation rather than on the park service to prove that there will be degradation (as is the case in the absence of such designations.)

Finally, such designation has administrative benefits for the Park Service. Both EPA and the appropriate state agencies issue a large number of wastewater discharge permits. The sheer number of permits makes it difficult for the staffs of individual parks to keep track effectively of all the actions that may result in impacts to park system units and their resources. Because ONRW designation for designated waters means more stringent standards, there may be less need for additional monitoring of permits by park service managers.

National Park Service Experience with ONRW. In 1986, the staffs of Buffalo National River, the Southwest Regional Office, and the Interior Department solicitor used Arkansas's designation of waters within the park as "Extraordinary Recreational and Aesthetic Value" (the equivalent of ONRW designation) as one of the bases for protesting the issuance of a permit for a landfill near the park. The park service believed, and was supported by available data, that because of the karst geology of the area, there was a significant potential for degrading waters within the unit if the landfill were to be constructed. ONRW-equivalent status for waters within Buffalo River provided a framework that was used as the basis for park service arguments concerning the need for enhanced resource protection. On appeal to the Arkansas Department of Pollution Control and Ecology, the permit was denied, based at least partially on the park service's arguments. An appeal is pending before the Arkansas Supreme Court.

In another case, a catfish farm in Oklahoma was discharging nutrient-laden effluent without a permit into a tributary of Lake of the Arbuckles, an ONRW in Chickasaw National Recreation Area, which also serves as the source of drinking water for several nearby towns. The discharge was located about one mile upstream of the park's boundary. In the permit proceedings, protection of the ONRW was the basis for much of the testimony. Unfortunately, the water quality standard applicable to the tributary was much less stringent than the ONRW classification for the lake. So even though the lake is designated ONRW, the discharges to the tributary could have adversely affected the recreation area's resources. The final decision of the Oklahoma Water Resources Board recognized the potential for adverse impact on the ONRW at Lake of the Arbuckles from discharges to the tributary. The Board put seasonal discharge limitations on the catfish farm that are designed to limit the addition of nutrients to the lake during the summer months when the potential for eutrophication is greater. The park service is continuing to monitor for adverse effects.

Guidance to Park Service Managers. The National Park Service has suggested that park managers take some, or all, of the following actions to facilitate ONRW designation for waters that are within or may affect park units.

- *Work with states.* There are wide variations in the programs and policies of the states. Some have prepared detailed guidelines on how to apply for such designations (Arizona, for example) with clearly delineated criteria that the water body must meet in order to be designated. In other states, the statutes implementing the Clean Water Act may mention ONRW or its equivalent and provide no information on how the bodies are selected or designated. In either circumstance, ONRW identification and designation requires working closely with state agency officials to prepare an application or petition for designation. Where the state has not established procedures already, the park service should participate in decisions that influence how the state goes about structuring and defining its application processes.
- *Develop information.* The park service should develop infor-

mation that clearly describes the role and importance of water quality in perpetuating park ecosystems. The more information provided to the state on the quality of the water resources, the ways in which the water functions as part of the park's ecosystem(s), and the ways in which visitors and wildlife use the water resources for which designation is being sought, the more likely the state will be able to act positively on the application for designation. If the uses of the water or purposes for which the unit was established are positively correlated with the quality of the water, for example, the park service should make that clear.

- *Seek consistency with plans.* Information should be developed as part of the park's planning process (Statement for Management, Development Concept Plans, General Management Plan, Resource Management Plan, Water Resources Management Plan, and others) that supports application for designation as ONRW. This information should be supported by park service actions as well. For example, if any park service activities, such as road or trail construction or use of pesticides, could adversely affect water resources, the environmental assessments or other documentation should make it clear that protection and preservation of high quality waters in the unit is of overriding importance to the service. If necessary, plans and specifications should be modified to ensure protection of water resources.

- *Develop public understanding.* The park service should make sure that its actions to have ONRW designated are clearly understood. Park service proposals should be shared with and explained thoroughly to local landowners, industries, civic groups, and other potentially interested parties. If there is resistance or opposition to ONRW proposals, the service may find it worthwhile to reconsider the way in which the information has been presented or how the proposal has been explained. The park service should work with the state agency to ensure that the two of them can function as partners rather than as adversaries in the designation process.

- *Develop broad-based support.* The park service manager needs to work as closely as possible with other groups that may be interested in protecting the water in the park, such as local hunting and fishing organizations, local Audubon chapters, and civic or environmental groups. Where waters of park system units serve as sources of drinking water, the local units of government or water management districts often support applications for ONRW status.

- *Convey support to the state.* The park service manager needs to apprise the states of service support for ONRW designations. In some circumstances, property owners whose lands are adjacent to or near waters that are candidates for ONRW may not support ONRW designation. On the other hand, it is difficult to imagine a circumstance in which a park service manager would not support ONRW designation. States that find themselves under pressure from EPA or the public to implement antidegradation policies may be unaware that the service supports such designations for park units.

Areas for Further Action on ONRW. Most of the states that have ONRW programs specifically address "national parks." When Congress or the National Park Service uses the term, it is synonymous with any unit in the National Park System as directed by the 1970 amendment to the Organic Act that calls for all units to be accorded the same degree of protection. When "national park" is used by the states, it may mean *only* national parks and may not include monuments, recreation areas, national lakeshores, national rivers, national historical parks, or other units of the national park system. Managers may find it useful to consult with the appropriate state agency to determine the reach of the state program. If park system units other than "parks" are not included as ONRW, the triennial review of each state's water quality standards is the time for service to raise the question and resolve the issue. In addition, some states have petition processes that allow individuals or agencies to propose changes to state standards and policies.

Many times, the "uses" for which water is valuable in National Park System units are not considered to be "uses" for the purpose of water quality standards. Or the uses in the system units represent a small segment of a longer or larger water system and thus are not accounted for in the state's water quality standards. For example, the San Antonio River links the Spanish colonial missions that make up San Antonio Missions National Historical Park in San Antonio, Texas. Indeed, the river's existence made possible the farming and pastoral activities that were at the heart of the decision to locate the missions. Upstream and downstream of the park, the river is used for light industrial purposes and the water quality standards reflect those uses. In spite of the standards, however, many park visitors wade, swim, and fish in the river—uses that clearly are not contemplated by the existing water quality standards. Greater protection of park visitors and resources could occur if the park service were able to identify the uses served by water in system units and to communicate those uses to the state. Cooperative efforts should enable mutually satisfactory accommodations.

It is not clear how ONRW designations affect state policies and programs concerning nonpoint source pollution. As of mid-1989, a suit was pending in the federal court for the Southern District of Florida brought by the U.S. attorney against the South Florida Water Management District and the Florida Department of Environmental Regulation. It alleges, among other things, that the Outstanding Florida Waters (OFW) designation (which is equivalent to ONRW) for Everglades National Park requires special efforts to abate sources of nonpoint pollution that threaten to change the composition and functioning of ecosystems that the park was established to preserve. It is not clear to what extent ONRW designations require special attention to potential nonpoint pollution or whether the designations relate only to point sources.

PROTECTING THE QUANTITY OF WATER

The regulatory scheme that protects the *quality* of water in park system units is, as the discussion above amply illustrates, a complicated one. Obtaining the *quantity* of water necessary to achieve the purposes for which units of the National Park System have been established is not only complicated, it is politically thorny as well. The federal government's activities in reserving lands for specific purposes can come into conflict with state systems for the adjudication of water rights because of the differing purposes and needs that water serves.

Rights to water in park system units generally are governed in accordance with one of two doctrines: the riparian or the prior appropriation. The riparian doctrine, generally applicable in the Eastern states where water is fairly plentiful, is based on English common law and gives owners of land bordering streams the right to reasonable use of water from the streams. The riparian water right is incident to ownership of the land and the use must remain in the watershed. The federal government's riparian rights as a landowner are no different from the rights of other landowners.

In the arid Western states, another doctrine developed that better suited the geography and climate of that area, that of prior appropriation. The basic principles of prior appropriation grew from the fact that there was not adequate water to supply completely the demands of industry—principally mining—and agriculture with the use of water control facilities at the time.

The phrase, "first in time, first in right," has been used to describe the prior appropriation system. An appropriation generally requires an intent to use, a diversion of water, and putting the water diverted to a "beneficial" use. For park managers, the prior appropriation doctrine poses difficulties. In parks, water is valued in situ, conserved as a part of the natural landscape. As such, the undiverted water in parks does not meet the tests enumerated above for an appropriation. In some prior appropriation states, instream or in situ purposes— such as for fishery or recreation—are recognized as beneficial uses, but generally they are not.

Reserved Federal Water Rights

Because of the inherent conflict between federal purposes, such as the needs of parks, and state prior appropriation laws, the doctrine of reserved federal water rights was first enunciated in *Winters* v. *United States*.[5] In that case, the U.S. Supreme Court stated, "The power of the Government to reserve the waters and exempt them from state laws is not denied, and could not be." In this case, the Court held that when the United States sets aside an Indian reservation, it impliedly reserves sufficient water to fulfill the purposes of the reservation. The Court further held that the priority date for the reserved water right is the date of the establishment of the reservation, not the date at which the water is put to use.

Fifty years elapsed after the *Winters* doctrine was articulated before its principles were extended to other lands reserved by the federal government for specific purposes, such as national parks and monuments and national wildlife refuges. In the landmark case, *Arizona* v. *California*[6], the Court agreed with the conclusion that "the United States intended to reserve water sufficient for the future requirements of the Lake Mead National Recreation Area, the Havasu Lake National Wildlife Refuge, the Imperial National Wildlife Refuge, and the Gila National Forest." The implied reservation of water was for the amount necessary to fulfill the purposes of the reservations, and no more.

Complicating factors for federal reserved water rights are how to quantify the rights and how to fit the reserved rights into state appropriative systems. In another major case, *Cappaert v. United States*[7], a reserved federal water right came into direct conflict with established uses under state water law. Devil's Hole was set aside as part of Death Valley National Monument by presidential proclamation in 1952 to protect an underground pool occupied by an endangered species of desert pupfish. In 1968, the Cappaerts began pumping water for irrigation from groundwater that had the same source as the water for Devil's Hole, which caused the water level in the pool to drop. With the drop in the water level, continued existence of the pupfish was in jeopardy because the habitat required for pupfish reproduction would be eliminated. The United States sued to enjoin the pumping, which was upheld by the Supreme Court. In the opinion, the Court stated: "Since a pool is a body of water, the protection contemplated is meaningful only if the water remains; the water right reserved by the 1952 Proclamation was thus explicit, not implied." The decision allowed for the water level in the pool to drop only to the extent that the scientific value of the pool as the habitat for the pupfish would remain unimpaired.

Reserving for Specific Purposes

The difficulty posed by the question of the quantity of rights that are to be reserved, regardless of the forum, is that the amount to be reserved is that amount necessary to achieve the purposes of the reservation and no more. The question of what constitutes federal purposes was directly addressed in *United States* v. *New Mexico*.[8] In its opinion, the Court drew a distinction between the "primary" purposes of the Gila National Forest—as enunciated in the Forest Service Organic Act—and "secondary" purposes—expressed in supplemental statutes enacted after the withdrawal of the forest. In this case, the primary purposes of forests were found to be timber production and securing favorable conditions of water flows; the secondary purposes included aesthetics, wildlife preservation, and recreation, among others.

The Court made clear, however, that the distinction between primary and secondary purposes for forests was not necessarily a distinction that would apply broadly to parks. Justice Rehnquist, writing for the majority, said:

Any doubt as to the relatively narrow purposes for which national forests were to be reserved is removed by comparing the broader language Congress used to authorize the establishment of national parks. In 1916, Congress created the National Park Service and provided that the "fundamental purpose of said parks, monuments, and reservations is to conserve the scenery and the natural and historic objects and the wild life therein and to provide for the enjoyment of the same unimpaired for the enjoyment of future generations."[9]

The Role of States

States have maintained repeatedly that state courts are the appropriate forum for the adjudication of all federal water rights. However, to protect the water in park system units and quantify the amount necessary to achieve the purposes for their reservation, the service must participate in state adjudication proceedings only where there is a general stream adjudication. The McCarran Amendment[10] enacted this limited waiver of sovereign immunity where there is a general adjudication of all the rights of various owners on a given stream or in a stream basin. The waiver of sovereign immunity does not apply unless all the owners of water rights in the stream to be adjudicated are included. The McCarran Amendment similarly is not applicable where a state or person may wish to sue the United States on a water rights issue unrelated to a general stream adjudication.

By their ability to determine when general stream adjudications will take place, the states are proceeding with efforts to quantify federal reserved rights and other water rights. This is because the prior appropriation system requires precision and predictability in order to ascertain what rights are senior to others. The federal reserved right militates against this precision and predictability until it is quantified. As a consequence, the next decade should see the initial quantification of park service reserved rights and other federal and Indian reserved rights in state courts. This process should result in whatever accommodations are necessary to provide the amount of water to achieve federal purposes, on the one hand, and to provide certainty for states and nonfederal appropriators, on the other.

PROTECTION OF WETLANDS

Wetlands include marshes, swamps, streambeds, bogs, mudflats, and other wet and water-influenced lands that currently amount to about 5 percent of the lands in the continental United States. Only about half of the original wetlands in the lower 48 states remain. And in spite of some regulatory measures that have been instituted to slow the rate of loss, some 300,000 to 450,000 acres of wetlands are lost annually.

Wetlands constitute critical components of most ecosystems managed by the park service. For example, wetlands are centers of primary production. Decomposition processes in wetlands convert the plant tissue produced into forms that are usable as food by higher organisms. Nutrients and debris flushed from wetlands into downstream systems increase riverine and estuarine productivity. Some of the other beneficial functions and values of wetlands include fish and wildlife habitat, flood control, erosion control, and water quality maintenance.

Executive Order 11990

The protection of wetland areas in National Park System units is provided primarily by Executive Order 11990, Protection of Wetlands, and by Section 404 of the Clean Water Act. The executive order directs federal agencies to "minimize the destruction, loss or degradation of wetlands, and to preserve and enhance the natural and beneficial values of wetlands." For the park service, this means that there must be a wetlands inventory of all lands subject to public use or development and where impacts are likely to be greatest. The purpose of wetlands inventories is to ensure that in parks, where there is a "practicable alternative," park service managers will seek to avoid any action with the potential for adversely affecting wetlands. Adverse impacts to wetlands can come from actions in wetlands, from actions external to wetlands that may nonetheless affect the wetlands, or from actions that otherwise, directly or indirectly, support wetland development. Park service guidance for complying with the executive orders, Floodplain Management and Wetland Protection Guidelines, was published in the *Federal Register*.[11]

As an example, at Jean Lafitte National Historical Park in Louisiana, another federal agency proposed a major flood levee alignment that would have paralleled the boundary of the Barataria Unit of the park that is located about 15 miles south of New Orleans. The Barataria Unit was established specifically to focus on the ecology of the Mississippi River Delta and consists of bayous, freshwater swamps, and marshes. It is composed almost entirely of wetlands and is one of the few such remaining wetlands in the region. The levee alignment would have deprived the unit of the sheet flow of water essential to the functioning of the wetland ecosystem. The agency changed its construction plans, at least in part because of the service's contentions regarding the potential for adverse impacts and the requirements to avoid adverse effects in the executive order on wetlands.

Section 404 Permits

Section 404 of the Clean Water Act gives the U.S. Army Corps of Engineers lead responsibility for regulating the discharge of "dredged or fill material" in the "waters of the United States." The Clean Water Act's definition of "waters of the United States" is a broad one that brings most waters, and many wetlands, under the regulatory purview of Section 404. Examples of regulated activities include filling to create development sites, most work in stream channels, and water resource projects such as dams or levees. Park service construction or development activities are subject to Section 404 to the same extent that any private construction or development activities would be.

Where activities regulated under Section 404 may have adverse effects on resources in parks, the park service may, like any other person, comment on or protest the issuance of a Section 404 permit. In some cases, such public comments result in modifications to the permits by requiring changes in the location of the dredge or fill activities or by requiring "offsets"—that is, by requiring the restoration or creation of other wetlands to offset the losses that would result from the permitted activity. In rare cases, public comments have resulted in the complete denial of Section 404 permits. The park service can successfully participate in Section 404 permitting processes by preparing comments that conclusively demonstrate the degree to which the permitted activity would adversely affect park resources.

In some respects, however, Section 404 is much less protective of wetlands than a superficial look at its provisions would suggest. It is primarily the discharge of dredged or fill materials that is regulated, rather than potential effects on wetlands. As a consequence, if an activity which is outside a wetland and which does not involve dredged or fill material would have an adverse effect on a wetland—such as groundwater pumping—it is probably beyond the regulatory reach of Section 404.

Because neither the executive order nor Section 404 has stemmed the accelerating loss of wetlands, President Bush proposed to the U.S. Congress, and EPA has adopted, a "no net loss" policy for wetlands. Although the policy has not yet been implemented, a no net loss program would establish a national goal of protecting both the acreage and function of the nation's remaining wetland resource. The program would aim toward the long-term goal of restoring the quality and quantity of the nation's wetland resource base. Achieving both of these goals will require not only that losses to existing wetlands be reduced significantly, but also that restoration, including mitigation or creation of new wetlands, be increased.

PROTECTION OF FLOODPLAINS

Federal policy respecting floodplains is founded on complementary bases—the need for protecting life and property, on the one hand, and the need for protecting the natural and beneficial values of floodplains, on the other. The foundation for floodplain protection and management resides in Executive Order 11988, Floodplain Management, signed May 24, 1977. The thrust of the executive order, like the one on wetlands, is to ensure that federal agency construction and development activities that may affect, or take place in, floodplains have been evaluated carefully and that there are no practicable alternatives. Where facilities already exist in floodplains, the executive order requires that floodproofing of structures or other flood protection measures be instituted. (Park service guidance for dealing with floodplain issues is found in the aforementioned Floodplain Management and Wetland Protection Guidelines.)

Floodplains can present significant issues for park resource managers. In the West, riparian zones near stream courses can be rare and unique ecosystems that provide shade, water, and protection from the wind. People naturally gravitate to such areas for picnicking and camping. Unfortunately, such areas are frequently high-hazard flood zones as well. In addition, it is not unusual for historic and cultural resource properties to be located in floodplains. Park service managers need to ensure that warning systems exist where they are warranted, that flood elevations are marked to increase public awareness of flood hazards, and that, to the extent possible, campgrounds and other public use facilities are floodproofed or located outside floodplains of concern.

CONCLUSION

Each of the tools for protecting water in national park system units described in this chapter—effluent limitations, antidegradation, securing water rights, protecting wetlands and floodplains—requires familiarity with complex legislative, regulatory, and legal systems. Effective use of these tools also requires understanding the equally complex physical, chemical, hydrological, and biological components and processes that characterize natural systems related to water and water-dependent resources in parks. The complexities of both, however, should not discourage park managers from making use of them.

There are significant difficulties in protecting park water resources, the most important being that the park managers have little direct regulatory control over the disposition of water resources. State pollution control agencies determine what discharges may occur within park boundaries and what discharges may take place near parks that can affect water resources within parks. State courts or other water agencies have initial control over determining the extent of water rights recognized for parks. As a consequence, the park service is often in the position of having to demonstrate how water functions in a park context. Thus, the more knowledge one has about the water in the park—the amount, its specific chemical make-up, its relationship to flora and fauna—the greater one's ability to realize park goals and objectives effectively in these sometimes hostile forums.

Moreover, intimate knowledge of the water resources of parks in scientific terms must be wedded to a negotiating strategy that aims at forging a partnership between the park service and the states. The service cannot achieve its goals for effective park management if accommodations with state regulatory agencies have not been reached. This is the challenge and advantage of working with the states: without state support, park service management of water resources falls short of the mark; with state agreement, park service management standards become the policy not only for the service itself but for the state as well.

The potential benefits of skillful use of the water quality and quantity regulatory systems are significant. Because of the importance of water to the very core of what many park units are and why they were created, successful use of the tools provided by these systems really is not an option for park managers; it is a necessity.

REFERENCES

1. 33 U.S.C. §1251, *et. seq.*
2. 33 U.S.C. §1251 *et. seq.* (1983); Pub. Law no. 92-500, Section 313.
3. P.L. 100-4, February 4, 1987.
4. U.S. Environmental Protection Agency, Office of Water Regulations and Standards (Dec. 1983), 2-13.
5. 207 U.S. 564 (1908).
6. 373 U.S. 546 (1963).
7. 426 U.S. 128 (1976).
8. 438 U.S. 696 (1978).
9. Ibid.
10. 43 U.S.C. §666.
11. 45 Fed. Reg. 35916, with minor revisions on 47 Fed. Reg. 36718.

Chapter 6

The Endangered Species Act

by Don Barry

The attorney who successfully blocked Tellico Dam in the snail darter case before the U.S. Supreme Court once said that when Congress enacts legislation, it launches an unguided missile. His analogy between legislation and missiles was quite accurate, especially in the context of a statute like the Endangered Species Act of 1973 (ESA).[1] During the passage of such legislation, the chief sponsors of a bill and various congressional committees attempt to define the bill's direction and impact through floor debates, committee report language, and other indicators of congressional legislative intent. When a bill is enacted into law, its legislative history is supposed to guide the bill's implementation by the executive branch and its interpretation by the courts.

Where a statute's legislative history is ambiguous or lacking, however, the issuance of implementing regulations, agency legal opinions, and judicial decrees begins to give the statute a life of its own, thereby allowing the legislative "missile" to veer off in directions that may not have been intended or foreseen by its authors. Some would argue that this has been the case with the ESA. In comparison with other modern environmental statues like the Clean Air Act or the Clean Water Act, the ESA stands out for its clarity and simplicity. Its goals seemed safe and laudatory—almost patriotic: the preservation of the nation's fish, wildlife, and plant heritage threatened with extinction. Originally viewed as noncontroversial and uncontentious, the ESA was passed by overwhelming margins in both the House and Senate.

However, in their haste to jump on the natural heritage preservation bandwagon, most members of Congress overlooked an innocuous paragraph tucked away in the middle of the bill under the vaguely optimistic heading of "Interagency Cooperation." Section 7 of the ESA[2] was little debated or discussed; the legislative history on the section is minimal. Yet section 7 and other sections of the bill that passed contain language that eventually was interpreted to make the ESA one of the most rigid and protective federal environmental laws in existence. The legislative guppy, as things turned out, was given the teeth of a piranha.

DEFINING KEY TERMS

Section 3 of the ESA[3] is the "definitional" section of the act and is a logical starting point for understanding how the ESA works. A few key definitions stand out in this section:

Conservation

Perhaps most important of all is the definition for the word *conserve* or *conservation*. The ESA defines this concept in exceptionally broad terms to mean the application of all modern natural resource management methods and procedures necessary to bring an endangered or threatened species back from the brink of extinction to a state of full recovery. This definition is the heart of the ESA, the primary purpose of which is to promote the "conservation" and recovery of species listed under the act.

Person

The definition of the word *person* is also important because it expressly includes departments or instrumentalities of a local, state, or federal government. The significance of this definition is that all of the prohibitions of the ESA apply to "persons" under the jurisdiction of the United States. Thus, the definition of the word *person* expressly applies the prohibitions and penalties of the ESA to governmental employees and agencies, in addition to members of the general public.

Not all environmental laws are interpreted as applying to agencies of the federal government. Quite to the contrary, there is an old rule of statutory construction that holds that laws of general applicability will not be interpreted as applying to the sovereign (post-1787 interpreted to mean the Executive Branch), unless the particular act expressly indicates a contrary intent. Thus, laws like the Bald and Golden Eagle Protection Act have been interpreted by the Interior Department as not applying to the federal government. By expressly including governmental agencies and instrumentalities in the definition of persons, however, Congress signaled its intent in the ESA to provide listed species with the broadest protection and coverage possible.

Species

Another important definition is of the word *species*. This includes plants and animals and not only subspecies, but also distinct "population" segments of any species of vertebrate fish or wildlife that interbreed when mature. This latter concept of "populations" provides considerable flexibility to the listing process by affording a declining isolated population of a species protection under the act, even though the species as a whole is still fairly stable; grizzly bears, bald eagles, and timber wolves in the lower 48 states, for example, have all been listed under the ESA on the basis of "populations," despite the presence of large numbers of these species in Alaska or Canada.

Secretary

The definition of the word *secretary* is also important because it splits primary jurisdiction under the ESA between the secretary of the interior (through the U.S. Fish and Wildlife Service) and the secretary of commerce (through the National Marine Fisheries Service), depending upon the particular listed species involved. Understanding this division of labor is important because one needs to know which "secretary" has the lead for law enforcement purposes, the listing process, and Section 7 consultation for a given species.

Take

The final key definition in Section 3 is of the word *take*. Under Section 10 of the ESA, no "person" may "take" an endangered species. Take is defined in exceptionally broad terms and could include, among other things, "harming" or "harassing" a listed species, whether intentional or not.

The concept of "harm" was not defined further in the ESA itself but was in subsequent regulations published to implement the act. Harm was defined to include, among other things, habitat or environmental degradation which resulted in the actual death or injury of a listed species.[4] Thus, a private developer or government agency could be guilty of a "taking" violation under the ESA as the result of habitat modifications which directly and adversely affected a listed species. In an extreme situation, the specter of a federal criminal prosecution resulting from the development of private property could raise interesting constitutional questions concerning the Fifth Amendment's prohibition on "taking" private property without just compensation, but so far these questions have been more hypothetical than real. The absence of much litigation on this point may be due more to cautious and restrained law enforcement in the area of private development rights than to any other factor.

LISTING SPECIES

With these key definitions in mind, one should next become familiar with the so-called listing process under the ESA. Species that are afforded protection under the act are designated by regulation into one or two categories—either "endangered" or "threatened," with the former category applying to species faced with the greatest danger of extinction.

Species are designated as endangered or threatened pursuant to informal rule-making procedures set out in Section 4 of the ESA.[5] Basically, the process involves the publication of a proposed listing regulation in the *Federal Register* with an opportunity for public comment. As a general matter, the "critical habitat" of a proposed species is also supposed to be delineated in the *Federal Register* proposed rule-making, unless the secretary concludes that the publication of critical habitat maps or location descriptions would affect the species' survival adversely.

The criteria in Section 4 for listing a species as endangered or threatened are based upon biological factors only and the best scientific and commercial data available. Significantly, the economic consequences of listing a species are not to be taken into account in the listing process itself, although economic considerations may influence the amount of critical habitat that is designated ultimately.

Strict time constraints apply to the listing process and were imposed by Congress in 1983 to ensure that the listing process continued to operate smoothly and efficiently without undue delays. Although more than 530 resident species in this country are currently on the endangered and threatened species list, another 3,883 species have been identified as "candidates" for listing. Of these 3,883 species, 885 have been classified into what is known as category I status, meaning that adequate biological data currently exist for actually listing the species, but that the limited bureaucratic resources of the U.S. Fish and Wildlife Service (FWS) and the National Marine Fisheries Service (NMFS) have created a backlog in the listing process for the species. Internal management goals for the FWS have set annual listing objectives under the ESA at around 50 new species per year, so the enormous backlog of species will constantly overwhelm the listing process.

PROTECTIONS AFFORDED BY LISTING

Assuming for a moment that a declining species "plunged to the top" of the priority candidate list and subsequently slugged its way through the listing process to the endangered species list, what then? What benefits flow to a species protected under the ESA?

At the risk of oversimplification, the primary benefits fall into one of three categories. First, the species qualifies for specific planning measures, including federal and state financial assistance for conservation programs to enhance its recovery. Section 5 of the ESA[6] directs the secretaries of the interior, commerce, and agriculture to develop and implement conservation programs for species listed under the act. Generally, this would include not only the drafting of a specific "recovery plan" for each species that is designed to restore it to full health and recovery but also could involve the acquisition of the habitat. State financial assistance and cooperation in this recovery effort would be encouraged via Section 6 of the act.[7]

Apart from whatever financial benefits might arise, a listed species is also accorded a second significant benefit under the ESA through the imposition of civil and criminal penalties of up to $25,000 for violating the prohibitions of the act. These prohibitions generally fall into one of two categories: prohibitions against commercial trade in the species and prohibitions against the "taking" of a listed species. If a species is listed as *endangered*, the prohibitions set out in Section 9 of the act[8] automatically apply as a matter of statutory law; the secretary is left with very little discretion to waive these prohibitions. If, however, a given species is listed as *threatened*, Section 4(d) of the ESA[9] grants the secretary broad regulatory discretion to fashion a set of prohibitions individually tailored to meet the particular needs of a given threatened species. Thus, the scope of protection under the ESA may vary, depending on whether it is listed as endangered or threatened.

Another difference in the level of protection turns upon whether the listed species in question is a plant or a listed species of fish or wildlife. Plants generally are accorded less protection under the ESA than wildlife, especially in matters involving takings. Thus, while Section 9 of the act protects endangered species of fish or wildlife from all forms of takings, it only protects endangered plants from takings in narrowly defined circumstances. In particular, it is only illegal to take an endangered plant on federal lands where it has been dug up and removed from the property or where it has been maliciously damaged or destroyed; the incidental or accidental destruction of an endangered plant on federal lands is not prohibited. Moreover, endangered plants are only protected from takings on nonfederal land where the taking was in knowing violation of any law or regulation of a state or in the course of any violation of a state criminal trespass law. Therefore, the degree of protection under the ESA is dependent not only upon whether a species was listed as endangered or threatened, but also on whether it is a plant or a species of fish or wildlife.

The third benefit associated with listing under the ESA generally has proven to be the most significant. Despite its inauspicious beginnings, Section 7 of the ESA[10] has become the most visible, effective, and controversial section of the act. As noted by former Chief Justice Warren Burger in the snail darter decision, *Tennessee Valley Authority v. Hill*,[11] Section 7 is painfully straightforward and to the point. It is directed at federal agencies and has two parts to it—one affirmative in nature and the other prohibitive in nature. Subsection 7(a)(1)[12] directs federal agencies to use their existing authorities in furtherance of endangered and threatened species conservation. Thus, federal agencies no longer can claim that endangered species enhancement is beyond their mission or authority.

The second part of Section 7, subsection 7(a)(2),[13] is prohibitive in nature and requires each federal agency to ensure that any action that it authorizes, funds, or carries out is not likely to jeopardize the continued existence of an endangered or threatened species *or* to result in the destruction or adverse modification of a listed species' designated critical habitat. Subsection 7(a)(2) has two distinct parts to it— the prohibition against "jeopardy" and the prohibition against the adverse modification or destruction of critical habitat. Each of these hurdles must be cleared separately and independently in order for a project affecting endangered or threatened species to move forward. Subsection 7(a)(2) also applies with equal protective force to threatened species as well as to endangered species and makes no distinction between listed plants or species of fish or wildlife. And while it is true that subsection 7(a)(2) only applies to the actions of federal agencies, the presence of the federal government in our daily lives is so sweeping that few activities affecting listed species will escape the impact of Section 7.

Mandatory Consultation

To assist federal agencies in assessing the impacts of their proposed actions upon listed species, Section 7 requires mandatory consultation with either the FWS or NMFS prior to taking final administrative action on a proposal which "may affect" a listed species or its critical habitat. An elaborate consultation process has been developed.[14] Most consultations are conducted "informally" between the agency proposing the action and the FWS or NMFS. Informal consultation is designed to provide a fast and flexible review of a project's potential impacts upon a listed species or critical habitat.

This part of Section 7 (part 402) also provides for "early consultation," which is a mechanism for getting a preliminary and tentative "biological opinion" regarding a proposal's impacts upon listed species at the earliest stages in an agency's planning process. Months later, as the action agency's decision making is brought to a close, the preliminary biological opinion from the FWS or NMFS prepared during "early consultation" must be reconfirmed and recertified for continued accuracy by the relevant federal wildlife agency.

Biological Opinions

In addition to "informal" and "early" consultation, part 402 sets out the procedures for "formal consultation" between the action agency and FWS or NMFS. Formal consultation generally must be completed within 90 days of its initiation and results in the issuance of a written biological opinion from the FWS or NMFS. A biological opinion contains the best biological judgment of the FWS or NMFS as to what the likely impacts would be on a listed species or its critical habitat as the result of a proposed federal activity. If the biological opinion concludes that a proposed activity is not likely to result in "jeopardy" or adverse modification or destruction of critical habitat, the federal action agency can move forward in its decision making fairly confident that its proposed action will withstand any legal challenge under the ESA. The reason for this is rather simple—the courts have accorded the biological opinions of the FWS and NMFS a great deal of deference and have been most reluctant to overturn a "no jeopardy" biological opinion. Thus, having a "no jeopardy" biological opinion in an agency's administrative record substantially enhances an agency's standing under the ESA, if a legal challenge claiming a violation of Section 7 is filed.

For the same reason, however, if a biological opinion concludes that a proposed action is likely to jeopardize the continued existence of a listed species or adversely modify or destroy its critical habitat, the proposing agency moves forward with the proposed project at its own peril and becomes very vulnerable to a legal challenge under Section 7. With only one very narrow and limited exception involving oil and gas leasing off the coast of Alaska (*Village of False Pass* v. *Watt*[15]; *Tribal Village of Akutan, et al.* v. *Hodel, et al.*[16]), the courts have never ignored the conclusions and advice in a "jeopardy" biological opinion from FWS or NMFS. Thus, while biological opinions are only advisory in nature, and Section 7(a)(2) does not provide the FWS or NMFS with an outright veto over agency decision making, a negative biological opinion can be the kiss of death, so to speak, in the administrative record for a proposed project or agency action, especially given the high degree of deference accorded biological opinions by the courts.

One clue for explaining this high degree of judicial deference might be found in former Chief Justice Burger's opinion in the snail darter case. In distinguishing appropriate judicial remedies for violations of the National Environmental Policy Act of 1969 (NEPA) versus violations of the ESA, Chief Justice Burger alluded to the fact that a judicial error in an endangered species case could result in the extinction of the species. Perhaps this most permanent of adverse consequences explains the reluctance on the part of the judiciary to ignore the biological advice from federal wildlife agency experts.

Alternatives and Exemptions

Despite the protectiveness of the courts, receiving an adverse biological opinion need not always spell outright doom for a given proposed project. Section 7 requires the FWS and NMFS to include within any "jeopardy" biological opinion such "reasonable and prudent alternatives" as may exist that would still allow the proposed project to move forward, albeit in modified form. In fact, the vast majority of projects that have received "jeopardy" biological opinions ultimately have been modified to the satisfaction of the FWS or NMFS.

In the rare case, however, where either reasonable and prudent alternatives do not exist, or where the action agency or project sponsor refuses to alter or modify the original proposal, the ESA was amended to contain an exemption process to deal with irreconcilable conflicts between proposed projects and endangered species conservation. Added in 1978 in response to the Tellico Dam decision, Sections 7(e) through (n)[17] establish an elaborate cabinet-level review committee—a so-called "God squad"—empowered to waive various provisions of the ESA, including Section 7. Since the decision is moved up to the highest levels of the agencies involved, an incentive is provided to the parties to reach consensus early on in the process.

Ironically, despite frequent complaints about the ESA from the development community and certain federal agencies, the exemption committee process has only been used twice since 1978. This would suggest that the ESA has not been the oppressive environmental law it was claimed to be by opponents of the act.

HABITAT CONSERVATION PLANNING

While the Section 7 process and severe criminal and civil penalties under the ESA have produced significant conservation benefits for years for listed species, a relatively new and promising conservation mechanism has evolved since 1983. Known as "habitat conservation planning" or HCP for short, the HCP process seeks to reconcile private development interests with the national goal of endangered species conservation. Formally added to the ESA in 1983, subsection 10(a) of the act[18] authorizes the FWS to negotiate a long-term conservation agreement for listed species with private development interests where a proposed private project would affect a listed species and its habitat. In exchange for a long-term commitment to fund a conservation program for the particular affected listed species and to set aside significant portions of the species' habitat, the private developer could be authorized by the FWS to develop the remainder of the habitat, even if it resulted in the incidental taking of a limited number of listed species.

The HCP process was first used in connection with a real estate development project on San Bruno Mountain in California and subsequently has been used in such diverse areas as the Coachella Valley in California and on Key Largo in the Florida Keys. From the FWS's point of view, the HCP process not only allows private sector funds to be tapped for endangered species conservation purposes (thereby supplementing limited federal funds available for this purpose), but also provides for the long-term conservation and preservation of important endangered or threatened species habitat.

In some respects, the HCP process has been viewed by the private sector as a less risky method for resolving endangered species conflicts than resorting to the exemption committee process. If the initial successes of the HCP process are duplicated, it could become a significant tool for promoting the long-term conservation of listed species.

PARKS AND ENDANGERED SPECIES

When viewed in its entirety, the ESA can affect and assist National Park System management in the following ways:

- *Enhanced law enforcement protection.* The severe civil and criminal penalties for prohibited activities affecting endangered and threatened species provide significant additional protection to national park wildlife and plant resources. The park service should maximize its use of these prohibitions wherever serious law enforcement problems exist and work cooperatively with the U.S. Fish and Wildlife Service to solve endangered species enforcement problems.

- *External threats to interagency consultation.* Given the sweeping responsibilities placed upon federal agencies under Section 7 of the ESA, the consultation process could result in an expanded level of environmental analysis for projects on adjacent federal lands, especially where those adjacent activities could adversely affect endangered or threatened park resources. Under certain circumstances, Section 7 could result in the significant alteration or abandonment of such activities. Therefore, the park service should not pass up opportunities to provide input into the Section 7 consultation process for external activities which could affect a park.

- *Internal threats to interagency consultation.* In some instances, the rigid provisions of the ESA may serve as the driving force behind politically unpopular—but biologically sound—park management decisions. To the extent that Section 7 eliminates some of a park superintendent's administrative discretion, it also shields that superintendent from political accountability for conservation actions taken as required by Section 7. Therefore, the park service should fully integrate endangered species conservation planning into park system management. To the extent that a park management program is consistent with the conservation responsibilities of the ESA, it most surely would be consistent with the park service responsibilities under the National Park Service's Organic Act.

- *Enhanced availability of appropriated funds.* Even during tight fiscal times, the appropriations committees of Congress have been fairly protective of endangered species conservation programs. The park service, therefore, should look for ways to merge endangered species conservation projects into budgetary proposals for the National Park System.

CONCLUSION

Several lessons can be learned from an analysis of the ESA. Politically, it is an immensely popular act that is here to stay—it is very unlikely that it will be repealed or significantly altered by Congress. Matching this protective attitude from Congress, the judiciary has been very supportive of the goals of the ESA and has shown great deference to the biological views of the FWS and NMFS, the lead federal agencies for implementing the act. Moreover, given the enormous backlog of candidate species, the number of listed species will continue to grow within this country with a resultant increase in the number of contacts or conflicts between listed species and proposed development projects.

From the perspective of a natural resource planner in an agency such as the National Park Service, the listing of an endangered species within a national park can be both a blessing and a burden. Given the high degree of protection afforded listed species under Section 7, the presence of a listed species can provide added protection to a park when dealing with external threats affecting the natural resources within the park. On the other hand, the listing of a species can influence the way the National Park Service conducts its own business in managing the affected national park. Situations arise, for example, where the park service has to seek the biological advice of FWS under Section 7 before taking final agency action. Based upon the conclusions of the biological opinion, modifications might be required in park service operations. Given the overall National Park Service mission, it is unlikely that any such changes would be dramatic or traumatic to the service.

For federal agencies with more of a development-oriented mission, however, or for developers in the private sector, the ESA can be a rigid environmental statute that does not allow for the usual balancing of competing environmental and economic interests that one finds under other statutes. Given the high risks and severe penalties associated with noncompliance with the ESA, past history would show that development-oriented agencies and the private sector are best served by addressing endangered species problems up front and early. By exhibiting flexibility in early planning stages and pursuing constructive approaches like the HCP process in good faith, development interests can discover that the ESA, although rigid, is not insurmountable.

Upon reflection, one would be hard pressed to identify another federal environmental law more compatible with and supportive of National Park System objectives than the Endangered Species Act. The primary purpose of the ESA is to preserve for the benefit of future generations endangered and threatened species and the ecosystems upon which they depend. Similarly, one of the primary purposes of the National Park System, as set forth in the park service's Organic Act,[19] is to "conserve" the "natural objects and wildlife therein and to provide for the enjoyment of the same in such a manner and by such means as will leave them unimpaired for the enjoyment of future generations." Thus, the goals of the two statutes are virtually interchangeable.

Given the ESA's emphasis on interagency consultation, and its rigid protective standards governing federal, state, and private activities, the act can be perhaps the most powerful ally the park service has in fending off external threats or implementing needed internal management improvements. The park service is engaged in a constant balancing act between preserving park resources for future generations and providing the public with an opportunity to view and enjoy those resources. When used to its fullest by park service employees, the ESA helps ensure that the administrative scales tilt in the direction of long-term preservation of park resources if they ever do tilt at all.

REFERENCE

1. 16 U.S.C. §1531-1543.
2. 16 U.S.C. §1536.
3. 16 U.S.C. §1532.
4. 50 C.F.R. 17.3.
5. 16 U.S.C. §1533.
6. 16 U.S.C. §1534.
7. 16 U.S.C. §1535.
8. 16 U.S.C. §1538.
9. 16 U.S.C. §1533(d).
10. 16 U.S.C. §1536.
11. 437 U.S. 174 (1978).
12. 16 U.S.C. §1536(a)(1).
13. 16 U.S.C. §1536(a)(2).
14. 50 C.F.R. Part 402.
15. 733 F.2d 605 (9th Cir. 1984).
16. No. 88-3610 (9th Cir. filed Oct. 5, 1988).
17. 16 U.S.C. §(e)-(n).
18. 16 U.S.C. §1539(a).
19. 16 U.S.C. §1.

Chapter 7

The National Historic Preservation Act

*by Michael A. Mantell**

The National Park System collection of historical and cultural resources is enormous, among the largest in the world. Nearly 60 percent of the units in the park system (although they constitute only a very small percentage of the land area) are primarily cultural or historical in nature. In addition, many of the other units—including Yellowstone, Yosemite, and Mount Rainier—along with more recently added units near urban areas, contain major cultural and historical resources. The service's List of Classified Structures, which identifies historic structures within the system, includes more than 10,000 entries, and the official estimate of "museum objects and artifacts of historical significance" comes to 10 million.[1]

The responsibilities of the National Park Service for cultural and historical resources date back to its beginning. The purpose of the parks, as set forth in the 1916 Organic Act, was to conserve not only scenery, natural objects, and wildlife but also "historic objects." This has been reiterated and expanded in key legislation that makes the park service the focal point of federal leadership in "preserving, restoring, and maintaining the historic and cultural environment of the Nation," both inside the parks (its "internal" responsibilities) and throughout the country (its "external" responsibilities).[2]

---

*This material is adapted from The Conservation Foundation, *National Parks for a New Generation: Visions, Realities, Prospects* (Washington, D.C.: The Conservation Foundation, 1985), and Christopher J. Duerksen, ed., *A Handbook on Historic Preservation Law* (Washington, D.C.: The Conservation Foundation, 1983).

Managing the national parks' collection of historical and cultural resources presents distinctive problems. Time, an ally in managing nature, is more of an enemy and less of a healer with historical resources. Fires, including those caused by lightning, burn down settlers' cabins; waves along the shore threaten to wash away historic dwellings; and other natural events, such as tornadoes, earthquakes, and severe fluctuations in temperature, may severely damage structures.

Experts often differ on answers to the distinct questions posed by managing cultural resources: Which features are worthy of "Cadillac" restorations? What are less costly options? Which features are not worth repairing if damaged? Given cost constraints, how can intelligent decisions be made between funding stabilization and renovation of buildings and research for surveys, cataloging, park histories, and the like?

Within the park service itself, the perceived core responsibility has long been natural areas, adding further to the difficulties of managing cultural and historical resources. In units not set aside specifically as historical, park staff have tended to regard archeological sites and old buildings—forts, settlements, ranches, taverns, outbuildings, and so forth—as "intrusions" on the landscape and to assume that these intrusions ultimately would be razed in favor of returning the land to a more natural state.

These tensions need to be recognized and reconciled more effectively. The historical resources within the park system are valuable and important. Moreover, the park service has lead responsibility for administering the nation's historic preservation programs as they affect other federal agencies, states, localities, and private landowners. If it cannot manage its own resources appropriately, it will be hard-pressed to require and expect others to do the same.

In addition to the Organic Act, various legal tools exist to protect historical resources and to grapple more intelligently with balancing the needs of these resources with natural ones. Foremost among them is the National Historic Preservation Act.

THE NATIONAL HISTORIC PRESERVATION ACT, AS AMENDED

The National Historic Preservation Act of 1966 (NHPA)[3] is the key federal law designed to encourage identification and preservation of the United States' cultural resources. The act commits federal agencies to a program of identification and protection of historic properties on land they own or control and establishes the National Register of Historic Places to designate public and privately owned resources and to encourage their consideration in planning and development activities affecting the properties. Properties not listed in the register because of owners' objections may be determined to be "eligible" for inclusion in the register and are given consideration in federal projects just as listed properties are.

The act coordinates federal efforts with those of the other sectors in the preservation spectrum: state historic preservation officers (SHPOs) are statutorily integrated into federal preservation activity, and local governments may be certified to carry out delegated responsibilities and apply for federal funds.[4]

Critical to the federal preservation effort is the Section 106 review requirement that agencies such as the park service afford the Advisory Council on Historic Preservation (ACHP) an opportunity to comment on their actions that may affect properties included, or eligible for inclusion, in the National Register. The agencies are required to "take into account" the comments of the ACHP.

Nevertheless, preservation of historic and cultural resources remains merely an encouraged goal and not a required action. Federal agencies ultimately have considerable discretion to undertake or approve projects that affect historic properties. The ACHP's review mechanism requires only that an agency first follow the prescribed consultation procedure. The ACHP can suggest alternatives to proposed actions but cannot require agencies to protect cultural resources. The NHPA is less stringent and far-reaching than some other environmental laws, such as the Clean Air and Water acts.

Identification and Listing of Resources

Section 101(a)(1)(a) of NHPA authorizes the secretary of the interior to "expand and maintain" a National Register of Historic Places, the official listing of the nation's historic properties and cultural resources found worthy of preservation.

Properties may be included in the National Register in one of four ways:[5]

- nomination by the SHPO, by qualified local governments, or by individuals in states where there is no Interior Department-approved state program;[6]

- nomination by federal agency head;[7]
- designation as a National Historic Landmark by the secretary of the interior;[8] or
- addition to the National Park System by act of Congress, if the area is determined by Congress to be of historic significance.

The register is to be composed of "districts, sites, buildings, structures, and objects significant in American history, architecture, archaeology, engineering and culture."[9] Properties listed in the register may be of local, state, or national significance. The register is administered by the Keeper of the National Register within the National Park Service.[10]

Qualifications for Listing in the National Register

To qualify for inclusion in the National Register, properties must meet the evaluation criteria in the Code of Federal Regulations.[11]

Once properties have been listed in the register, they may be removed only in certain situations: if a mistake in professional judgment as to eligibility is proved; if procedures for listing were not followed; if the property has been altered so that it no longer meets the National Register criteria; or if additional information shows that the property does not satisfy the criteria. Section 101(a)(1)(B) of the 1980 NHPA amendments, however, legislatively recognizes all properties listed on the register or designated as national landmarks as of December 12, 1980. Only alterations subsequent to this date constitute grounds for removal from the register.

Nomination Procedures

Nominations are reviewed by the National Register Branch of the Interagency Resources Division within the National Park Service for technical and professional sufficiency and conformance with National Register criteria, and, on approval, they are listed in the National Register.

The staff of the National Register monitors properties in the register to ensure that the listed properties maintain the qualifications and the integrity for which they were listed. Changes or revisions to the boundaries of a property and proposed relocations of the property must be reviewed and approved by the National Park Service if the property is to be kept in the register.

The 1980 NHPA amendments codified the requirements placed on federal agencies in Executive Order 11593 that each federal agency establish a program to nominate to the register all apparently eligible properties under that agency's ownership or control.[12] Aided by the secretary of the interior and the SHPO, each agency must establish a program to locate, inventory, and nominate such properties. Summaries from the regional offices in 1987 showed, for example, some 36,000 sites and some 15,000 structures, most of which were eligible for register listing if they were not, in fact, already listed. Section 110(c) requires agency designation of a "preservation officer" to coordinate all activity under the act.

Nominations by the federal preservation officer are submitted to the appropriate SHPO for comment.[13] The chief elected county or municipal officials also must be notified and allowed 45 days in which to comment. The federal officer may choose to forward the nomination to the Keeper of the National Register for a final determination of whether to include the property in the register.

For a nomination he or she supports, the federal officer also must include an opinion of the property's qualifications as well as comments received on the nomination. The keeper may approve or disapprove the nomination following publication in the *Federal Register* for a 15-day comment period. During the nomination process any person or organization may petition the keeper either to accept or to reject a nomination. The keeper must then substantively review the nomination under the same procedure as if it were a nomination from the state.

Effects of Listing

Inclusion in the National Register or a determination of eligibility for inclusion plays three major roles. First, it creates an inventory of properties that can be used as a planning tool by government, private organizations, and persons to help identify cultural resources worthy of preservation. Second, it is a legal instrument that ensures that federal, federally assisted, or federally licensed undertakings affecting properties listed in, or eligible for listing in, the National Register undergo Section 106 review and comment. Third, it makes listed properties eligible for benefits such as tax incentives and National Historic Preservation Fund grants and loans, if the programs are implemented by the Interior Department and if there are appropriations available.

Section 106 of NHPA requires that federal agencies take into account the effect of their undertakings on included or eligible properties and that the ACHP be given the opportunity to comment on such undertakings.

Although Section 106 applies only to federal, federally funded, federally subsidized, or federally licensed undertakings, these activities often involve actions by private parties—for example, private contractors hired by a federal agency or recipients of federal funds or licenses. Consequently, injunctions for noncompliance with Section 106 may be issued against nonfederal parties and municipalities involved in federal actions.[14]

Section 106, however, is a procedural requirement that does not prohibit a proposed undertaking that has a negative effect on register properties. A federal agency only can be made to consider the effects of its undertakings, including undertakings or effects identified by the ACHP, and to provide the ACHP with an opportunity to comment. Having done so, the agency has complied with Section 106 and may proceed with its planned action, including demolition of National Register buildings if desired. An agreement between the agency and the ACHP on how to treat historic properties, however, is enforceable as a contract.

Properties may be determined "eligible" for inclusion in the National Register, on federal agency request, for purposes of Section 106 of NHPA. Eligible properties are protected by Section 106 review just as properties included in the register are.

CONCLUSION

The NHPA pulls together four basic activities that comprise the federal historic preservation program:
  • identification of historic and cultural resources;
  • evaluation and registration of resources that meet the evaluation criteria for determining significance;
  • protection of resources; and
  • encouragement of preservation activities at the state and local levels of government.

However, the act provides very limited protection from adverse private actions and only procedural safeguards for adverse federal effects on cultural and historic properties. Listed or eligible properties fall under the Section 106 review only if there is some federal involvement. Further, the federal undertaking must include an element of discretion if adverse effects are to be avoided. Properties not specifically listed in the National Register, included in a district listed in the register, or eligible for listing receive no protection under the act.

The ACHP review process covers a broad range of federal actions from a single perspective. The make-up of the governing board of the ACHP is unusual, and its comments and recommendations are advisory only. Perhaps the most significant protection offered by the Section 106 process rests in the light that the ACHP's review process can shed on proposed federal activities. The procedures of the ACHP are flexible and provide no rigorous standard of review that all agencies must meet.

Clearly, the National Park Service has legal responsibilities to comply with the NHPA in managing park cultural and historical resources. Given its leadership in historic preservation efforts nationwide, it also has compelling political reasons for adhering to NHPA's goals and procedures.

REFERENCES

1. The Conservation Foundation, *National Parks for a New Generation* (Washington, D.C.: The Conservation Foundation, 1985), p. 112.

2. Ibid.

3. 16 U.S.C. §470 (1976 and Supp. IV 1980).

4. All of the states and territories have enacted historic preservation laws. James P. Beckwith, Jr., "Appendix of State and Territorial Historic Preservation Statutes and Session Laws," *North Carolina Central Law Journal* 11 (1980):308-40. In addition, at least 832 historic district or landmark commissions had been created as of 1981. Stephen N. Dennis, ed., *Directory of American Preservation Commissions* (Washington, D.C.: National Trust for Historic Preservation, 1981), p. iii.

5. 46 Fed. Reg. 56,211 (1981) (proposed rule to be codified at 36 C.F.R. 60.8) provides for nominations by persons or local governments in states without approved state historic preservation programs. All states have approved programs as of the date of this writing. Note that the interim rules, 46 Fed. Reg. 56,184 (1981), no longer allow SHPO nomination of properties under federal ownership or control. See 46 Fed. Reg. 56,191 (1981) (to be codified at 60.6[y]).

6. 16 U.S.C. §470a-d (Supp. IV 1980).

7. Executive Order No. 11593 2(a), 36 Fed. Reg. 8,921 (1971), reprinted in 16 U.S.C. §470h-2 (Supp. IV 1980).

8. 16 U.S.C. §461-69 (1976).

9. Ibid. at 470a(b)(2).

10. The Heritage Conservation and Recreation Service (HCRS) administered the federal historic preservation program between 1978 and 1981. Pursuant to Secretarial Order No. 3060, Amendment No. 1 (February 19, 1981), HCRS was abolished, and the National Park Service reassumed responsibility.

11. 36 C.F.R. 60.15 (1980).

12. According to National Register staff estimates, there were 3,342 listed properties owned or managed by federal agencies and bureaus as of 1988. Almost one-third of these are overseen by the park service. The next most active agencies were the Postal Service, Fish and Wildlife Service, Bureau of Land Management, and Coast Guard. See "Guidelines for Federal Agency Responsibilities under Section 11 of the National Historic Preservation Act," 53 Fed. Reg. 31,4727-4746 (1988).

13. 36 C.F.R. 60.9.

14. See, for example, *Biderman* v. *Morton*, 497 F.2d 1141, 1147 (2d Cir. 1974); *Jones* v. *Lynn*, 477 F.2d 885 (1st Cir. 1973); *Save the Courthouse Committee* v. *Lynn*, 408 F. Supp. 1323, 1344 (S.D. N.Y. 1975).

Chapter 8

Planning for Forest Service and Bureau of Land Management Lands

by William E. Shands*

In many places, especially in the West, national park neighbors include national forests managed by the Forest Service within the U.S. Department of Agriculture (USDA) and public domain managed by the National Park Service's sister Interior Department agency, the Bureau of Land Management (BLM). Both the national forests and public domain lands are, by law, managed for many different uses and values: wilderness preservation, outdoor recreation, provision of habitat for game and nongame wildlife, and the production of timber, range forage for livestock, and minerals. How these multiple-use neighboring lands are managed can have a significant impact on National Park System resources and use. Because of these cross-boundary influences, it is important that park managers understand the legislative mandates, policies, and planning processes of these other federal land-managing agencies. Just as the Forest Service and BLM can express their views on national park management plans, there are abundant opportunities for park service personnel to comment on Forest Service and BLM policy and program proposals.

---

*Parts of the following section on the USDA Forest Service are adapted from William E. Shands and Thomas E. Waddell, *Below Cost Timber Sales in the Broad Context of National Forest Management* (Washington, D.C.: The Conservation Foundation, 1987) and William E. Shands and V. Alaric Sample, "National Forest Plan Implementation: An Overview," unpublished paper, The Conservation Foundation, 1988.

THE FOREST SERVICE

The Forest Service is the largest agency in the U.S. Department of Agriculture, with about 39,000 permanent employees. Altogether, it manages some 191 million acres of National Forest System lands in 156 national forests and grasslands in 45 states and Puerto Rico. In addition to the management of the national forests, the Forest Service conducts the world's largest forest and range research operation and provides funding and technical assistance to state forestry agencies and small private landowners.

Just as the park service traces its institutional ethos to its founder, Stephen T. Mather, the Forest Service still bears the imprint of its founder and first chief, Gifford Pinchot. Pinchot set out the principles of national forest management in a famous letter which he wrote for agriculture secretary James Wilson to himself upon taking over control of the then forest reserves (the forerunners of the national forests) in 1905:

> In the administration of the forest reserves . . . all land is to be devoted to its most productive use for the permanent good of the whole people and not for the temporary benefit of individuals or companies. All the resources of the forest reserves are for use and this must be brought about in a thoroughly prompt and business-like manner, under such restrictions only as will insure the permanence of these resources. . . . Where conflicting interests must be reconciled the question will always be decided from the standpoint of the greatest good to the greatest number in the long run.[1]

Pinchot's principles endure in Forest Service law, policies, and tradition to this day.

Administratively, the Forest Service is organized in much the same way as the National Park Service, with broad direction for the national forests provided by the chief of the Forest Service and deputy chief for the National Forest System (NFS), through nine regional foresters, to the 126 national forest supervisors (a supervisor may administer more than one national forest), and through the supervisors to district rangers responsible for all activities in a specific area of a national forest. There are staffs at the Washington headquarters, regional, forest, and district levels that parallel one another (for example, a timber staff, recreation staff, etc.), with each staff providing policy and program guidance and technical assistance to the staff below it within the organizational hierarchy. Although some differences in size and workload emphasis undoubtedly exist, the basic responsibilities of all forest supervisors and district rangers are essentially the same.

Perhaps the greatest organizational difference between the National Park Service and the Forest Service is that the latter does not administer the tremendous variety of units that exist in the park system.

Unlike the National Park System, which has seen significant growth since World War II, the National Forest System has grown only slowly during the past four decades. There have been modest additions to some forests through Land and Water Conservation Fund acquisitions and land exchanges. In 1987, however, an exchange of land between the Forest Service and the Bureau of Land Management netted the Forest Service more than 600,000 acres in Nevada.

National forest landownership patterns differ significantly from those of the large, traditional national parks. National forest boundaries (legally, the area within which land can be proclaimed or acquired for the national forest) typically include large amounts of private land. These may include towns, valley farmland, or land owned by forest products companies interspersed with public land in a checkerboard pattern dating back to 19th-century railroad land grants. Only in a few instances, such as at the Sawtooth National Recreation Area in Idaho, has Congress given the agency some authority to control private land use and to acquire scenic easements over land within national forest boundaries.

Major Laws Governing National Forest Management

The Organic Administration Act of 1897 established the purposes of the national forests: (1) to "improve and protect the forest"; (2) to "maintain water flow"; and (3) to "provide a continuous supply of timber." There are, of course, many laws governing management of the national forests. However, the lodestar law for national forest management is the Multiple-Use Sustained Yield (MUSY) Act of 1960.[2] The MUSY Act simply wrote into law long-standing management policy for the forests, providing the Forest Service with explicit authority to manage the national forests for outdoor recreation, wildlife and fish, and range forage, in addition to water and timber.

In the 1960s, pressure on the national forests intensified, fueled by the pressures for economic development on one side and burgeoning recreation demands and the growth of the environmental movement on the other. The clash of competing interests led in the 1970s to passage of two laws providing for long-term, comprehensive planning at the national and forest levels—the Forest and Rangeland Renewable Resources Planning Act of 1974 and the National Forest Management Act of 1976, which amended the 1974 act.

The Resources Planning Act

The Resources Planning Act (RPA)[3] established a national planning process that was to be comprehensive, long-range, and continuous. The act requires the Forest Service to prepare an "RPA Assessment" of the nation's forest and range situation every 10 years and a long-term plan for the Forest Service called the "RPA Program" every 5 years. (The Forest Service now updates the assessment every five years in synchronization with the program.) Each program—which details plans for the next 40 years of Forest Service management of the national forests, forest and range research, and assistance to state and private forestry—must respond to the findings of the assessment. The president sends the program to Congress with an accompanying statement of policy, and Congress can revise the statement if it wishes to do so.

The RPA Program, then, amounts to a broad, *national* plan for Forest Service activities. Although it is too general to provide useful information on the management of any specific national forest, the program does establish broad policy and program direction for the National Forest System as a whole, and this direction should ultimately influence management of individual forests. The RPA Program is in transition, and it is envisioned that the 1990 program will be a powerful policy-setting document for the Forest Service. For the park service, the upcoming 1990 program will bear analysis since it will describe, for example, the role the Forest Service is to play in the production of commodities, how national forests should relate to adjacent landowners, and the Forest Service's role in the production of outdoor recreation and other noncommodity resources and uses. For park service managers, the RPA Program will signal directions that will influence the policies, programs, and attitudes of their Forest Service counterparts.

The National Forest Management Act

The RPA did not quell dissatisfaction over national forest management. Noncommodity interests especially were distressed over what they saw as an emphasis on timber production to the disadvantage of recreation, wildlife, and scenic qualities of the forests. When a suit filed by noncommodity groups brought timber sales to a halt in the central Appalachians and Alaska, Congress responded with the National Forest Management Act (NFMA). The NFMA required the Forest Service to prepare plans for each of the national forests and, in specifying how the public was to be involved in the preparation of these plans, amplified the applicable public participation provisions of the National Environmental Policy Act (NEPA).

The national forests' land and resource management plans (informally called "forest plans") under the NFMA determine activities on specific areas. The Forest Service did develop forest-level multiple-use plans throughout the 1960s, but these plans rarely addressed fundamental questions of how uses were to be sorted out and distributed across a national forest. Indeed, they were much criticized for often seeming to imply that no such sorting out was necessary, that most uses could be accommodated simultaneously everywhere. The forest plans developed pursuant to the NFMA will determine management emphasis on specific areas of a forest and, ultimately, on the ground projects and management activities. Regulations detailing the NFMA planning process, including provisions for public participation, are set forth at 36 C.F.R. 219.

Regional Guides

Though not required by either the RPA or the NFMA, the Forest Service decided in 1979 that "regional guides" were necessary to link national-level RPA planning and field-level forest planning. Prepared by each Forest Service region, the regional guides set forth broad management standards and guidelines for a region's forests, covering, for example, the size of clearcuts. However, the guides have not fulfilled earlier expectations that they would establish the broad context for management of a forest in a region and its relationships with nearby national forests and other landowners. With the RPA in transition, and forest plans now being implemented, the role of the regional guides also is likely to be reappraised. As of 1989, at least one Forest Service region—the Rocky Mountain—has begun work to revise its regional guide.

Forest Planning and Plan Implementation

A national forest's land and resource management plan (forest plan) is to chart the direction for management of the forest for a 10- to 15-year period. Developed with the participation of local constituents of the forest, such a plan amounts to a contract in which the Forest Service says, in effect, "Here's what we promise to do." While providing broad direction for forest management, each plan also states explicitly how much timber is expected to be harvested, how many miles of trail are to be built, how many campsites are to be developed. The plans, however, do not determine on-the-ground activities. This is left to the implementation phase.

The best introduction to a forest plan is the regional forester's "record of decision" that accompanies each plan. In it, the regional forester explains, typically in straightforward terms, his or her reasons for choosing a particular plan direction. The plans themselves describe the resources and the management environment, set out a management direction chosen from among various alternatives, and detail a program for monitoring plan implementation.

Plan direction is translated to the field through management prescriptions for specific geographic areas termed "management areas." Just as a city may have several noncontiguous areas zoned for commercial development, many portions of a forest may be assigned to a single management-area classification. The management areas are the bridge to on-the-ground activities to implement the plan. Officials of national parks adjacent to a national forest should be familiar with the prescriptions for management areas lying near the park or in areas where management could affect resources such as wildlife and water quality.

The implementation phase of planning is now under way in most national forests. Plan implementation focuses on projects and activities required to achieve the objectives of the plans. The debate turns from questions such as "How much timber will be cut?" to "Where will timber be cut, when, and using what harvesting technique?"; from "Which lands will emphasize wildlife habitat?" to "What projects are required to enhance habitat?"; from "How many miles of trail will be built, and how many new campgrounds will be constructed?" to "Where will trails be built and new campgrounds constructed?" Park service officials should be alert to proposals for site-specific activities in management areas critical to park resources.

The NFMA requires that each forest plan be revised every 15 years. Managers of most forests, however, anticipate that their plans will have only a 10-year life. All plans are intended to be dynamic and flexible, responding to new information, the identification of new issues and opportunities, and other changes in the management environment. Thus, plans are to be amended as plan implementation proceeds.

Implementation is highly decentralized. Whereas a forest plan is prepared in a forest supervisor's office, primary responsibility for plan implementation analysis and decision making rests with the district ranger and his or her staff. Thus, park service personnel concerned about what is going on in a forest should maintain close contact with district rangers and their staffs.

The Forest Planning Process and Outside Participation

The NFMA, combined with the public participation requirements of the NEPA, provides numerous opportunities for government agencies—federal, state, and local—and the public to become involved in forest planning. In addition to the specifications of law and regulation, Forest Service officials typically stand ready to discuss policies, programs, or plans informally. Moreover, Forest Service officials may invite other agencies and knowledgeable members of the public to participate in interdisciplinary planning teams working on the forest plan.

Both NFMA and its implementing regulation set forth some minimal requirements for coordination with other federal agencies, state and local governments, and Indian tribes. Forest Service officials are required to meet with federal, state, tribal, and local officials as planning begins to arrange procedures for coordination. "At minimum, coordination meetings must be held after public issues and management concerns have been identified and before the Forest Service recommends a preferred alternative."[4] Moreover, regulations require that the environmental impact statement (EIS) accompanying the forest plan consider the planning and policy objectives of other government agencies. Forest officers are to seek other agencies' comments and ideas on alternatives to resolve identified conflicts between forest plan proposals and the plans of other agencies.

As a rule, opportunities for comment on plans or proposed activities are widely publicized by the Forest Service in the area or region affected. Forest Service field offices maintain extensive lists of agencies, organizations, and individuals to whom announcements are sent routinely. News releases are sent to local news media. A Forest Service official who failed to notify a major interest group of some proposed action or did not actively solicit the participation of major players would be seen as failing an important element of his or her job.

Similarly, a park service official would be remiss not to establish a good working relationship with his or her counterpart at a nearby or adjacent national forest. It is probable that some, perhaps many, park service concerns can be addressed early on through informal communications. The Forest Service places a premium on containing and resolving issues at the lowest possible level of the management hierarchy. There is no advantage to a Forest Service official's letting an issue boil to the point where it has to be decided by his or her superior. Of course, this does not obviate a park service official's need to participate actively in the formal process too, filing official comments on draft EISs, speaking out forcefully at coordination meetings, and presenting park service views at formal public meetings.

In February 1988, the director of the National Park Service and chief of the Forest Service signed a memorandum of understanding intended to promote cooperative management and research, and the exchange of information between the two agencies, identify potential conflicts, and establish a framework for ongoing coordination and communications.[5] The memorandum provides examples of a number of current and potential activities that might be carried out. Twice-yearly coordination meetings of regional officials of the two agencies are required, and regional officials are encouraged to develop supplemental agreements to implement the master memorandum.

These procedures give National Park Service officials numerous opportunities to raise and express concerns regarding Forest Service plans for activities that might affect adjacent or nearby parkland.

Considerations for Success

Final decisions on forest plans and actions affecting park resources are, of course, still up to individual forest supervisors and regional foresters. The effects of such communications depend, however, on a variety of factors, some personal, some technical, some political, and some having to do with the Forest Service's institutional ethos, goals, and objectives. Some Forest Service officials are more sensitive than others about management impacts on parks and their resources.[6] The Forest Service's response also may depend on the detail and technical accuracy of the comments and on whether they address a specific action or are so general that they raise questions about overall management of a forest.

Political factors relate to the prominence of a national park or a specific resource—demonstrated by the concern over Yellowstone and the fate of its grizzlies. Not the least important is the Forest Service's institutional ethos. Congress has mandated that the national forests are to accommodate many different—even conflicting—uses. Accordingly, the Forest Service places a high value on *use* of the forests for many purposes and strives to satisfy a variety of demands—from campers to wilderness backpackers, from hunters to birdwatchers, from timber companies to small towns that see timber as the lifeblood of their economies. Typically, the Forest Service resists the exclusion of some activities without good cause. Similarly, high value is placed on the maintenance of management flexibility, which the Forest Service perceives as enhancing its ability to ensure goods and services for present and future generations. Thus, it generally opposes actions that curtail flexibility and its own management discretion.

Personalities and politics aside, the Forest Service's response to comments from an outside agency such as the National Park Service will hinge to a large extent on how realistic the outside agency's proposals are, the technical adequacy of the comments, and the degree to which the agency's proposals are compatible, or do not conflict, with what Forest Service officials see as their national, regional, and forest mandates, goals, and objectives. For example, an emotional plea not to cut timber over any part of a national forest visible from any place in a national park probably would not get a particularly sympathetic response. Similarly, a general plea for management of a national forest to protect park values is unlikely to be persuasive. On the other hand, opposition to a discrete timber harvest on an area visible from a popular park viewpoint or parkway or a well-documented technical presentation supporting a contention that a timber sale could result in disruption of wildlife or siltation of a stream would have far better chances of a favorable reaction. A park superintendent's case will be strengthened by an approved plan for the park system unit, particularly if the plan discusses the implications of activities on an adjacent or nearby national forest.

THE BUREAU OF LAND MANAGEMENT

With fewer personnel (8,500 permanent) than either the Forest Service or National Park Service, the Bureau of Land Management administers more land—272 million acres—than the other two agencies combined. Some 174 million acres are in 11 western states and the Dakotas, and nearly all the remainder are in Alaska. In a number of states, BLM-administered land is significant. For example, 69 percent of Nevada, 41 percent of Utah, and 21 percent of Idaho are BLM-managed public domain. While some BLM land is fairly well consolidated (particularly in Alaska), much of it exists in scattered blocks or strips between higher-altitude forest land (often in national forests) and more fertile valleys or better rangeland. Because of this pattern of ownership, fewer national parks than national forests border BLM lands, though some of the spectacular national parks of the Southwest and Alaska count BLM lands as their neighbors.

For the most part, BLM manages the remnant public domain—land unwanted by settlers and lacking qualities warranting its reservation for national parks or forests. The so-called Oregon and California lands in northern California are notable exceptions. Reclaimed by the federal government when the railroad entrepreneurs to whom the lands had been granted failed to construct the line, these lands produce high-quality, high-value Douglas fir. The remainder of BLM's lands in the contiguous 48 states are largely desert, brushland, and grassland. Though once considered of little value except for livestock grazing, these lands are increasingly being discovered by recreationists of all kinds and those seeking to exploit their minerals. Like the Forest Service areas, BLM lands are the subject of intense pressure by competing users.

Some BLM land has been recognized by Congress as having exceptional ecological and recreational values. These are the 12.5-million-acre California Desert Conservation Area, the King Range Conservation Area (both in California), and the Birds of Prey Conservation Area along the Snake River Gorge south of Boise, Idaho. Some 450,000 acres of BLM land have been designated wilderness, and another 24.6 million acres are under study for wilderness designation. BLM also administers some 2,000 miles of wild and scenic rivers. BLM also bears primary responsibility for administering federally owned minerals beneath 300 million acres, an activity that also can affect some national parks. (See chapter 9 for a discussion of BLM's role in mineral activities affecting parklands.)

As a government agency, BLM traces its bureaucratic lineage back to the establishment of the Cadastral Survey in 1785 and thus can boast that it is the oldest of the federal land management agencies. However, the modern-day BLM dates back only to 1946, when the Federal Grazing Service and General Land Office were combined by executive order to create the new Bureau of Land Management.

Organizationally, BLM parallels the Forest Service, with a director and staff in Washington, 12 state offices (comparable to National Park Service or Forest Service administrative regions), districts (comparable to a national forest), and resource areas, the smallest management unit (comparable to a ranger district).

The Public Land Law Review Commission and FLPMA

For more than two decades following its creation, BLM operated with no clear direction as to the future of the public domain. Its mandate—if it could be called that—was a conflicting array of 19th-century statutes and 20th-century amendments. In 1964, Congress charged the Public Land Law Review Commission (PLLRC) with making sense of the chaos of public land statutes. PLLRC's 1970 report, *One Third of the Nation's Land*, set the stage for the enactment six years later of the Federal Land Policy and Management Act (FLPMA)—an organic act for the Bureau of Land Management.[7] Although the report's commodity orientation and recommendation for continued disposal of the public domain drew a barrage of criticism, the report did spotlight numerous public land issues and the need for reform.

The FLPMA responded to some of the PLLRC recommendations and repudiated others. Of considerable importance, it gave BLM the same congressionally designated status as the National Park Service and the Forest Service. In directing that the public lands be retained, it rejected a key PLLRC recommendation and long-standing national policy. Moreover, the public domain was to be managed for multiple use, making explicit the multipurpose role of lands that historically had emphasized livestock grazing. Not the least important, BLM also was given authority and direction to protect its lands and resources from inappropriate uses and to identify and designate "areas of critical environmental concern" for special management.

Planning in the Bureau of Land Management[8]

Seven years before the FLPMA, BLM had initiated a new land-use planning system with a multiple-use focus. It involved the preparation of "management framework plans" (MFPs) for relatively small planning units within BLM districts. By the time the FLPMA was enacted, MFPs had been prepared for some 80 percent of BLM's public domain outside Alaska. The system had serious problems, however, and, by the early 1980s, it had been buried by an avalanche of critical studies and reports.

Congress set out principles and criteria in the FLPMA for a new BLM planning process. That the first substantive section of FLPMA dealt with planning indicated the value Congress put on long-range planning to resolve issues and assure the long-term sustainability of the land and associated resources.[9] Key sections included adherence to the principles of multiple use and sustained yield; priority attention to identification and planning for areas of critical environmental concern; the inventory of the public lands, resources, and values as the basis for planning; consideration of present and potential uses and the weighing of long-term public benefits against short-term benefits; and conformance with pollution control laws. Finally, BLM plans are to be *consistent* with other federal, state, and local plans *so long as [the plans] are also consistent with the purposes, policies, and programs of Federal laws and regulation applicable to the public lands*[10] (emphasis added).

Based on the FLPMA's mandate, BLM developed a new planning process that intended, according to BLM Chief Planner David C. Williams, to be issue-driven and comprehensive and to integrate fully FLPMA requirements with those of the NEPA. The planning process is to result in resource management plans (RMPs) for each of BLM's resource areas. The plans are to be prepared by area staff and to be the direct responsibility of the area managers—a deliberate decision aimed at building field-level ownership of the plans. Though BLM has no national-level planning effort like the Forest Service's RPA, the RMPs are to be responsive to national direction that is relayed, presumably, through policy and program directives from the BLM director and annual budgets and appropriations.

As of January 1989, some 54 RMPs have been completed, covering about 42 percent of BLM's public domain in the lower 48 states. Another 46 are in various stages, with a few not yet even begun. BLM regulations provide for either amendment or revision of the RMPs. Amendments are relatively minor adjustments to the plan and occur frequently. Revisions, on the other hand, entail a major reworking of the plan and require that the resource area staff go through all the steps for plan preparation, including compliance with the NEPA. Unlike the Forest Service, which is required by the NFMA to revise a forest plan at least every 15 years, there is no statutory life for RMPs. The first revision of an RMP (a plan that was completed in 1984) is now in process.

In sum, RMPs, like forest plans, are intended to be dynamic, ever-changing documents. Where RMPs are in preparation, national park managers would be well advised to maintain close contact with BLM area and district managers to take advantage of opportunities to express views in both formal and informal settings. But the fact that an adjacent resource area has completed its RMP does not relieve a national park manager from maintaining close contact with his or her BLM counterpart to keep abreast of proposed RMP amendments.

A Special Opportunity: Areas of Critical Environmental Concern

The FLPMA directs BLM to identify Areas of Critical Environmental Concern (ACECs) and develop special protective approaches. ACECs are defined as places where "special management attention is required to protect and prevent irreparable damage to important historic, cultural, or scenic values, fish and wildlife resources or other natural systems or processes, or to protect life and safety from natural hazards."[11]

Late in 1988, BLM adopted guidelines for the designation of ACECs.[12] Under the guidelines, BLM lands adjacent to lands of other federal and state agencies must be examined to see if the "special values" of the other lands extend to BLM's domain. If so, ACEC designation may be warranted. The proposed RMP for the San Juan Resource Area in Utah demonstrates how ACECs might be used to help protect national park values. Three ACECs, ranging in size from 12,000 to 62,000 acres, have been proposed for areas around Canyonlands National Park. Two of the ACECs protect landforms that extend from the park onto BLM lands and views from and into the park. The third is intended to protect valuable wildlife habitat lying between the national park and the MantiLaSal National Forest.[13] The RMP also proposes a 1500-acre ACEC surrounding a small unit of the Hovenweep National Monument to protect outlying cultural resources, and another along the main highway entry to Natural Bridges National Monument to protect the view of the monument. In three of the ACECs, no mineral development will be allowed; in four of them, no ORV use; and in the wildlife-sensitive ACEC, grazing will be prohibited.

Procedures for Federal Agency Participation

The FLPMA emphasizes that BLM plans are to be prepared with involvement of the public, other federal agencies, and state, local, and tribal governments. Section 1739(e) of the act states:

> The Secretary [of the Interior] shall establish procedures . . . to give . . . federal, state, and local governments and the public adequate notice and the opportunity to comment on the formulation of standards and criteria for, and participate in, the preparation and execution of plans and programs for, and the management of, the public lands.[14]

Accordingly, BLM has promulgated regulations prescribing actions to be taken to foster public and agency involvement. The regulations require that BLM's state directors and its district and area managers know what is in the plans of other federal agencies and that those plans be considered in the development of RMPs. Any inconsistencies between another agency's plan and BLM plan proposals are to be resolved "to the extent practicable."[15] Any agency that believes a BLM plan is not consistent with its own officially adopted plan is to notify BLM in writing, calling attention to specific inconsistencies. BLM must then document how the inconsistencies were addressed. Overall, BLM must "provide for meaningful public involvement of other Federal agencies,"[16] and other federal agencies are to be given opportunities to provide advice and suggestions on "issues and topics which may affect or influence other agency or other government programs."[17]

However, the cold wording of regulations simply establishes *minimum* requirements aimed at satisfying the letter of the law. As in the case of the Forest Service, BLM officials at all levels may be open to informal meetings with anyone who wishes to discuss the agency's policies or programs.

Ensuring Consistency

The FLPMA's consistency requirement provides a special opportunity for National Park Service managers to influence BLM planning. Echoing the language of the act, BLM regulations state that RMPs "shall be consistent with *officially approved or adopted* resource related plans, and the policies and programs contained therein, of other federal agencies, . . . so long as the [RMPs] are also consistent with the purposes, policies, and programs of Federal laws and regulation applicable to public lands"[18] (emphasis added). Thus, it is critically important that a national park's plans be officially approved or adopted if park officials are to contest a BLM plan on the grounds of inconsistency. When notified of a possible inconsistency between an approved plan for another federal unit and the RMP, the burden falls on BLM planners to "show how those inconsistencies were addressed, and, if possible, resolved."[19]

Conflict Resolution

As with the Forest Service, the National Park Service's director has signed a memorandum of understanding with the director of BLM that commits the two agencies to the improvement of planning and program coordination and communications.[20] The memorandum encourages informal communications at all levels but specifies that deputy directors of the park service and BLM are to meet at least twice a year, as are park service regional directors and their counterpart BLM state directors.

The park service-BLM memorandum also introduces conflict resolution mechanisms. Recognizing "the potential for conflicts in their respective missions, plans, and programs," the two directors acknowledged that "it is in the best interest of both agencies to anticipate these conflicts early, avoid them if possible, and resolve them if possible."[21] The memorandum pledges the agencies to experiment with innovative dispute-resolution techniques, such as mediation by neutral third parties. Every attempt is to be made to resolve disputes at the lowest organizational level possible; if this fails, it will be sent to the next highest level of authority. Presumably, the two agency directors would resolve especially prickly differences.

CONCLUSION

The multiple-use lands managed by the Forest Service and BLM have far broader purposes than do lands in the National Park System. The uses and values of Forest Service and BLM lands encompass both preservation and development of economically valuable resources. Forest Service and BLM managers strive to satisfy highly diverse constituencies and are held personally accountable for carrying out agency policies and programs and meeting production targets for the lands in their charge. Expecting multiple-use lands to be managed exactly like adjacent national parks would be unreasonable. Nevertheless, park service managers can achieve much through watchfulness, open communications with their Forest Service and BLM counterparts, arguments based on sound scientific knowledge, and solid, up-to-date park management plans.

REFERENCES

1. Quoted in Samuel T. Dana and Sally K. Fairfax, *Forest and Range Policy* (New York: McGraw-Hill Book Co., 1980), p.82.

2. 16 U.S.C. §528.

3. 16 U.S.C. §1601.

4. 36 C.F.R. 219.7(d).

5. Memorandum of Understanding Between the Forest Service and the National Park Service for Planning and Program Coordination, dated February 22, 1988.

6. For a good case study of Forest Service attitudes towards a national park, see Joseph L. Sax and Robert B. Keiter, "Glacier National Park and Its Neighbors: A Study of Federal Interagency Relations," *Ecology Law Quarterly* 14, no. 2 (1987):207-49.

7. Public Land Law Review Commission, *One Third of the Nation's Land* (Washington, D.C.: U.S. Government Printing Office, 1970).

8. The primary sources for information on the Bureau of Land Management's planning process are two unpublished speeches by BLM's chief of planning, David C. Williams: "Planning Approaches in the Bureau of Land Management," September 1987, and "Integrating Impact Assessment into Resources Planning: the Bureau of Land Management," July 1988. A condensed version of the first speech appeared in *Trends* magazine (National Park Service and National Recreation and Parks Association) 24, no. 2, 1987.

9. 43 U.S.C. §1701.

10. 43 U.S.C. §1712(c)(9).

11. 43 U.S. 1702(a) (1985).

12. *BLM Manual*, Sec. 1613, Areas of Critical Environmental Concern (Bureau of Land Management).

13. David Williams, Bureau of Land Management, personal communication, June 1989.

14. 43 U.S.C. §1739(e) (1984).

15. 43 C.F.R. 1610.3-1(a).

16. 43 C.F.R. 1610.3-1(a); 43 C.F.R. 1610.3-1(b).

17. 43 C.F.R. 1610.3-1(b).

18. 43 C.F.R. 1610.3-2(a).

19. 43 C.F.R. 1610.3-1(e).

20. "Memorandum of Understanding between the Bureau of Land Management (BLM) and the National Park Service (NPS) for Planning and Program Coordination," September 15, 1987.

21. Ibid.

Chapter 9

Mining Laws and Regulations and the National Park System

by Frank Buono, Carol McCoy, and Barbara West*

Congress charged the National Park Service with the responsibility of managing the 354 units that comprise the National Park System so as to preserve and protect the resources and values of those units for current and future generations. In carrying out this mandate, the park service must contend, at times, with existing land uses that pre-date the establishment of the units. A primary example of such land uses is the existence of nonfederal ownership of mineral rights within the boundaries of certain units. Congress also has allowed the creation of new mineral rights through the issuance of federal mineral leases in three national recreation areas, subject to certain conditions.

Based on available data, individuals have rights to minerals in more than 200 units of the National Park System. However, active mineral development currently occurs in approximately 27 units. Examples of mineral rights include 1872 mining claims for talc in Death Valley National Monument (California/Nevada) and for gold in Denali National Park and Preserve (Alaska); oil and gas subsurface rights in the Big Cypress National Preserve (Florida); an open pit haydite (used in making cement) mine in Cuyahoga Valley National Recreation Area (Ohio); and federal mineral leases at Glen Canyon National Recreation Area (Utah/Arizona). Mineral development activities

---

*Natural Resources Report Series 86-2, "Regulating Mineral Activity in NPS Units," prepared by Frank Buono and Barbara West, was revised by Carol McCoy to form this chapter.

include oil and gas wells, pipelines, open-pit mining, gold dredging in stream beds, and mineral exploration.

Depending on the type of mineral right, the activity proposed, and the language that established the individual unit, the park service can employ a variety of tools, ranging from regulation to land acquisition, to protect park resources and values inside park boundaries. The service also works with adjacent land managers (such as the Forest Service, the Bureau of Land Management, and states) to protect parks from proposed mining activities. To do so, the park service monitors proposed and active mineral operations adjacent to park units. When a given activity is considered a threat to park resources or values, the service is expected to take all appropriate steps to protect park resources. These steps might include:

- recommending the adoption of measures to mitigate the adverse effects associated with a proposed operation (for example, required containerized drilling mud disposal in connection with nonfederal oil and gas development at Big Cypress National Preserve);
- requesting the selection of alternative mineral lease tracts (for example, federal coal leasing adjacent to Theodore Roosevelt National Park); and
- seeking a legal injunction to have a proposed or existing activity stopped when all other efforts fail to produce a satisfactory outcome (for example, preclusion of rock blasting at Buffalo National River).

This chapter provides a brief overview of the types of mineral rights that exist in units of the National Park System, the laws and regulations governing the development of those rights, and, where no regulations exist, some of the options available to park resource managers to protect park resources and values from mineral development inside park boundaries. It also briefly highlights some of the opportunities available to work with neighboring land managers to protect parks.

TYPES OF MINERAL RIGHTS EXISTING IN PARK UNITS

Three types of mineral rights exist within park units: mining claims, federal mineral leases, and nonfederally owned minerals. Each of these mineral rights constitutes a legally recognized and constitutionally protected property interest. Thus, if the park service seeks to acquire these interests, it must observe the due process requirements of the

U.S. Constitution and provide just compensation to the owners.

Mining Claims

Under the Mining Law of 1872, individuals may enter federal public domain lands that are open to claim location and stake a claim to such lands if they discover a valuable mineral.[1] Enacted back in the days when most mineral development was conducted by prospectors with pickaxes and mules, this law has remained virtually unchanged.

Claims can be located for certain types of minerals such as gold, silver, tin, lead, and uranium, generally known as "hardrock" or "locatable" minerals. There are two general types of claims: lode claims, associated with vein or ore deposits; and placer claims, associated with minerals deposited in the beds of streams. In addition, claimants can establish millsites for processing minerals taken from claims. Both lode and placer claims are approximately 20 acres in size; millsites cannot be greater than 5 acres in size. Claimants can locate as many claims as they wish. Claims located contiguously by one claimant are known as a claim group.

A properly located claim, if valid, gives the claimant a property right to the minerals in the claim and the right to use as much of the surface and its resources as are necessary to extract the minerals. In addition, the Mining Law of 1872 provides claimants an implied right of access to their claims. When a claim is located, the United States retains ownership of both the minerals and the surface. Title to the minerals passes to the claimant when the minerals are extracted. This is known as an unpatented claim.

The Mining Law of 1872 also establishes a process by which a claimant may bring the claim to patent. When patented, actual ownership of (title to) the minerals, and in most cases the surface and its resources, passes from the United States to the claimant.

With a few exceptions, when Congress and the president have created national park units, they have closed those units to mineral entry under the mining laws. Thus, persons could no longer locate new claims on these lands and any claims filed would be null and void. Nonetheless, there are approximately 2,300 mining claims in a total of 24 park units today. This is so because:

- Congress previously allowed claim location in a handful of units, such as Death Valley and Organ Pipe Cactus national monuments, and Crater Lake and Mount McKinley (now Denali)

National Parks, even after the units were established; and
- when certain units were established or expanded, those units incorporated lands that were already encumbered with existing mining claims. Among such units are Denali and Wrangell-St. Elias national parks and preserve, and Great Basin National Park.

Seventy-four percent of the mining claims within park units are found in Alaska on lands that came under park service jurisdiction in 1978 and 1980. In the lower 48 States, Death Valley National Monument and Great Basin National Park contain the majority of mining claims within park units.

Federal Mineral Leases

Nearly 50 years after establishing the mining claim method of transferring federally owned minerals into private hands, Congress created another method for disposing of certain federally owned minerals that would return substantially greater revenues to the federal government. This method, known as the federal mineral leasing system, is governed by the Mineral Leasing Act of 1920 on public domain lands and by the Mineral Leasing Act for Acquired Lands of 1947 on acquired federal lands. Under the leasing system, a citizen obtains a lease that constitutes a right to develop certain federal minerals in exchange for paying the United States a royalty (a percentage of the value of the minerals produced). In addition, if a citizen obtains a lease through the competitive leasing process, an up-front bonus bid payment must be made to the federal government. The United States decides which lands and minerals will be leased.

Under this system, as with mining claims, the United States retains ownership of both the lands and minerals. The party leasing these minerals receives title only to those minerals actually extracted. The minerals that can be leased include oil and gas, tar sands, oil shale, coal, potassium, phosphate, and sodium. These minerals are generically known as the "leasables." The line between the leasable and locatable (that is, mining claim) minerals is not always firm; Congress occasionally has authorized the leasing of locatable minerals, which normally are subject only to the mining laws.[2]

Approximately nine park units contain federal mineral leases. These leases exist because Congress specifically authorized leasing of federal minerals in the enabling acts for three units (Lake Mead, Whiskeytown, and Glen Canyon national recreation areas) and because lands already encumbered by existing federal leases were incorporated into the National Park System when several units were created or enlarged. Examples of such units are Chaco Culture National Historical Park and Dinosaur National Monument. Such leases, like a valid mining claim, are legally recognized and protected property interests.

Nonfederally Owned Minerals

The United States now holds title to almost all lands within park boundaries in units created before 1961. Between 1961 and 1980, however, the park system underwent rapid expansion. Unlike during earlier periods of expansion, many of the newer units were not carved from existing federal lands, and contained lands and mineral rights that could thus be devoted to nonpark purposes such as mineral development by their nonfederal owners.

In addition, Congress specifically limited the park service's ability to acquire nonfederal mineral rights in the enabling legislation of several of these newer units. For example, legislation establishing Big Cypress National Preserve provides: "No improved property . . ., nor oil and gas rights, shall be acquired without the consent of the owner unless the Secretary, in his judgment, determines that such property is subject to, or threatened with, uses which are or would be, detrimental to the purpose of the Preserve."[3] Other units with statutory provisions limiting the service's acquisition authority include Big Thicket National Preserve, Texas; Jean Lafitte National Historical Park, Louisiana; Fort Union National Monument, New Mexico; and Padre Island National Seashore, Texas.

The enabling legislation of some of these units contains statutory provisions pertaining to the exercise of nonfederally owned mineral rights. In Big Thicket National Preserve for example, Congress directed the secretary of the interior to "promulgate and publish such rules and regulations . . . as he deems necessary and appropriate to limit and control the . . . exploration for, and extraction of, oil, gas, and other minerals."[4] Other units with similar authority include Padre Island, Big Cypress, Jean Lafitte, Gateway, New River Gorge, and Big South Fork.

While outstanding mineral rights exist in more than 200 park units, whether those rights will ever be developed depends on a variety of factors, such as concentration and extent of mineral deposits, overburden ratios (depth and thickness of deposit), available transportation, proximity to markets, price, labor cost, and environmental mitigation requirements. Currently, active nonfederal operations occur in 19 parks units: 561 nonfederal oil and gas wells and/or pipelines in 10 parks, 1 coal-mining operation at New River Gorge National River, and 22 nonfederal solid mineral operations in 11 parks.

LAWS AND REGULATIONS GOVERNING MINERAL DEVELOPMENT IN PARK UNITS

Mining Claims

The Mining in the Parks Act of 1976 closed the last six units of the National Park System that were open under its enabling legislation or other statutes to the location of mining claims. This law also directed the secretary of the interior to regulate all activities within park units in connection with the exercise of mineral rights on patented and unpatented mining claims.

The park service promulgated regulations under the authority of the Mining in the Parks Act.[5] The regulations are designed to permit claimants to exercise their rights while preserving the integrity of units of the National Park System. The primary method the park service uses to enforce these regulations is to require a service-approved plan of operations for all mineral exploration and development activities proposed for patented and unpatented mining claims within park units. The park service also requires that operators post a bond to ensure that mining operations conform to the plan and to ensure that reclamation will be completed. In some cases, the park service may not be able to approve a plan as submitted, but may be able to approve an alternative one.

If, because of the presence of sensitive environmental resources, no level of mineral development would be acceptable, the park service can extinguish the property interest in a mining claim through acquisition.

Federal Mineral Leases

In the three units of the National Park System open by law to federal mineral leasing and development (that is, Lake Mead, Glen Canyon, and Whiskeytown national recreation areas), leasing may be permitted only if the park service determines that the subsequent development will not have a significant adverse effect upon the resources or administration of the unit.

The appropriate regional director must make this determination before the Bureau of Land Management (BLM) can issue a lease or permit in one of these units. In addition, every lease issued in such units must contain a stipulation that the park service must approve the conduct of all site-specific activities. For combined hydrocarbon leases, the park service also must determine that the issuance or development of such leases within Glen Canyon National Recreation Area will not have a significant adverse effect on any contiguous units of the National Park System.

The regulations that control activities on federal mineral leases within park units are the same as those that apply to all federal mineral leases on any federal lands: 43 C.F.R. 3100 for the leasing and development of federal oil and gas, including tar sands, and 43 C.F.R. 3500 for the leasing and development of federal solid minerals other than coal and oil shale. Both parts of the regulations cited above require park service concurrence and approval before the BLM may take any action with respect to a lease or permit on lands under the service's jurisdiction. In practice, this means that the park service is able to attach special stipulations and operating conditions to leases and permits in its units, making it possible to preserve and protect park service resources to the maximum extent compatible with congressional direction to permit mineral leasing and development.

Nonfederally Owned Minerals

Congress, in the Organic Act and in unit-specific enabling legislation, has authorized the secretary of the interior to develop regulations for the park units under his or her jurisdiction. In addition, Congress has specifically authorized the secretary to promulgate regulations for the development of nonfederal oil and gas in units such as Big Thicket and Big Cypress national preserves, Padre Island National Seashore, and Jean Lafitte National Historical Park.

Based upon these authorities, the park service has promulgated regulations governing the exercise of nonfederal oil and gas rights in all of its units.[6] The regulations for nonfederal oil and gas, just as those for mining claims, require park service approval of a plan of operations before the nonfederal party may conduct operations. Plans of operations and reclamation bonds form the basis for park service regulatory control of these nonfederal mineral rights. The service has not yet promulgated regulations governing the development of non-federal minerals other than oil and gas. (Figures 9.1 and 9.2, at the end of this chapter, contain an overview of the laws and regulations governing federal and nonfederal mineral development in units of the National Park System, respectively.)

MINERAL DEVELOPMENT IN PARK UNITS
NOT SUBJECT TO PARK SERVICE REGULATIONS

The National Park Service currently does not regulate several types of mineral development, either because it concluded that there was a lack of clear congressional direction to control those specific activities or because no significant adverse effects to unit resources had resulted from such activities. These views are changing and efforts are under way to develop regulations to control such activities.

Mineral activities presently unregulated by the park service are nonfederal oil and gas where access is not on, through, or across federal lands. These activities also include nonfederal minerals other than oil and gas.

The regulations that control activities associated with nonfederal oil and gas rights within park units apply only when the potential operator must cross federally owned or controlled lands or waters in order to exercise those nonfederally held mineral rights.[7] At present, these rules—if diligently enforced—appear sufficient to protect park resources and values. The possibility remains, however, that the exercise of nonfederal oil and gas rights could cause unacceptable damage to unit resources in those instances where operators may gain access to their nonfederal oil and gas within a park without crossing federally owned or controlled lands or waters.

The enabling statutes for the various park units containing nonfederal oil and gas do not condition the authority of the park service to regulate nonfederal oil and gas activities within those units on access over federally owned or controlled lands or waters. However, park service regulations currently restrict service regulatory authority even though the Congress has conferred on the service the general authority to control the exercise of nonfederal oil and gas activities within its units irrespective of the operator's means of access.

The park service is currently considering regulatory changes to address this issue. The service is also contemplating developing regulations governing nonfederal minerals other than oil and gas.[8]

Park Service Options for Controlling These Mineral Operations

Until the National Park Service revises existing regulations and promulgates new ones to control development of these types or classes of nonfederal minerals in units of the National Park System, park resource managers must be inventive and draw upon alternative means to protect park resources and values. In some units, park resource managers have used special use permits to authorize and regulate the extraction of nonfederal sand and gravel. Several of the general park service regulations also may be used to control certain aspects of potential nonfederal mineral operations.[9] In addition to special use permits and use of these general park service regulations, park resource managers can use the following options:

- Pursue *formal agreements* (such as memoranda of understanding or other agreements) with state and local agencies to resolve nonfederal mineral problems. Such agreements could result in enforcement of state regulations and procedures where applicable. At a minimum, park resource managers should pursue continuous, informal coordination with such agencies. This is particularly important in those cases where operators have abandoned wellsites within the boundaries of a unit contrary to state regulations. Those operations best handled by close cooperation with the multiple authorities include diking of tanks, cleanup of pits, and placement of identification and warning signs.
- Pursue *voluntary surface use agreements* with operators. Surface use agreements may be of limited utility if operators do not benefit directly from such agreements and, in practice, only incur costs. However, park managers might be able to work out agreements, for example, to fix wells; eliminate junkyards and trash sites; remove unused surface flow lines; fence and dike tanks; clean up pits; put up signs; and reclaim abandoned well pads.
- Secure *funds* from government accounts such as the park service's Cyclic Maintenance Fund and the Natural Resource Preservation Program. Monies from these and other government sources could be used to remove abandoned equipment, including surface flow lines, and to clean up abandoned pits and wellsites.
- Seek *injunctive relief* against nonfederal mineral operators. Negligence and nuisance are the most likely causes of action that the park service could bring against these operators. Injuctive relief must be obtained from a court judge. In requesting such relief,

a showing must be made that irreparable injury will result if the activity is not halted or precluded. A court judge will evaluate the showing and other factors in determining whether to grant this extraordinary remedy.

- Initiate *acquisition proceedings* to preclude nonfederal mineral development if the proposed development is in derogation of unit resources and/or values. With one exception—Jean Lafitte National Historical Park—the park service can acquire nonfederal mineral rights even in those units where Congress placed limitations on acquisition, such as Big Cypress and Big Thicket.[10] In many cases state-owned nonfederal mineral rights may be acquired only by exchange or donation. A park unit's enabling act will delineate any restrictions on acquisition that may apply.

OPPORTUNITIES TO WORK WITH ADJACENT LANDOWNERS TO PROTECT PARK UNITS

Opportunities to protect park resources and values from the adverse impacts associated with mineral development extend beyond park boundaries. Key federal agencies that the park service needs to work with include the BLM, the Forest Service, and the Office of Surface Mining Reclamation and Enforcement (OSMRE). While the OSMRE does not have land management responsibilities, it does oversee the implementation of the Surface Mining Control and Reclamation Act,[11] which regulates surface coal mining on federal and nonfederal lands. The park service also needs to work with appropriate state agencies.

At the federal level, the park service has entered into memoranda of understanding with both the BLM and the Forest Service to promote better resource management through planning and program coordination (see chapter 10). Through these formal mechanisms, the park service can educate the BLM and Forest Service to the importance of accounting for and mitigating the spillover effects associated with mineral development on lands adjoining park units. The park service can also use them as an additional springboard for raising its concerns regarding proposed rule makings. Strong working relationships need to be established at the Washington headquarters and field levels. Information needs to be exchanged regarding land-use planning, proposed and final rule making, and site-specific authorizations of mineral development proposals.

At the state level, park service resource managers need to establish similar working relationships with pertinent staff. Institutional arrangements will vary state by state. In most cases, park resource managers will need to work with state staff in natural resource management and mineral development to get national park protection concerns addressed in state land-use plans, regulations, and permitting activities concerning minerals.

REFERENCES

1. 30 U.S.C. §21 *et seq.*.
2. In the Combined Hydrocarbon Leasing Act of 1981 (30 U.S.C. §81 *et seq.*), Congress redefined oil and gas to include tar sands, thus adding tar sands to the list of leasable minerals. For a limited period, which has expired, this act allowed persons with existing oil and gas leases within areas designated as Special Tar Sand Areas (STSAs) to convert their leases to combined hydrocarbon leases. One of the designated STSAs, known as the Tar Sand Triangle, lies partially within the Glen Canyon National Recreation Area and adjacent to Canyonlands National Park. Also, this act authorizes the secretary of the interior to lease federal tar sands competitively.
3. 16 U.S.C. §698f.
4. 16 U.S.C. §698(c).
5. 36 C.F.R. 9(A).
6. 36 C.F.R. 9(B).
7. Ibid.
8. If promulgated, such regulations will be codified at 36 C.F.R. 9(C).
9. 36 C.F.R. 1, 2, 4, 5, and 14.
10. In Jean Lafitte, Congress limited the secretary's authority to acquire nonfederal oil and gas to only those situations where the park service has obtained the consent of the owner (16 U.S.C. §230a[a]).
11. 30 U.S.C. §1201.

Figure 9.1
Laws and Regulations for Federally Owned Minerals
Within National Park Service Units

LAWS	NOTES	APPLICABLE REGULATIONS
MINING CLAIMS		
Mining Law of 1872 (30 U.S.C. 21 *et seq.*)	*General* Allows claims on public domain lands; claimants have mineral rights to unpatented mining claims, claimants gain fee title to surface and subsurface only through patent claims.	BLM 43 C.F.R. 3800
	Park Service Units All park service units now closed to location of mining claims (mineral entry); approximately 2300 unpatented and patented mining claims exist in 24 units, mostly in Alaska.	
Mineral Oil Placer Claim Act of 1897 (30 U.S.C. 101)	*General* Allows placer claims for oil (law superseded by Mineral Leasing Act of 1920).	
	Park Service Units Old oil claims may exist in some units.	NPS 36 C.F.R. 9(A)[1]
	Some claims were eligible for conversion to combined hydrocarbon leases only within special tar sand areas (STSAs), primarily in Utah.	BLM 43 C.F.R. 3140.7
Mining in the Parks Act of 1976 (16 U.S.C. 1901)	*Park Service Units* Closed last six units open to mineral location (Mount McKinley, Death Valley, Organ Pipe Cactus, Coronado, Crater Lake, Glacier Bay).	
	Authorizes secretary of the interior to regulate 1982 unpatented and patented mining claims within all park service units.	NPS 36 C.F.R. 9A

[1] 36 C.F.R. 9(A) is section 36, *Code of Federal Regulations,* Part 9 Minerals Management, Subpart A-Mining and Mining Claims.

LAWS	NOTES	APPLICABLE REGULATIONS
MINERAL LEASES		
General Laws		
General Leasing Act of 1920 (30 U.S.C. 181) 1926 1927 1947 1960 1981	*General* Authorizes secretary of the interior to issue leases for leasable minerals on public domain lands. *Park Service Units* No mineral leasing allowed in park service units.	BLM 43 C.F.R. 3100.0-3(a)2(i) (oil and gas) BLM 43 C.F.R. 3400.2(a)(1) (coal) BLM 43 C.F.R. 3500.8(a) (all solid leaseable minerals except oil shale and coal)
Acquired Lands Mineral Leasing Act of 1947 (36 U.S.C. 351)	*General* Allows mineral leasing on acquired lands that were not covered by 1920 Mineral Leasing Act. *Park Service Units* No mineral leasing allowed in park service units.	BLM 43 C.F.R. 3100.0-3-(b)(2)(1) (oil and gas) BLM 43 C.F.R. 3400.2(a)(1) (all solid leasable minerals except oil and shale coal)
Atomic Energy Act of 1954 (43 U.S.C. 2097)	*General* Allows secretary of energy to issue leases or permits for uranium on public domain lands. *Park Service Units* Secretary of energy may issues leases or permits in park service areas only if President declares a national emergency.	None None
Geothermal Steam Act of 1970 (30 U.S.C. 1001) as amended in 1988	*General* Allows secretary of the interior to issue leases for geothermal resources. *Park Service Units* Law prohibits leasing in all park service units and near some units.	BLM 43 C.F.R. 3201.1-6

LAWS	NOTES	APPLICABLE REGULATIONS
Federal Coal Leasing Amendments Act of 1976 (30 U.S.C. 201)	*General* Adds significant environmental protection measures to coal leases issued under the mineral leasing acts of 1920 and 1947.	BLM 43 C.F.R. 3400.2(a)(1) (coal)
	Park Service Units This act specifically prohibits coal leasing in park service units and national recreation areas authorized by law.	
Combined Hydrocarbon Leasing Act of 1981 (30 U.S.C. 181)	*General* Amends Mineral Leasing Act of 1920; owners of oil and gas leases or placer oil claims in special tar sand areas (STSAa) may convert to combined hydrocarbon leases. Also allows for competitive tar sand leasing.	BLM 43 C.F.R. 3140 BLM 43 C.F.R. 3140.4-1(b) BLM 43 C.F.R. 3140.6(c) BLM 43 C.F.R. 3140.7 BLM 43 C.F.R. 3141.4-2(b)
	Park Service Units This act does not modify the general prohibition on leasing in park service units; however, lease conversion can be issued in only park service areas open to leasing by their enabling legislation, with park service approval. Although 3 units are open to mineral leasing by their enabling acts, an STSA has only been designated within Glen Canyon National Recreation Area.	
Special Enabling Laws		
Act of 10/8/64 (16 U.S.C. 460[n])	*Park Service Units* Created *Lake Mead* National Recreation Area; secretary of the interior may issue mineral leases.	Present regulations allows leasing in these 3 NRAs.

LAWS	NOTES	APPLICABLE REGULATIONS
Act of 9/8/65 (16 U.S.C. 460[q])	Created *Whiskeytown* National Recreation Area; secretary of the interior authorized to permit removal of leasable federal minerals under mineral leasing acts of 1920 and 1947 and nonleasable federal minerals under the Reclamation Act of 1939.	1. Oil and gas BLM 43 C.F.R. 3100.0-3(g[4]) BLM 43 C.F.R. 3109.2 2. Solid minerals (other than coal[2] & oil shale[3])
Act of 10/27/72 (16 U.S.C. 460[dd])	Created *Glen Canyon* National Recreation Area; secretary of the interior may issue mineral leases.	BLM 43 C.F.R. 3500 BLM 43 C.F.R. 3582
Act of 1988 (P.L.100-68)	Allows the sale of sand & gravel from *Lake Chelan* National Recreation Area to the residents of Stehekin.	
Reclamation Act 1939[4]	*General* Allows secretary of the interior to permit removal of sand, gravel, and other minerals and building materials from federal lands in federal reclamation projects. *Park Service Units* The phrase "other minerals" has been interpreted to include hardrock minerals in the 3 park service units.	
Leases on Indian Trust Land		
Allotted Lands Leasing Act of 1909 (25 U.S.C. 396)	*General* Allows leases to be issued for any minerals by the Bureau of Indian Affairs or allottee in certain circumstances. *Park Service Units* Allows leases to be issued for any minerals by the Bureau of Indian Affairs.	BIA 25 C.F.R. 272

[2] Coal leasing is prohibited.
[3] Oil shale regulations do not exist.
[4] This act is cited in the enabling legislation for each of the above units except Lake Mead.

LAWS	NOTES	APPLICABLE REGULATIONS

MINERAL MATERIALS

LAWS	NOTES	APPLICABLE REGULATIONS
Mineral Materials Disposal Act of 1947 (30 U.S.C. 601 as amended in 1954 1955 1962)	*General* Authorizes secretary of the interior to sell or donate to local governments sand, gravel, stone, pumice, pumicite, cinders, clay, and petrified wood.	BLM 43 C.F.R. 3600.0-3(a)(3)
	Prior to 1955, these mineral materials were subject to claim or sale; prior to 1962 petrified wood was subject to claim, sale, or donation.	
	Park Service Units Act prohibits sale of materials in park service units.	
	No pre-1962 mining claims of these materials exist in park service units. If any exist, regulate via:	NPS 36 C.F.R. 9A

Figure 9.2
Nonfederally Owned Minerals in the National Park System (NPS)
(by Mineral Type)

MINERALS TYPE	LAWS	UNITS	APPLICABLE REGULATIONS
Oil and Gas	Enabling Acts for Several NPS areas; NPS Organic Act (16 U.S.C. 1)	Some units' enabling acts or agreements contain language regarding the acquisition of nonfederal (private or state) oil and gas rights or their development (e.g., Lake Meredith, Padre Island, Big Cypress, Big Thicket, Jean Lafitte). Nonfederally owned oil and gas exist in many other NPS units (e.g., Cuyahoga, Chickasaw national recreation areas).	NPS 36 C.F.R. 9(B), but only if access to oil and gas is on through, or across federally owned or controlled waters. If access can be obtained otherwise, 36 C.F.R. 9B does not apply.
Coal	Surface Mining Control and Reclamation Act of 1977 (30 U.S.C. 1201)	This law prohibits surface coal mining on any lands in any unit subject to valid existing rights.	OSM 30 C.F.R. 761.11
		Valid existing rights defined via regulations. For federal lands in NPS areas, the Office of Surface Mining (OSM) makes the valid existing rights determination. For nonfederally-owned lands in NPS areas, the state regulatory authority under an OSM-approved program makes the valid existing rights determination.	OSM 30 C.F.R. 761.5 OSM 30 C.F.R. 740.0(a)4 OSM 30 C.F.R. 745.13.(o)
		The NPS must be notified of valid existing determinations on its lands.	OSM 30 C.F.R. 30 761.12(b)(2)

Figure 9.2
Nonfederally Owned Minerals in the National Park System (NPS)
(by Mineral Type)
(continued)

MINERALS TYPE	LAWS	UNITS	APPLICABLE REGULATIONS
Nonfederal Minerals Other than Oil and Gas	Nonfederally owned minerals developed by owners or their lessees subject to federal, state, and local laws	Nonfederally owned mineral rights exist in many units.	No specific NPS regulations exist. However, conditions may be attached to permits issued under 36 C.F.R. 5.6 for commercial vehicles used in connection with developing these nonfederal minerals. Other means also exist for protecting unit resources and values from such development.

Part III

The Nonfederal Setting

The kinds of development occurring outside most park boundaries that affect park resources are typically ones within the domain of state and local government. Virtually all subdivisions, commercial structures, strip developments, and tourist attractions go up on private lands, outside the control of federal agencies and beyond the reach of federal laws. Many of these developments—a shopping center here, small housing lots there, and so forth—may go relatively unnoticed on their own; their cumulative effect over time, however, can have serious consequences for park resources.

The strong tradition of private property rights in this country, coupled with the lack of federal involvement in how these lands are developed, make these especially thorny issues for the National Park Service as it attempts to protect park resources. Moreover, even if land-use controls have some degree of acceptability at the local level, there is generally tremendous antagonism toward federal involvement in these issues. Yet in a very real way, the success of the parks and the condition of park resources will rest increasingly on decisions made by nonfederal officials. The great risk is that as the park service seeks to get more active in state and local decisions about private land uses, it will be perceived more as a bossy neighbor and less as a helpful and concerned partner.

As a result, those concerned with park resources will need to take several steps to ensure that the needs of park resources are reflected in decisions states, localities, and private parties make about neighboring land uses. Discussed in detail in the following chapters, these include:

- becoming familiar with the way states and local governments make land-use decisions;
- showing greater sensitivity to local needs and the problems they face;
- seeing the nonprofit private sector as a necessary partner for advancing park resource needs in local forums concerning development on private land; and
- developing solid information and data about the condition of park resources and the potential impacts of developments outside the boundaries on them.

Chapter 10

Park Resources and State Programs

by Michael A. Mantell

State programs regarding land and distinctive resources provide some important opportunities to protect National Park System lands. The Tenth Amendment of the U.S. Constitution has reserved to each state the power to protect and enhance the public health, safety, and general welfare of its citizens. Some states have, in turn, delegated portions of these so-called police powers to local governments, yet nearly every state has retained some degree of jurisdiction over land, especially over critical areas such as floodplains, wetlands, cultural resources, and the coastal zone. State involvement in these lands has increased significantly over the past two decades, caused, in part, by local actions that cut across community boundaries and by rising demands for fiscal and technical resources.

Governments can often be major offenders of a land protection program. Constructing public facilities, supplying services or other infrastructure, or lending capital for large improvements near National Park System lands are all government activities that can undermine resource protection efforts. In this regard, state laws provide a significant tool for requiring government compliance with these programs. In most states, local and even state agencies are subject to state laws and regulations.[1]

State activities in regulating land uses that affect national park units are numerous. The approaches states have taken are marked by their diversity and responsiveness to individual concerns. State roles range from providing a link between federal and local programs, to authoriz-

145

ing and initiating local programs while planning and developing their own, to performing significant information-gathering and enforcement functions. Yet some basic similarities exist among the laws and regulatory activities. Both the common elements and differences are highlighted in this brief look at state-level programs. Of course, the variety of state laws and programs requires the reader to assess the applicability of a specific point to his or her particular situation.

STATE ENABLING LEGISLATION

Traditionally, land-use regulations have been the province of local governments, with the state providing the authority to regulate and retaining the power to assist in the effort through coordination and technical advice. Many localities are creatures of the state and have only those powers that are granted to them. In these jurisdictions, powers to regulate floodplains, wetlands, and other land areas may be found in state enabling legislation. A 1977 report for the U.S. Department of Housing and Development found that:

> with minor exceptions existing enabling statutes provide sufficient authority for municipal adoption of zoning, subdivision controls, and building codes in all States. No court has found broad enabling authority insufficient for the adoption of regulations.[2]

As part of enabling authority, states often require that local zoning be "in accordance with a comprehensive plan" that is locally developed. Some 15 states have made such planning mandatory, with 9 (including the District of Columbia) legally requiring consistency between zoning and the plan.[3] In many cases, local plans must address various goals under state enabling law, including the protection of natural, cultural, and recreational resources.

Home rule is another source of local power. Most states permit home rule, in which case a local government itself drafts its own charter and determines its power. Because each community drafts its own charter, the distribution of home-rule powers varies significantly among localities. Yet all of the states granting municipalities home-rule powers also authorize them to adopt zoning, subdivision regulations, and, in most instances, building codes. Thus, home-rule powers provide an independent basis for the adoption of such regulations and, depending on the nature of home rule, may allow home-rule communities to go further than other localities that are only subject to state enabling legislation.

State enabling legislation is the most indirect method for state involvement in land-use activities that affect national parks. Nonetheless, the broad police power language in most state enabling statutes is generally sufficient to provide localities with the power to regulate land uses in areas where activities outside park boundaries could affect national park resources. Local authority to protect and enhance aesthetic, historic, and open-space resources has been strengthened by numerous U.S. Supreme Court rulings, including those in *Penn Central Transportation Co.* v. *New York City*,[4] and *Agins* v. *City of Tiburon*.[5] (See chapter 11, "Local Governments and Park Resources," for a discussion of local legal powers.)

STATEWIDE GROWTH MANAGEMENT PROGRAMS

Several states have attempted to provide localities with a comprehensive framework for managing growth and protecting key assets. These programs have met with varying degrees of success, but all offer promise and have proved important in building awareness and strengthening local capabilities to manage growth. Following a relatively quiet period after much activity at the state level in the 1970s, there has been a recent resurgence of interest in state growth management programs. Since the mid-1980s, several eastern states have either developed new programs or refined existing ones.

Park managers can participate in the implementation of these laws to ensure that park resources are adequately protected in decisions made under them at the state and local levels. A sampling of these programs follows.

Oregon

Oregon's comprehensive statewide land-use management program was established by Senate Bill 100, the Land Use Act of 1973.[6] Protection of the state's agricultural and other sensitive natural lands was a prime motivation behind the program. The act established the Land Conservation and Development Commission (LCDC), which was charged with formulating statewide planning goals and policies. By 1975, LCDC had established some 15 goals, encompassing such areas as agricultural land, open space, urban growth, forestry, and housing.

Following the adoption of state goals, cities and counties had to develop comprehensive plans and implement development regulations consistent with the state goals and policies. As part of this, local governments also delineated boundaries of areas appropriate for future urban growth and those that are to remain rural for a 20-year planning period. State agencies were also required to adopt plans consistent with state goals, subject to review by the LCDC.

The delegation of authority within the program—with local planning and zoning regulations guided by general statewide goals and objectives and subject to state approval—has become a model for programs in other states, including Maine, Georgia, New Jersey, and Maryland.

By most accounts, Oregon's program has been effective in providing a consistent framework for local growth management efforts.[7] The program has received consistent and increasing public support in a series of statewide referenda. A statewide nonprofit land-use organization—1000 Friends of Oregon—has been instrumental in improving the program's effectiveness, building a constituency for it, and bringing about consistency among various levels of government.

Vermont

Vermont's Act 250, the Land Use and Development Law, was enacted in 1972 in response to rapid growth and particularly to second-home development.[8] It established a program of direct state development permitting to protect Vermont's environment. Under Act 250, the State Environmental Board reviews all projects that are likely to have a greater than local impact.

New legislation enacted in 1988—called Act 200—does not require towns to develop comprehensive plans. Rather, the state provides technical and financial assistance to local governments for planning. Access to the state's Geographic Information System is conditioned on local planning. Cooperating local plans must be consistent with regional plans. In turn, regional plans must be consistent with state guidelines. State agency actions must also be consistent with regional plans.

In addition to encouraging local comprehensive planning, Act 200 contained noteworthy funding inducements for a wide constituency. It alloted $20 million to the Vermont Housing and Land Conservation Trust Fund, created a milk price subsidy, and implemented a 95 percent tax-relief program for working farms. The legislature also increased the state's real estate transfer tax, with the proceeds to be divided between funding local and regional planning efforts and supporting the Vermont Housing and Land Conservation Trust Fund.

Florida

Florida has enacted a series of increasingly ambitious growth management statutes. In 1972, the state enacted the Environmental Land and Water Management Act, which established critical area and development-of-regional-impact (DRI) regulatory programs. These programs apply state oversight to a limited number of development proposals or a limited geographic area.[9] The state experience in both programs, however, was important to the later expansion of the state role in the 1980s.[10]

In 1975, the state enacted the Local Government Comprehensive Planning Act. This statute required all cities and counties in the state to adopt comprehensive plans, but it provided for little state review.

In 1984 and 1985, as a result of continuing rapid growth, increasing traffic congestion, and inadequate infrastructure, Florida passed new legislation requiring local governments to adopt comprehensive plans and development regulations. These local plans are reviewed by the state for consistency with the state plan. Communities that refuse to bring their policies into conformance with the state plan face financial sanctions. The legislation also provides great latitude for citizens to challenge plans in administrative hearings and to appeal plans to the governor and cabinet.

Perhaps the most significant state policy requires "infra-structure concurrency": no new development will be approved until and unless the necessary public facilities are in place to serve the development. The legislation also requires the state's 11 regional planning councils to develop Comprehensive Regional Policy Plans to implement the state plan. These regional plans are the basis for review of developments of regional impact. State agencies must also adopt "functional plans" to implement the state plan.

Following Oregon's experience, a new group—1000 Friends of Florida—has been formed to ensure that the state's growth management program is enforced and that a broad constitutency exists for its success.

New Jersey

New Jersey, the nation's most densely populated state, has grappled for years with the consequences of urban and suburban sprawl. In 1986, the state legislature passed the State Planning Act, creating the New Jersey State Planning Commission and its staff arm, the Office of State Planning. The Office of State Planning was placed within the Department of the Treasury, which is seen as neither pro- nor anti-development, to help demonstrate the relationship between state planning and spending.[11] The commission has prepared a State Development and Redevelopment Plan to provide an integrated, comprehensive plan for the state's development and conservation needs. The plan establishes planning objectives for land use, housing, economic development, transportation, natural resources, conservation, agriculture, farmland retention, recreation, urban and suburban redevelopment, historic preservation, public facilities and services, and intergovernmental coordination.

An innovative aspect of New Jersey's law is a process called "cross-acceptance." Cross-acceptance is defined as a "process of comparison of planning policies among governmental levels with the purpose of attaining compatibility among local, county, and state plans." The act requires the proposed state plan and land-use map to be submitted to the counties and municipalities to negotiate cross-acceptance of the plan. Consistency between state and local plans is to be achieved through these negotiations between state and local officials.

Localities are not absolutely required to prepare plans that conform to the state plan, but the commission is authorized to withhold state highway, transit, sewer, water, park, and open space spending in localities that do not bring their local policies into conformance with the state plan. The state plan also contemplates enforcement of the plan through its environmental permitting.

Maine

Maine also adopted comprehensive statewide land-use planning legislation in 1988. The Maine Comprehensive Planning and Land Use Regulation Act, based on the Oregon model, has three major components.

First, the statute creates statewide land-use goals "to provide overall direction and consistency to the planning and regulatory actions of all state and municipal agencies affecting natural resource management, land use and development."

Second, the law mandates local comprehensive planning and growth management programs. Localities must submit their plans and programs to the newly created Office of Comprehensive Land Use Planning to be reviewed for consistency with state goals and policies. As in New Jersey, the penalty for a community's failure to adopt a certi-fied local growth management program within the mandated time frame is denial of funds to the locality under various planning, open-space acquisition, and community development block grant programs. Local plans must include an inventory and analysis of local and regional resources, a policy development section that relates the find-ings of the inventory and analysis to the state goals, and an implemen-tation strategy that includes a timetable for implementation. The guidelines in the statute are rather specific: Each municipality must establish growth areas and rural areas; policies to implement this distinction; a capital investment plan; and ordinances and policies to protect water quality, natural resources, access to coastal waters, agricultural and forestry resources, historic and archeological resources, and access to outdoor recreational oportunities. Each municipality must also ensure that local policies encourage the provision of afford-able housing within the community.

Third, the law requires the state to provide technical and financial assistance and local training to assist localities in implementing the program. In addition, the program creates an innovative municipal legal defense fund, in which the state attorney general assists munici-palities with the defense of approved local land-use ordinances.

STATE FLOOD-HAZARD PROGRAMS

Suppose part of a National Park System unit is in a floodplain and that this area extends outside the boundary onto privately owned land. Or that flood-prone land exists solely outside the park's boundary but that development on it could affect park resources. Are there any state-level handles that can be used to ensure that the adverse impacts to a park of a proposed development in this area are considered and minimized?

In recent years, many states have enacted floodplain programs, creat-ing specific flood-hazard mitigation responsibilities for state agencies and assuming direct police power authority over land uses in flood-plain areas. This increased state involvement in floodplain land use is part of a larger state role in protecting "critical environmental areas." Moreover, the recognition that flooding poses severe threats to its citizens' health, safety, and general welfare; that these threats almost never respect local government boundaries; and that regulating land use can be an effective tool have helped spur state initiatives in this area.

Various types of state controls exist for flood areas, coastal and inland wetlands, lake and shore areas, and coastal areas in a majority of states. Some 24 states have authorized regulations or standard-setting for floodway areas, while 17 have programs for both the floodway and floodfringe areas. State floodplain regulations generally follow one of two forms:
- direct state regulation through permit procedures; or
- state adoption of standards for local regulations and direct state regulation of floodplain uses only if there is local failure to adopt and administer controls meeting state standards.

A third, less direct approach authorizes a state agency to aid local governments through planning, studying, and coordination activities in regulating hazard areas.

Direct State Regulation of Floodplains

Basically, five types of programs exist that require direct state regulation of flood hazards.
- Over three-fourths of the states have permitting programs for dams, reservoirs, levees, and other flood-control works and for obstructions to navigable water (that is, fills and docks) to ensure their safety and the protect flood-flow capacity. Plans and designs to guarantee safety are usually required for proposed dams.
- A small number of states exercise varying degrees of direct control over floodway areas by requiring permits for structural uses. Examples include Connecticut, Indiana, Maryland, and Pennsylvania.
- At least seven state programs require state permits for structural uses in both the floodway and floodfringe areas. Hawaii, Illinois, Massachusetts, and Michigan provide examples.
- A growing number of state programs (for example, Michigan, California, and Wisconsin) require subdividers to submit subdivision plats for state approval in areas potentially subject to flooding. These programs involve both interstate land sale and state-level subdivision review acts.
- A significant number of states have permitting programs over structures or fills in coastal waters or adjacent lands. These programs apply to both coastal and inland wetlands, dune and beach areas, and activities that may affect shoreland erosion.

State Standard Setting for Localities

At least 15 states have statutes that authorize a state agency to adopt standards and criteria for local regulation of flood hazard areas. The programs differ in scope, with some applying to both floodway and floodfringe areas. Generally, the state standards are a minimum that the local regulations must meet; state agency approval of the local program is usually required. A few state agencies are authorized to regulate floodplains directly when the localities fail to adopt or administer regulations. Other states use incentives such as financial aid to induce localities to comply with state-designed programs.

Common Statutory Elements

Regardless of the exact approach taken, state floodplain regulatory programs generally contain the following similar provisions:
   • a statement of purposes or policy;
   • definitions that, among other things, can determine the scope of the statute;
   • enumeration of specific powers—
      1. Planning, surveys, mapping
      2. Special power such as regulation of structures in tidal waters, eminent domain powers, and coordination of flood-control works
      3. Permit requirements for new structures
      4. Provisions to regulate existing structures
      5. Establishment of encroachment lines, floodplain limits, or other delineations
      6. Standards for issuing permits and subdivision plat review;
   • procedural requirements (notice, hearings, and appeals);
   • sanctions and penalties; and
   • state requirements for local regulations (if applicable).
   Staff in parks that contain or are near floodplain areas should be aware of what state programs are available to mitigate against flood hazards and protect park resources from the harmful effects of inappropriate development in these areas.[12]

WETLAND PROGRAMS

Wetlands are among the most valuable and sensitive of lands. As noted in chapter 5, they serve as food providers, spawning sites, and sanctuaries for many forms of fish and bird life. They also serve as storage areas for storm and flood waters, reduce erosion, provide for ground-water retention, and at times purify polluted waters. As with flood-plains, when they are adjacent to park boundaries they are particu-larly important areas in terms of wildlife habitat, open space, and other valued ecological conditions.

A number of states have established permitting programs for development and activities that threaten wetlands. (See figure 10.1 at the end of this chapter.) To date, coastal wetlands have received far more attention from state programs than have inland wetlands.

Coastal and Inland Wetland Programs

As with floodplains, states generally have addressed coastal wetland protection in one of two ways—either through specific regulatory acts or as part of a larger regulatory program. At least 13 states have coastal wetland regulatory acts that require a permit for fill and structures in these areas. Statutory or administrative requirements provide the basis for granting or denying permits. State agencies are authorized in 6 states to adopt wetland zoning-like regulations and determine permitted and prohibited wetland uses. The remaining coastal states have broad regulatory programs with wetland protection as one com-ponent. These regulatory efforts may include a coastal zone plan, power plant siting controls, or shoreland zoning programs.

Inland wetlands generally are treated separately from coastal wet-lands, in part because of their different physical characteristics and use potential. Only some 7 states have adopted specific inland wet-land protection acts. In most state programs, the protection of inland wetlands is generally the result of regulatory efforts concerning other areas such as shorelands, floodplains, and wild and scenic rivers.

Common Statutory Elements

Like state floodplain regulatory programs, coastal and inland wet-land regulatory statutes have a common form. They either may require a state to establish standards for local government regulation or may provide for direct state regulation. Generally, these statutes contain the following provisions:
- findings of fact regarding wetland losses and the need for protection;
- statement of statutory purposes and policies;
- definitions;
- authorization of a state agency to gather data and map areas;

- authorization of power to an agency either to regulate wetland uses directly or to establish standards for local government regulation;
- requirement of permits for specified land uses in wetland areas from either the local government or state agency—the statute may contain criteria for evaluating permits;
- procedures for issuing or denying permits;
- penalties for violating standards; and
- appeal procedures.

In addition to federal programs to conserve wetlands, such as Section 404 of the Clean Water Act, many states have important policies that park personnel should not neglect in seeking to ensure that these sensitive resources are protected adequately.[13]

CRITICAL AREA PROGRAMS

Some states have attempted to solve problems surrounding floodplains and wetlands by enacting legislation over "critical areas" or areas of special statewide concern. This type of legislation generally seeks to regulate ecologically fragile areas and areas subject to intense development pressures. At least six states have comprehensive critical areas programs while a few others have identified and protected such areas on an individual basis. Generally, a program authorizes a state agency to identify areas in need of protective land-use practices. Some programs require localities to prepare development plans for identified areas and to submit the plan for approval to the state agency. Florida is an example of one such program.

COASTAL ZONE MANAGEMENT

Many park system units—seashores, lakeshores, and recreation areas, in particular—are on the coastline or quite close to it. Apart from the wetlands and floodplains that may exist in these areas and be subject to the programs discussed above, parks in most coastal areas come under the purview of specific coastal zone management programs.

The preservation, protection, development, and, where possible, restoration or enhancement of coastal resources is the goal of the federal Coastal Zone Management Act (CZMA). This goal, which was part of the CZMA as originally enacted in 1972, was reaffirmed by Congress as part of the act's reauthorization in 1986.

The CZMA is largely an act to fund state management programs; funding and other federal assistance is provided to states for planning and implementing coastal zone management programs. State participation is completely voluntary. States wanting federal support must comply with federal standards and regulations in developing their plans. To date, more than 78 percent of the coastline—including the Great Lakes—is covered in 28 federally approved state programs.

Federal Role and Consistency

The CZMA does not provide for direct federal land-use regulation. However, the implementing agency—the National Oceanic and Atmospheric Administration (NOAA) and its Office of Coastal Resources Management (OCRM)—within the U.S. Department of Commerce is involved in both the process and content of state program development and administration. OCRM responsibilities include publishing regulations, supervising and approving grant programs, and preparing studies and technical assistance material. The Commerce Department has the power to withdraw approval and funding for programs that are not making "satisfactory progress."

If not regulated, federal actions in the coastal zone can disrupt and undermine state preservation, protection, and enhancement programs. In coastal areas, federal agencies may wish to construct facilities, permit and license projects, or fund development programs that run counter to CZMA plans. The CZMA requires various federal actions to be consistent "to the maximum extent practicable" with approved state plans. This is the so-called consistency provision. Federal consistency regulations cover a wide range of federal activities in the coastal zone and seek to balance the need to provide federal programs with the need to ensure consistency.[14] Detailed procedures to follow when conflicts arise are in both the federal regulations and the state plans.

State Programs

The CZMA establishes the minimum program requirements for participating states. For example, concern for floodplains and wetlands is specifically addressed in the act since state programs must provide for:

- the protection of natural resources, including wetlands, floodplains, estuaries, beaches, dunes, barriers islands within the coastal zone; and
- the management of coastal development to minimize the loss of life and property caused by improper development in flood-

prone, storm surge, geological hazard, and erosion-prone areas and in areas of subsidence and saltwater intrusion, and by the destruction of natural protective features such as beaches, wetlands, and barrier islands.

The CZMA provides grants to states to administer their federally approved programs. States have been required to use up to 30 percent of their federal grants to address these and other objectives.

Seeking Protection for National Park System Units Under the Act

There are a variety of ways park officials can help to ensure effective decisions under the CZMA. These include:

- Examine the action that threatens park resources within the coastal zone. Is the National Park Service-proposed action consistent with the CZMA? Will the action on the coast by others outside the park boundary affect park resources adversely?
- Review the applicable state and local plans. State and local programs are at the heart of CZMA. Even consistency disputes require state government cooperation to be resolved. Thus, attention must be directed toward state and local plans, permitting decisions, and laws. Does the program define coastal zones and identify boundaries broadly enough to encompass the area in question (federally owned land is excluded from the reach of state and local programs)? Should the affected land be designated for special management as an area of particular concern? Is it a part of an estuarine sanctuary or the shoreline erosion protection provisions?
- Participate in the administrative process. It is far more likely that an agency decision protecting a coastal area will be upheld than it is that an agency action that permits harmful development will get reversed. Moreover, a thorough record at the administrative level will help the reviewing court.[15]

STATE ENVIRONMENTAL POLICY ACTS

Sometimes, a development may be proposed for outside a national park unit that could have major adverse impacts on park resources. Such a development may involve no federal funding or permitting, and there may not be any wetlands or floodplains. In such a case, the National Environmental Policy Act (NEPA), other federal environmental laws, and various state programs would not be applicable. In addition to participating in the local government development process, are there any other legal handles that can be used to minimize the adverse consequences to a park of such a proposal?

State environmental policy acts (SEPAs) have been enacted in one form or another by some 30 states. Modeled largely after the NEPA, they typically apply to a broader range of impacts than the NEPA and generally require the state or local government to consider and minimize the adverse environmental effects of projects they fund, approve, or license. Thus, because it would require local approval, any private development in an area may be subject to a SEPA.

Projects that threaten, use, or affect national park units are generally subject to a SEPA process to some degree. Most laws require the relevant government body to document and provide public access to its consideration of environmental effects through an impact statement. Therefore, park personnel should be familiar with SEPA requirements in a particular state and be prepared to comment on and participate in the process used to implement it.[16]

ACQUISITION POWERS

State and local government acquisition of sensitive and recreation lands is an important tool. By acquiring such lands, these governments can promote multiple goals such as waterfront revitalization, providing open space, or increasing recreational opportunities. In many cases, however, fiscal considerations can cause governments to be reluctant to use acquisition rather than regulatory and other mechanisms. Even acquiring easements or other less-than-fee interests may be beyond the budgets of state and local governments. Nevertheless, acquisition efforts continue to play an important role in land protection efforts, assisted in part by funds from various federal programs. For example, the Land and Water Conservation Fund, Coastal Zone Management Act, and Housing and Community Development Act all grant money to state and local governments to acquire recreation lands, floodplains, and wetlands.

Powers

Most states authorize relevant state agencies to acquire park lands, flood-prone areas, wetlands, and other critical areas. Localities may have acquisition powers through state enabling legislation or as part of home rule. Local acquisition powers also may be implied when they are necessary to exercise other powers expressly granted.

Acquisition, including less-than-fee interests, generally occurs by one of two ways: through negotiated purchase, through voluntary sale, or by eminent domain. Purchase simply refers to a buyer selling land to the state at a mutually agreed upon price. On the other hand, eminent domain is the sovereign power of the government to condemn property against the wishes of the owner.[17] In such a case, a state or local government must pay "just compensation," with the amount determined by a court as part of a judicial proceeding.

Limitations

Two key limitations exist in the acquisition powers of governments:
- *Public use*. State and local governments can only acquire lands for "public use." The facts of each case determine whether an acquisition is for public use, but generally the community, or at least some segment of it, must receive a benefit. Moreover, the acquisition power can only be used to further lawful government purposes. For example, land cannot be acquired for investment or speculative purposes or for purposes beyond the scope of a particular agency. Therefore, courts hearing an acquisition case routinely examine the number of people to be benefited and the legislative purpose behind the acquisition. Lenient standards of review are applied.[18]
- *Just compensation*. In exercising eminent domain powers, federal and state constitutions require the government to pay "just compensation." The specific amount varies with each parcel and is determined by the court.

CONCLUSION

States are involved in overseeing land-use activities that affect national parks in a variety of ways. Moreover, states are continuously designing new approaches to controlling the adverse impacts of development in these areas. As the needs for protection, technical expertise, and financial resources become greater, and as the role of the federal government in these areas continues to change, states will likely become even more important partners in protecting park resources from the adverse impacts of activities outside park boundaries.

REFERENCES

1. See, generally, B. Rose, "Intergovernmental Zoning Disputes: A Continuing Problem," *Land Use Law and Zoning Digest* 32, no. 7 (1980):6.

2. U.S. Department of Housing and Urban Development, *Statutory Land Use Control Enabling Authority in the Fifty States* (Washington, D.C.: U.S. Government Printing Office), pp. 2,17.

3. Mandelker and Netter, "A New Role for the Comprehensive Plan," *Land Use Law and Zoning Digest* 83 (1981):54.

4. 438 U.S. 104 (1978).

5. 100 S.Ct. 2138 (1980).

6. Oregon Revised Statutes Section 197.225.

7. Jeffrey H. Leonard, *Managing Oregon's Growth: The Politics of Development Planning* (Washington, D.C.: The Conservation Foundation, 1983).

8. 10 V.S.A., chapter 151.

9. In the critical area program, a particular geographic area can be selected for special management attention, including review and approval of local land-use plans and regulations within the critical area and review and modification of local development permits. The development-of-regional-impact program applies to development projects meeting certain threshold sizes and characteristics. State-established regional planning councils review local government development permits for these projects, with the review being somewhat similiar to an environmental impact statement.

10. John M. DeGrove and Nancy E. Stroud, "State Land Planning and Regulation: Innovative Roles in the 1980s and Beyond," *Land Use Law and Zoning Digest* 39, no. 3 (1987).

11. Barbara L. Lawrance, "New Jersey's Controversial Growth Plan," *Urban Land* 47, no. 1 (1988):19.

12. See U.S. Army Corps of Engineers, *A Perspective on Flood Plain Regulations for Flood Plain Management* (Washington, D.C.: U.S. Government Printing Office, 1976), pp. 95-97; U.S. Water Resources Council, *Regulation of Flood Hazard Areas to Reduce Flood Losses*, vol. 1, parts I-IV (1970), pp. 59-66, 126-175.

13. See Jon A. Kusler, *Strengthening State Wetland Regulations* (Washington, D.C.: U.S. Fish and Wildlife Service, 1978), and Jon A. Kusler, *Our National Wetland Heritage* (Washington, D.C.: Environmental Law Institute, 1983).

14. See 15 C.F.R. Section 930 *et seq.* (1983).

15. See 16 U.S.C. §1457-64 (1984): 15 C.F.R. 923 *et seq.* (1984); *Coastal Zone Management Newsletter* 17, no. 14 (1986); Coastal Zone Management Improvement Act of 1980, P.L. 94-404, 94 Stat. 2060 (October 17, 1980).

16. See Michael Mantell, "State Preservation Law," in The Conservation Foundation and the National Center for Preservation Law, *A Handbook on Historic Preservation Law* (Washington, D.C.: The Conservation Foundation, 1983); and Council on Environmental Quality, *Environmental Quality—1979: The Tenth Annual Report* (Washington, D.C.: U.S. Government Printing Office, 1979), pp. 595-602, table 10-13.

17. See Nichols, *On Eminent Domain*, rev. 3d ed. (New York: Matthew Bender, 1979); David R. Godschalk et al., *Constitutional Issue of Growth Management* (Chicago: American Society of Planning Officials Press, 1979), pp. 28-31; E. Meidinger, "The 'Public Uses' of Eminent Domain: History and Policy," *Environmental Law* 11 (1980):1.

18. State and local government spending powers are similarly limited by public use or public purpose criteria. In reviewing public expenditures, courts will generally ask two types of questions: (1) Is the object being promoted reasonably related to a valid government purpose?; and (2) Does the expenditure promote the general welfare?

Figure 10.1*
Summary of State Wetland Regulatory Programs

STATE	Filling	Draining	Excavating	Diverting Water	Clearing	Flooding	Diverting Sediment	Shading	Adjacent Activities	Changing Nutrient Levels	Introducing Toxics	Grazing	Disrupting Populations	NOTES/COMMENTS
Alabama														
-Coastal	x	.	x	x	.	.	.	.	.	x	.	.	.	
-Inland	.	.	.	.	.	.	.	.	.	.	.	.	.	
Alaska														
-Coastal	.	.	.	.	.	.	.	.	.	.	.	.	.	Coastal Management Program regulates economic activities and their effects: recreation, energy facilities, transportation and utilities, seafood processing, mining and mineral processing, timber harvest and processing. Habitat Protection Program: regulates all activities but includes only designated areas: streams with resident fishes, streams with anadramous fishes, critical habitats, or game refuges. Only applies to wetlands when they are associated with streams or in protected areas.
-Inland														

*This figure was prepared by The Conservation Foundation in 1987 as part of its work for The National Wetlands Policy Forum.

Arizona
-Inland · · · · · · · · · · · · — Floodplain regulation covers activities that alter floodplain or floodways.

Arkansas
-Inland · · · · · · · · · · · · — Natural or Scenic Rivers Program covers associated wetlands.

California
-Coastal x · x · · · · · · · · · — Regional Coastal Management Programs: some regions regulate any activity that might impact a coastal wetland; all regulate dredge and fill.
-Inland · · · · · · · · · · · ·

Colorado
-Inland · · · · x · · · · · · · — Floodplain regulation focuses on water allocation.

Connecticut
-Coastal x x x x · x · · x · · ·
-Inland x · x x* · · x x · · · · — *includes water usage regulations.

Delaware
-Coastal x x x · x · · · · · · ·
-Inland · · · · · · · · · · · ·

Florida
-Coastal and Inland x · x · · · · · · · · ·

Georgia
-Coastal x x x · · · · · · · · ·
-Inland · · · · · · · · · · · ·

STATE	Filling	Draining	Excavating	Diverting Water	Clearing	Flooding	Diverting Sediment	Shading	Adjacent Activities	Changing Nutrient Levels	Introducing Toxics	Grazing	Disrupting Populations	NOTES/COMMENTS
Hawaii														
-Coastal														
-Inland	·	·	·	·	·	·	·	·	·	·	·	·	·	Floodplain regulations cover placement of structures.
Idaho														
-Inland	·	·	·	·	·	·	·	·	·	·	·	·	·	No state regulatory programs affecting wetlands.
Illinois														
-Coastal														
-Inland	·	·	·	·	·	·	·	·	·	·	·	·	·	Floodplain regulations cover construction in floodways.
Indiana														
-Coastal	x	·	·	x	·	·	·	·	·	·	·	·	·	
-Inland	·	·	·	·	·	·	·	·	·	·	·	·	·	Floodplain regulations cover dredging, filling, and construction.
Iowa														
-Inland	·	·	·	·	·	·	·	·	·	·	·	·	·	Floodplain regulation covers channel straightening.
Kansas														
-Inland	·	·	·	·	·	·	·	·	·	·	·	·	·	Construction permits program regulates stream channel changes. Floodplain regulations cover construction in floodplains.

Kentucky
-Inland — No state regulatory program affecting wetlands.

Louisiana
-Coastal — x x x · x — Natural and Scenic Rivers Program regulates all activities that could impact designated streams. Water Bottom Use Program regulates construction in and reclamation of bottomlands.
-Inland — · · · x x

Maine
-Coastal — x x x
-Inland* — *Freshwater Wetlands law specifically regulates construction and, generally, covers all activities that impact wetlands.

Maryland
-Coastal — x · x · x x — Stormwater discharges included in filling regulations.
-Inland

Massachusetts
-Coastal and Inland — *Wetland Protection Act provides authority for regulation of activities that "alter" wetlands, both coastal and inland.

Michigan
-Coastal — x x x
-Inland — x x x — Floodplain regulations cover all "disruptions" in designated wetlands.

Minnesota
-Coastal — Floodplain regulations cover filling, construction, and alteration in floodplains.
-Inland — · x — Protected Waters Permit Program regulates activities that change the course of public waters and wetlands.

STATE	Filling	Draining	Excavating	Diverting Water	Clearing	Flooding	Diverting Sediment	Shading	Adjacent Activities	Changing Nutrient Levels	Introducing Toxics	Grazing	Disrupting Populations	NOTES/COMMENTS
Mississippi														
-Coastal	x	·	x	·	x	·	·	·	x	x	x	·	·	
-Inland														
Missouri														
-Inland	·	·	·	·	·	·	·	·	·	·	·	·	·	Governor's executive order instructs state agencies to avoid unwise use of floodplains.
Montana														
-Inland	·	·	·	·	·	·	·	·	·	·	·	·	·	Floodplain regulations restrict activities that would alter stream flows and include a dredge-and-fill program for floodplain areas.
Nebraska														
-Inland	·	·	·	·	·	·	·	·	·	·	·	·	·	Drainage regulations directed at agriculture industry. Floodplains regulated by local government.
Nevada														
-Inland	·	·	·	·	·	·	·	·	·	·	·	·	·	Dredging and filling regulated for navigable waters and Lake Tahoe.

New Hampshire
-Coastal and
Inland*   *Coastal and Inland Wetlands law prohibits activities that will "impair statutory wetlands."

New Jersey
-Coastal*   *Coastal Wetlands law provides authority for regulation of "alteration" of coastal wetlands.
-Inland*   *New Jersey Freshwater Wetlands Act regulations pending, which may be interpreted broadly to include many of these.

New Mexico
-Inland   . . . .   No state regulatory programs affecting wetlands.

New York
-Coastal   x x . . . . . . x x .
-Inland*   *Inland Wetlands law provides authority for regulation of all activities that "substantially impair wetlands."

North Carolina
-Coastal   x x x x x . . x x . .
-Inland   . . . .

North Dakota
-Inland   . . . .   Draining, channel modification, and construction are regulated in certain wetlands contiguous with state waters; isolated wetlands are not covered.

Ohio
-Coastal   . . . .
-Inland   . . . .   Scenic Rivers Program regulates all activities in designated river systems.

STATE	Filling	Draining	Excavating	Diverting Water	Clearing	Flooding	Diverting Sediment	Shading	Adjacent Activities	Changing Nutrient Levels	Introducing Toxics	Grazing	Disrupting Populations	NOTES/COMMENTS
Oklahoma -Inland				x										Programs direct water allocation (surface and underground sources). Construction in floodplains is regulated.
Oregon -Coastal and Inland*														*Removal-Fill law provides authority for regulation of "removal, filling, or alteration" of wetlands.
Pennsylvania -Coastal and	x		x			x			x					Dam Safety Encroachment Act regulates construction and use of water control structures, allowing a 300-foot buffer zone around important wetlands.
Inland	x		x			x			x					
Rhode Island -Coastal	x		x											*Freshwater Wetlands Act provides authority for regulation of any activity that alters a wetland, including sedimentation impacts.
-Inland*										x	x			
South Carolina -Coastal*													·	*Coastal Management Act regulates all coastal and freshwater wetlands in coastal counties and permits only activities with no feasible alternative.
-Inland														

State			Description
South Dakota			
-Inland	·	·	Floodplain regulations cover dredging and filling in floodplains and lake bottoms.
Tennessee			
-Inland*			*Governor's executive order "Providing for the Protection of Wetlands" covers all activities affecting wetlands; establishes policy but doesn't increase regulation.
Texas			
-Coastal	x · x · · · · · ·		
-Inland	· · · · · · · ·		
Utah			
-Inland	· · · · · · · ·		No state regulatory program affecting wetlands.
Vermont			
-Inland*			*Inland Wetlands law covers any activity expected to affect the values and functions of significant wetlands.
Virginia			
-Coastal and Inland*			*Wetlands Act provides authority for regulation of any activity that would disturb wetlands of ecological significance.
Washington			
-Coastal*	· · · · · · ·		*Shoreline Management Act sets standards for local jurisdictions to adopt regulations.
-Inland	x · · ·		State hydraulics code regulates water diversion and alteration of streambeds.

STATE	Filling	Draining	Excavating	Diverting Water	Clearing	Flooding	Diverting Sediment	Shading	Adjacent Activities	Changing Nutrient Levels	Introducing Toxics	Grazing	Disrupting Populations	NOTES/COMMENTS
West Virginia -Inland	·	·	·	·	·	·	·	·	·	·	·	·	·	Natural Streams Preservation Act provides authority for regulating modification to streams, including flooding; wetlands protected if association with streams.
Wisconsin -Coastal and Inland	x	x	x	x	·	x	·	·	·	x	x	·	·	Several programs combine in regulating.
Wyoming -Inland	·	·	·	·	·	·	·	·	·	·	·	·	·	No state regulatory programs that extend federal coverage.

Chapter 11

Local Governments and Park Resources

by C. Luther Propst, Dwight Merriam, and Christopher J. Duerksen

A developer proposes to build a "campus-like" office park and a small neighborhood shopping center on a 542-acre parcel immediately adjacent to the Manassas National Battlefield Park in Virginia. This proposal brings immediate local objections, as well as concern from the National Park Service. Nevertheless, citizens, county supervisors, and the park service all agree to this development proposal with modest restrictions to reduce the impacts on the battlefield.

Several months later, the same developer announces a new plan to build instead, on the same parcel, a 1.2-million-square-foot regional shopping mall, 1.7 million square feet of office space, and 560 residential units. County supervisors vigorously support the expanded proposal on the basis of the tax revenues that the project will generate. The county supervisors decide that no new zoning permits or approvals are necessary and that no public hearings will be held on the new proposal.

When the park service requests a review of the matter, a Prince William County, Virginia, official responds, "The Service should confine its activities to matters within its jurisdiction. . . . [Service] intrusion is neither useful nor wise."

In Pima County, Arizona, county supervisors debate a controversial Buffer Overlay Zoning Ordinance, conceived by local park protection advocates, that would protect Saguaro National Monument and other public open-space preserves in the Tucson area. The original proposal would have imposed restrictions on new development within one mile of the monument and other public preserves to reduce the wildlife and visual impacts of the development. Park service staff participate extensively in the debate, meeting and talking with local decision makers—both supporters and opponents—almost daily to obtain the greatest possible protection for the monument and its wildlife, while they also carefully work to ensure that there is no negative backlash against the monument.

After a rancorous public hearing, the county supervisors adopt a much weakened version of the proposal but decide to fund wildlife movement studies undertaken by Saguaro National Monument and the University of Arizona. Local officials have an eye toward using this wildlife movement information to identify and protect critical wildlife corridors leading out from the monument, refining the initial proposal.

For better or for worse, these situations are becoming more common in many units of the National Park System. In the system's earlier years, resource managers rarely needed to pay much attention to development on private land around national parks. Most parks were so remote that there was little chance that adjacent developments would even be proposed, let alone have an impact on park resources. But times have changed—and often dramatically so.

Now, many communities adjacent to parks are not only growing, but booming as the nation's population grows and demand increases for second homes, recreational opportunities, and natural resource development. Areas around several parks, especially battlefield units in the mid-Atlantic states, are fast becoming suburbs and major adjuncts to metropolitan centers. Familiar gateway communities such as Jackson Wyoming; West Yellowstone, Montana; Front Royal, Virginia; and Gatlinburg, Tennessee, are, in effect, the welcome mat put out for the parks, creating a strong first impression of what the visitor can expect. Committed to shoring up their local economies, some local governments in several areas have ignored sound land-use planning policies and have allowed unsightly strip developments, huge billboards, and ecologically damaging projects to shoulder up against park boundaries.

Poorly planned private land development near parks may not only be unsightly and ruin scenic views from within the park. It can also threaten park resources by degrading water and air quality and increasing noise that detracts from the park experience. Adjacent land development can encroach on wildlife habitat or migration routes and increase confrontations between people and park wildlife.

The growing impacts of development on private land adjacent to parks make it mandatory that park managers learn how to work within the local land-use regulatory systems; but that is not the only reason for learning the ins and outs of growth management. The rise of so-called greenline parks such as Santa Monica Mountains National Recreation Area and Cape Cod National Seashore—where Congress has directed that park goals be reached through partnerships among various levels of government and a combination of land acquisition and regulation—make it imperative that park service personnel familiarize themselves with development control techniques. Indeed, in some units such as Cape Cod, park managers are not limited to working informally with local governments through the zoning process. They have legal authority to review and approve local plans that regulate private development. As a practical matter, local land-use controls may be the only tools to reduce the impacts of development of private lands within park boundaries if funds for land acquisition are not available.

The local land-use regulatory process and the myriad tools used for growth management often seem mysterious and inaccessible to many park managers who are not used to dealing with private developers or local government officials. While they vary from state to state and locality to locality, the process and regulatory tools are actually quite similar in major respects in most communities. Using a variety of development management techniques, local governments, depending on state enabling authority, usually can regulate most major aspects of projects on private land that might affect a national park. They can control size and density of development (including the height and bulk of buildings), the type of land use allowed (for example, single family, commercial, industrial), the environmental costs or impacts of a project, the location and pace of growth, and, particularly in historic areas, the design of new construction and preservation of older buildings.

Ideally, each local development management program should be based on and integrated into the local land-use planning process. Such a planning process includes background studies of social, economic, fiscal, and environmental conditions affecting a community, much as is done in preparing a general management plan for park units. Based on the planning process, a community should then implement a development management program using a variety of tools—including zoning, site planning, and subdivision control—that are designed to accomplish the plan's goals.

If a community's comprehensive plan and development management program fail to consider park needs, it may permit or even encourage projects that harm park resources. By contrast, if a community carefully plans and controls its growth, much can be done to reduce adverse impacts on park units. Thus, a familiarity with the tools available to foster well-designed, ecologically sensitive projects at the local level and a working knowledge of how a local land-use regulatory process operates can be enormously helpful to the modern-day park manager.

PARTICIPATING IN THE LOCAL LAND-USE PROCESS

Involvement by national park managers in a local land-use planning process can be a politically very sensitive and time-consuming task. If park managers are perceived as dictating to local officials in a heavy-handed way, involvement may turn out to be counterproductive. And if park managers think that they can be successful simply by appearing at an occasional public hearing on a project that affects their unit, they will quickly discover that being effective requires a long-term investment of time in the community's planning and regulatory process.

Participation in the local development management process is always more effective, be it by citizens or the National Park Service, if it occurs early in the process of creating or revising a comprehensive plan and growth management program rather than responding to a specific development proposal. Once a local plan is adopted and regulations put into place, forces are put into motion and expectations created that are difficult, if not impossible, to stop at the project stage. As a result, park managers should involve themselves at the earliest possible moment in the planning process. This can be done in a variety of ways.

It can sometimes be accomplished informally by working with local planning staff to provide information about park goals and potential development problems. In case after case, the courts have told municipalities that the key to success in lawsuits is a strong data base resulting from local planning studies that support a well-reasoned comprehensive plan implemented through carefully considered and drafted regulations. Park managers may have resource information that will persuade the local planning staff of the need to conserve areas around a park or keep densities at a relatively low level. Particularly in smaller jurisdictions where staff and money for local studies are scarce, this kind of information can be particularly effective.

Park staff should assess what uses of adjacent lands are most compatible with park objectives. Influencing adjacent land uses is often not as simple as supporting only open space or low-density residential uses for adjacent lands. A park manager may conclude that park resources would be better protected by adjacent development proposals that are opposed by some residents of an area. For example, a sensitively designed resort or clustered development might better protect wildlife habitat than would poorly designed, low-density residential development or ranching. Prior to participating in the local growth management process, it is important that park managers clearly understand the feasible alternatives and the likely impact of various development scenarios on park resources.

Park staff can also help supply information about what other communities are doing to grapple with similar park-related growth management issues and provide examples of model ordinances that might be used to protect special areas (such as a historic district around a park unit). Some units, such as Sleeping Bear Dunes, have authority in their enabling legislation to provide planning grant funds to localities to help draft better local plans. If that is not possible, park managers might accomplish the same goal by exploring whether offering the help of park planners to research or study an issue of mutual concern would be beneficial.

In addition, individual development proposals often can be dealt with informally through negotiations between park personnel and the developer and local planners. In numerous instances, after park managers have approached the proponents of a proposed development, these proponents have agreed to ameliorate adverse impacts on a park unit voluntarily. By the time a project reaches this stage, the chances of negotiating some mitigation measures are far more promising than stopping a development outright at the local level. For example, through negotiation with local officials and a developer, the superintendent of Fredericksburg-Spotsylvania National Military Park was successful in securing the redesign of a shopping center being built near the park's headquarters to reduce its visual impact. The superintendent recognized that there was little hope politically of stopping the project in a county that had been courting commercial growth assiduously. In such situations, where significant local opposition to a project does not exist, quiet diplomacy often is the most effective approach.

In addition to this type of informal cooperation, park personnel should participate in the formal hearing process that is almost universally required before a comprehensive plan and development regulations become law or a project is approved. This participation is important for several reasons. First, on appeal, courts generally review only the record developed at the public hearings and at other public deliberations in reviewing the validity of a local authority's action. Evidence supporting the decision and an appellant's contentions must be found in the public record. Second, courts give land-use regulatory boards broad discretion and rarely upset their decisions on substantive grounds. If all procedural requirements have been complied with, the courts most often uphold the local decision. It is therefore important that interested parties, including the park service, present evidence at the public hearing, rather than wait for an unfavorable decision and then make an appeal. In making such a presentation, park managers should come armed not only with information about the impact of a development but also with testimony detailing the positive economic contributions that the park has on the local economy. (Figure 11.1 provides tips for making effective presentations at local land-use public hearings.)

While an appearance and direct testimony by park personnel can be helpful if done carefully, park managers often find that the park's interests are better advanced by local citizens and "friends of the park" groups that are strong supporters of park protection. These citizens often have more direct influence on local officials than would a federal government representative, and they can take positions that a park manager might have to avoid due to political considerations. (Chapter 12 discusses in greater detail how these "friends" can be called on to help advance park goals.)

LOCAL DEVELOPMENT MANAGEMENT TOOLS

Local governments can use a variety of tools to create effective development management programs. The most important of these are planning and development regulations. The latter includes the traditional local regulatory devices of zoning and subdivision regulation as well as several innovative techniques that frequently are used as supplements. Land acquisition, public spending, and local taxation are other important tools for development management.

Figure 11.1
Effective Participation at Local Hearings

To be an effective witness at a local hearing:

DO	DON'T
• state clearly at the beginning of the statement whether you support or oppose the hearing issue	• provide a detailed history of the National Park Service and its mission
• make a short statement	• make a long, rambling statement
• be calm and composed	• lose your cool
• stay within the time limit specified	• go over the time limit
• divide up the work among several speakers or groups	• have so many speakers that the hearing panel loses interest
• use local examples to bolster your position	• use examples from out of state unless there are no others available
• be specific about the issue at hand	• pad the statement with cliches and repetitious language
• say "I don't know," if you don't	
• say you must consider a suggested compromise	• bluff your way through questions
• compliment the hearing panel and agree with their goal or policy in conducting the hearing	• say you will or won't support a compromise if you're unsure
• have a summary of your statement available for the hearing panel and the press	• castigate the hearing panel
• attach data, facts, etc., to support your position	• speak extemporaneously
	• make unfounded general observations
• conclude your remarks with a memorable quote from the Constitution, Town History, or Lincoln—but not John Muir or Jane Fonda	• threaten the hearing panel
• stress local economic benefit of good planning	

Planning

Land-use planning is a broad term. According to the American Planning Association:

> Planning is a comprehensive, coordinated and continuing process, the purpose of which is to help public and private decision makers arrive at decisions which promote the common good of society. This process includes:
> (1) Identification of problems or issues;
> (2) Research and analysis to provide definitive understanding of such problems or issues;
> (3) Formulation of goals and objectives to be attained in alleviating problems or resolving issues;
> (4) Development and evaluation of alternative methods (plans and programs) to attain agreed upon goals and objectives;
> (5) Recommendation of appropriate courses of action from among the alternatives;
> (6) Assistance in implementation of approved plans and programs;
> (7) Evaluation of actions taken to implement approved plans and programs in terms of progress towards agreed upon goals and objectives; and
> (8) A continuing process of adjusting plans and programs in light of the results of such evaluation or to take into account changed circumstances.[1]

Ideally, a local comprehensive plan is a product of this planning process. In addition, a comprehensive plan is not static but must be updated regularly as part of a continuous process that reflects the evolution of a community itself.

A comprehensive plan should embody a community's vision of what it wants to become and how it intends to get there. This vision should serve as an overall policy guide for public and private decisions that affect community development, including the implementation of land-use regulations and other growth management strategies. Frequently, however, the implementation of zoning ordinances and other growth management strategies precedes or coincides with the initiation of revisions to a comprehensive plan. Consequently, the degree of inconsistency between plans and other growth management techniques varies considerably from community to community.

Planning is but one of the numerous local tools available to manage growth. Preparation and adoption of a comprehensive plan are, in fact, only the first steps in the growth management process. Plans are not self-executing but must be implemented through land-use regulations, capital facilities spending, land acquisition, and other growth management strategies. Although the techniques commonly appear as discrete options, most effective local growth management programs combine several separate techniques.

Zoning

Zoning is the most commonly used local device for regulating land use. Initially developed in the early part of this century basically to insulate residential neighborhoods from the negative impacts of industrial development, the essence of the traditional zoning ordinance remains the physical separation of potentially incompatible land uses.

Zoning regulates the use of land and structures—for example, commercial versus residential—and the dimensional characteristics of permitted uses, such as minimum lot sizes, the placement of structures on lots (that is, minimum setbacks from street or property lines), the density of development, and the maximum height of buildings. In addition, zoning ordinances increasingly regulate nondimensional aspects of development such as landscaping, architectural design and features, signage, traffic circulation, and stormwater management.

Zoning ordinances consist of a text and a zoning map. The text describes permitted and prohibited uses in the various districts, establishes standards for uses within these districts, and provides for administration and enforcement. The map divides the jurisdiction into districts. Changes to a zoning ordinance text or map occur through an amendment process that is initiated either by the local government or by landowners.

Conventional Zoning Devices

Conventional zoning promotes strict segregation of uses and predictable dimensional and density regulations. From this orderly and static pattern, land-use regulation has evolved into a system of numerous techniques designed to balance the predictability of conventional zoning with administrative flexibility, discretionary review of individual developments, and specialized techniques to meet particular local needs.

Large-Lot Zoning. Large-lot zoning or minimum lot size zoning—requiring, for example, that lots in a residential zone be at least 5 acres and in some cases as much as or more than 100 acres—is often used to reduce the density of residential development. The environmental and economic effects of large-lot zoning vary with the specific situation. When used judiciously in areas with significant development constraints, often in combination with regulations that accommodate market demand in other, more suitable areas, large minimum-lot-size zoning can effectively reduce the negative impacts of development on park resources or sensitive landscapes. Overreliance on large-lot zoning, however, often encourages land consuming and inefficient low-density sprawl.

Agricultural Zoning. Agricultural zoning establishes minimum parcel sizes large enough to ensure that each parcel can sustain a viable agricultural operation. Agricultural districts often prohibit land uses that are incompatible with agriculture. Although exclusive agricultural zoning is often considered desirable, certain agricultural practices— such as feed lots, pesticide use, and barbed wire fencing—may be detrimental to park resources.

Height Limits. Localities often limit building heights either townwide or by zoning district. Height restrictions are sometimes used in conjunction with site-specific standards to prohibit structures that would be visible from scenic roads, trails, or viewpoints. These restrictions also may be used to prohibit structures from rising above specified ridge lines.

Sign Regulation. Zoning (or sometimes other local regulations) may control the size, type, design, setback, height, spacing, and number of signs permitted on a lot and sometimes include provisions for the ultimate removal (or amortization) of existing signs without compensation. Courts generally permit a locality to prohibit off-premise commercial signs and to impose strict standards for on-premise commercial signs, in the interest of improving community aesthetics.

Because signs in strip commercial districts outside national parks can detract significantly from the experience of park visitors, sign control can be a useful tool for those concerned with development around national parks. Not only can sign regulations significantly enhance the aesthetics of communities, they can also improve a commercial district's economic viability. As a result, business owners often will support a comprehensive regulatory program.

Zoning Devices that Provide Flexibility

Most municipalities now also use zoning techniques that provide flexibility and local review of individual development proposals. These devices generally supplement the conventional division of a municipality into several zones or districts.

Special Permits. Special permits (also referred to as conditional uses or special exceptions) are the most widely used device allowing individual review and approval of proposed developments that require individual scrutiny to avoid or alleviate particular problems. In most zoning ordinances, uses are permitted within a district either "by right," with no individual discretionary review of the proposed development, or by special permit, in which case a zoning board reviews individual proposals in accordance with standards set forth in the ordinance. A special permit is granted only if a proposal adequately complies with the provisions in the ordinance, which typically deal with traffic and other impacts of the proposal.

Floating Zones. Floating zones serve the same purpose as special permits but provide a locality with more discretion. The standards for a floating zone are set forth in the text of a zoning ordinance, but the district is not mapped. Rather, the district "floats" above the community until a second, later ordinance brings the zone to the ground by affixing the zone to a particular parcel that meets the standards set forth in the zoning text for the district. For example, a zoning ordinance may create a shopping mall district with various requirements to ensure that a proposed mall is appropriate for a site. Later, when a developer proposes a shopping mall at a particular site, the developer must apply for an amendment to the zoning map to have the designation of the site changed to allow the shopping mall.

The floating-zone technique gives a locality greater discretion over a proposed use than does a special permit. A decision on a proposed rezoning to apply the floating zone is a legislative function in most states and is rarely overturned by the courts; a special permit application is an administrative function and must be granted if a proposed use is shown to meet the stated criteria.

Overlay Zones. Overlay zones apply a common set of regulations and standards to a designated area that may cut across several different pre-existing conventional zoning districts. These regulations and standards apply in addition to those of the underlying zoning district. Two common examples of overlay zones are the flood zones created under the National Flood Insurance Program and many historic districts.

Flood zones often are described in local zoning ordinances, but are not mapped on a zoning map. Rather, a local ordinance provides that flood district regulations apply to areas within a 100-year floodplain, as designated in federal flood insurance rate maps. An overlay flood zone may allow whatever uses and densities are permitted in the underlying zone but impose additional construction and flood-proofing requirements.

Overlay historic districts often permit the uses and densities permitted in the underlying zone but require that structures within the historic district be maintained in conformity with regulations to ensure historic compatibility. Overlay zones can also be used effectively to protect mapped wildlife corridors or critical wildlife habitat around national parks.

Conditional Zoning and Contract Zoning. Sometimes a landowner may seek a rezoning, but a locality is unwilling to permit the whole range of uses or densities that the proposed zoning classification would allow. Instead of denying the rezoning, the local government may wish to impose conditions on the prospective rezoning. With conditional zoning, a local government may make a rezoning provided an applicant agrees to concessions or conditions that are not otherwise imposed in the proposed zoning district. The applicant undertakes these concessions in exchange for the rezoning; however, the local government makes no formal, reciprocal obligation to the applicant to rezone the property. Rather, the local government simply makes the necessary zoning amendments in its normal course of business. Many states have upheld the use of conditional zoning, while several others have rejected its use.

Contract zoning also permits a locality to impose individual conditions on a rezoning, but, unlike conditional zoning, a local government, in exchange, enters into an enforceable agreement to grant the desired zone change. In many states, contract zoning has been held invalid, because the locality bargains away its police power without state enabling legislation to do so. A growing number of states (among them, California, Maine, and Hawaii), however, have enacted legislation authorizing contract zoning or "development agreements" to regulate large-scale development. These agreements typically are enforceable agreements between a developer and a local government, which lay out precisely the land uses and densities a developer may place on a large parcel and the public benefits the developer must provide as a condition of approval. The use of development agreements allows a single "master" approval for a large-scale, phased development. This approach provides developers and lending institutions the certainty of knowing early in the development process the amount and type of development authorized. Development agreements often also provide that a developer's right to complete all phases of a project vests earlier than it would in the absence of the agreement, a provision that benefits developers when arranging financing. In exchange for this regulatory certainty, the local government may negotiate with the developer for a better package of public benefits and resource protection measures than it may obtain otherwise.

Bonus or Incentive Zoning. Bonus or incentive zoning allows a developer to exceed a zoning ordinance's dimensional limitations if the developer agrees to fulfill conditions specified in the ordinance. The classic example is when an ordinance authorizes a developer to exceed height limits by a specified amount in exchange for providing open spaces or plazas adjacent to the building.

Zoning Based on Performance Standards. Zoning regulations often use performance standards to regulate development based on the permissible effects or impacts of a proposed use rather than simply the proposed dimensions. The complexity and sophistication of these standards vary widely, depending on the objectives of the program and the capacity of the locality to administer a complex program. Performance zoning may supplement or replace traditional zoning districts and dimensional standards.

Under performance zoning, proposed uses whose impacts would exceed specified standards are prohibited. Performance standards are widely used to regulate noise, dust, vibration, and other impacts in industrial zones, and they are increasingly used to regulate environmental impacts, such as to limit the stormwater runoff resulting from development. Proposed uses exceeding maximum permitted impacts are prohibited. For environmentally sensitive lands, such as areas in and around many national parks, these controls can be used to specify maximum levels of permissible stress on natural systems such as aquifers, watersheds, and wetlands.

Perhaps the best-known performance-based zoning ordinance is that of Sanibel Island, Florida, which has adopted standards for development based on the characteristics and thresholds of the island's different ecological zones. An applicant for a development permit must demonstrate that a proposed use will not interfere with the vegetation, wildlife, coastal processes, geology, or hydrology of the ecological zone in which it is situated.[2]

Variances

Zoning variances permit land to be used in a manner expressly prohibited by a zoning ordinance, if approved by a board of adjustment or board of zoning appeals. This board must consider several factors in determining whether to grant a variance. Typically, an applicant is expected to show that strict compliance with the zoning ordinance would impose undue hardship on the property owner. The claimed hardship should be unique to the property rather than a general characteristic of the area. The hardship also should result from application of the zoning ordinance to the property rather than from the actions of the property owner. The landowner should not have known of the hardship when the property was purchased. In addition, the board should consider whether the variance would violate the intent and purpose of the zoning ordinance and how significantly the variance would affect the use of adjoining property and the character of the neighborhood.

In practice, however, boards in many communities grant variances under circumstances that do not meet these strict requirements.

Moratoriums and Interim Development Regulations

Moratoriums and interim regulations are designed to substantially restrict development for a limited period. They can impose a complete temporary moratorium on all development or on specific types of intensive development. A moratorium can apply to zoning approvals, subdivision approvals, and building permits.

Courts usually permit a development moratorium or other strict interim growth management controls that temporarily eliminate all economically reasonable use of property. To be legally defensible, a moratorium must generally promote one of two objectives:

- allowing a community to undertake a planning process or to revise land-use controls without the pressures of reviewing pending applications that may be incompatible with the new plan or growth management program; or
- preventing critical public facilities (such as a sewer treatment plant or traffic circulation network) from becoming dangerously overburdened.

A moratorium should have a limited and clearly defined duration, so that it does not prohibit, but only delays, use of property. For the most part, the duration of the moratorium must not exceed the time required to complete the necessary planning studies or growth management revisions or to correct the public facilities capacity problem.

Erosion and Sedimentation Control

Most states have established programs to control surface water run-off and erosion from construction sites and the resulting sedimentation of streams and other surface waters. These programs generally require a developer to submit a sedimentation control plan to a state or local agency before undertaking land-disturbing activity. Most programs exempt small land-disturbing actions and mining, farming, and forestry.

Subdivision Regulation

Subdivision regulations are widely used to regulate the conversion of land into building lots. In rural communities, they are often the principal or only means by which a community regulates residential development.

Originally, subdivision regulations were enacted primarily to facilitate land transfer by providing a method for landowners to file a subdivision plat with numbered lots, rather than with the traditional lot descriptions that rely upon compass directions and distances of the lot boundaries (that is, a "metes and bounds" description). In the 1920s and 1930s, cities began to use these regulations to manage the quality of streets, storm drainage systems, lot layout, and adequacy of utility services. Typically, subdivision ordinances articulate design standards and materials for streets and utility systems, site topography, sidewalks, curbs and gutters, stormwater management, landscaping, open space, and recreational facilities. More recently, subdivision regulations have been widely used not only to improve the engineering and physical design of on-site public improvements but also to require the provision of dedicated recreational lands, off-site road improvements, and other necessary public services.

Municipal review of subdivision plans, like review of special permit applications, is an administrative function in which the planning board determines whether a proposed subdivision complies with its subdivision ordinance. The board must approve the application if it does comply but may refuse to grant approval if the subdivision would cause negative off-site impacts (environmental damage or increased flooding) or would overload public facilities, such as roads or sewer treatment capacity.

Consideration of off-site impacts and effects on public facilities may be important for protecting national park resources for at least two reasons. These considerations promote compact development rather than "leap-frog" subdivisions that require major expenditures for public infrastructure. And they can make development in environmentally sensitive areas contingent on the availability of facilities, such as sewerage, reducing the environmental impacts of development.

Cluster Development and Planned Unit Development

Cluster zoning and planned unit development (PUD) are land-use control devices that allow flexible design and clustering of development in higher densities on the most appropriate portion of a parcel in order to provide increased open space elsewhere on the parcel. These techniques, which exist in many forms, have become increasingly popular, as more communities have realized that conventional zoning and subdivision regulations often result in inefficient and land-consuming development patterns. These alternative clustering techniques can offer several benefits relative to conventional zoning, including:

- limiting encroachment of development in and adjacent to environmentally sensitive areas;
- reducing the amount of open land disturbed by development, thereby encouraging the preservation of agricultural lands, woodlands, and open landscapes; and
- reducing the amount of roads and utility lines needed for new development, which can reduce the cost of housing and public services.

Cluster development techniques typically do not allow increased development density. Rather, they simply rearrange development to preserve open land and improve site design. This concept can be demonstrated by a simple example of cluster development: A developer has 100 acres in an area zoned for one-half-acre residential lots. The area could be developed into 200 one-half-acre lots, using up the entire 100 acres. Or, under a cluster zoning program, the developer could cluster the 200 units on 50 acres, for example, and permanently dedicate 50 acres of open space for public use.[3]

Although cluster or PUD alternatives typically are available only for tracts of land covering at least 10 or 15 acres, they can be of significant assistance in controlling development near national parks. They can, for example, be used to create undeveloped park buffers or, when paired with stringent density limitations, to limit encroachment into environmentally sensitive areas.

Transfer of Development Rights

Transfer of development rights (TDR) is an innovative growth management technique based on the real property concept that ownership of land gives an owner many rights, each of which may be separated from the rest and transferred to someone else. One of these separable rights is the right to develop land. With a TDR system, landowners are able to retain general ownership of their land but sell the right to develop the land for use on another property. Regarding the National Park System, TDR has been used most extensively in the Pinelands National Reserve in New Jersey.

Under a typical TDR program, a local government awards development rights to each parcel of developable land in the community or in selected districts, based on the land's acreage or value. Persons can then sell their development rights on the open market if they do not want to develop their property or are prohibited by regulation from developing the property at a desired density. Land from which development rights have been sold cannot be developed.

There are many possible variations on TDR, but a system can work in the following way. Suppose "A" owns four acres of land that has been allocated two development rights. If local regulations require "A" to have one right per acre to develop the land fully, "A" has three choices. "A" can develop just two acres and expend all the development potential for the parcel, "A" can buy two development rights on the market and develop the entire four acres, or "A" can sell the two rights at a market-determined price and preclude any development of the property. If the land is in an agricultural or historic district, regulations may restrict development of the parcel, in which case "A" can only develop the parcel at a low density and sell the balance of the development rights for use on another site.

TDR substantially eliminates the value shifts and economic inequities of restrictive zoning. For example, it can allow the market to compensate owners whose land cannot be developed because of its environmental, scenic, or historic significance. By selling development rights, a landowner can receive profit from property appreciation without developing the parcel.

TDR requires a high level of staff expertise to design and administer. The novelty of the TDR concept and the sophistication required to make it work properly reduces its attractiveness and political acceptance in many communities.

Development Exactions and Impact Fees

"Development exaction" is a generic term that describes a variety of mechanisms by which communities require dedication of land or facilities, or payment of a fee in lieu of land or facilities. Exactions are either explicitly mandated in development regulations or imposed informally on a case-by-case basis in development negotiations. Impact fees require a developer to pay an amount of money determined by a uniform formula rather than through negotiations.

Traditionally, exactions have required subdivision developers to provide on-site infrastructure such as roads, parks, sewer lines, and drainage facilities. Realizing that to require certain on-site improvements such as recreational facilities might be inefficient or inequitable, many communities have required developers to pay fees in lieu of improvements in certain situations. These fees are then earmarked for providing those facilities to serve the development.

Recently, municipalities also have begun imposing impact fees to finance an expanding variety of public facilities and services in virtually all regulatory contexts. Martin County, Florida, for example, has enacted a Beach Impact Fee Ordinance, which requires developers to contribute to a fund, based on the projected recreational demand resulting from the proposed development, to purchase and maintain public beachfront property. (The legal limitations on the use of exactions and impact fees are discussed later in this chapter.)

Annexation

Annexation is the means by which a municipality increases its land area. It often results when landowners within an area perceive a need for better public services. Generally, an annexing city's ability to provide services and the need of an area for such services determine when and whether annexation is proper. Annexation is particularly useful to manage growth when used in conjunction with a utility extension policy.

Cities usually are not compelled to annex an area. Because annexation is discretionary, a municipality may use it to direct growth to areas best suited for development. A municipality might, for example, use annexation to direct growth away from a national park unit or other area of environmental or scenic significance.

Capital Programming

The provision of municipal services is an important tool for managing development. A community's decision whether to extend or expand public utilities or facilities strongly influences the economic feasibility of most large private development projects. The extension of municipal services is generally governed by a city's capital improvements program (CIP), a timetable by which a city indicates the timing and level of municipal services it intends to provide over a specified duration. Generally, the CIP covers a 5- to 10-year period, although it may be shorter or longer depending on the municipality's confidence in its ability to predict future conditions.

Capital programming, by itself, influences land development decisions. By committing itself to a timetable for expansion of municipal services, a locality influences development decisions, especially in areas where on-site sewage disposal or water supply is unusually expensive or infeasible. A capital program may also be used effectively as part of a more comprehensive program to manage development. In addition to formulating a timetable for the provision of services, a municipality can regulate the extension of and access to municipal services. A decision not to extend services to a specified area or not to expand current public facilities can make development prohibitively expensive or limit growth of the area. By properly coordinating its utility extension policy with its comprehensive plan, a community can guide the location and direction of development—another potentially useful tool for directing growth away from park boundaries.

Adequate Public Facilities Ordinances

Communities can use adequate public facilities ordinances to manage growth by conditioning development approval on a finding that adequate public facilities are available to serve a proposed development. These ordinances set quantitative standards for required public service levels and link development approval to the ability of public services that serve a proposed development to comply with the standards. The public services that have the most significant impact on development decisions—and are therefore most commonly used in these ordinances—are water supply, sewerage, and traffic circulation networks. Other public services sometimes linked to development approval are stormwater management facilities, parks and recreational lands, emergency response time, and mass transit.

Local Taxation

Although local taxation is not primarily a land-use control device, it can significantly affect private land development decisions. Municipalities have no inherent power to levy taxes. Rather, they possess only the powers specifically granted by the state.

One local taxation policy that is widely used to influence land development is preferential assessment of property, or use-value assessment. Almost every state has enacted preferential assessment of farmland. Most states also provide for preferential assessment of other specified land uses, including forest lands, open-space lands, lands available for public recreational use, and land of scenic or ecological significance. Most preferential assessment programs include a recapture penalty that must be paid when land that has received preferential tax treatment is converted to a more intensive use.

Preferential assessment of open-space land is useful as part of a comprehensive program to encourage low-intensity land uses within or around national parks. It often can relieve the financial burdens of holding land subject to strict development regulations and can also allow landowners to profit from continued farming, forestry, or other nonintensive use.

Land Acquisition

Local governments enjoy broad authority under state enabling legislation to acquire real property interests, either through voluntary sale or condemnation, for any legitimate public purpose. Land acquisition is an important supplement to land-use regulations as a means of managing growth and protecting critical resources.[4] Although localities generally use land acquisition to control directly the use of a specific parcel acquired, several communities have used land acquisition to influence the community's general growth policies. For example, Boulder, Colorado, has acquired a large amount of land in the foothills outside the city to prevent environmentally destructive and fiscally unsound development of these areas.

Local land acquisition programs are generally funded either by bond issues or real estate transfer taxes. Nantucket, Massachusetts, for example, imposes a 2 percent conveyance tax on most transfers of real estate to fund its open-space acquisition program. The federal Land and Water Conservation Fund has been an important supplemental source of revenues for recreational land acquisition and development.

Fee-Simple Acquisition

Land ownership is often said to constitute ownership of a "bundle of rights," including, for example, the right to control access to the land, the right to develop property, the right to mine coal from beneath the land, the right to hunt on the land, and so forth. (Each of these is subject to reasonable police power regulations.) When one person owns all the rights associated with a parcel (the entire bundle), this person is said to own the land "in fee simple"; however, these rights can be owned separately, in which case an owner is said to own a "less-than-fee interest."

Local governments generally acquire fee-simple ownership for parks and other property needed for public use or other municipal uses, such as for schools or landfills. Fee-simple acquisition provides the greatest level of control over the use of a parcel; however, it is also usually the most expensive method of land acquisition. For this reason, localities and land trusts often consider other private land protection techniques when full ownership is unnecessary. In addition to the substantial acquisition costs, fee-simple acquisition removes property entirely from local tax rolls and can result in significant maintenance costs.

Easements

The acquisition of easements constitutes a particularly useful tool for many local governments and local land trusts. Easements are effective devices for preserving sensitive lands, providing public access along rivers or greenways, and allowing landowners to obtain income and estate tax benefits for land stewardship while they continue to live on their land.

Easements are among the distinct property rights that may be sold separately from the other rights (in other words, separated from the fee). An advantage of easements is that the land remains on the tax rolls, albeit at a reduced value. Easements, however, may create long-term administrative, enforcement, and maintenance costs.

Conservation easement statutes clarify the ambiguities and remove the barriers to enforcement of certain easements. These statutes set forth rules governing the definition, creation, transfer, and enforcement of easements created to conserve land or buildings. Conservation easement statutes vary from state to state.

LEGAL PARAMETERS AND REQUIREMENTS FOR LOCAL DEVELOPMENT MANAGEMENT ACTIONS

In June 1987, the U.S. Supreme Court decided two important cases that have heightened concerns over the legal limits to local efforts to regulate land use and manage growth.[5] Initial reactions to these decisions among local officials, developers, planners, lawyers, and journalists suggested that the Court had announced major changes in land-use law, tilting the balance far in the direction of development interests.

While the actual ramifications of these decisions are still unclear, and their impacts may be far less important than first thought, they demonstrate the major role courts and constitutional doctrines play in defining growth management strategies. In fact, few activities of local government raise as many significant legal issues as the regulation of land use. Traditional notions that permit landowners to do as they please with their land can run head-on into government efforts to protect and promote the public health, safety, and general welfare. When attempting to manage growth and protect key resources effectively, local officials must accordingly be sensitive to the legal rights of property owners.

At the same time, thoughtful good faith efforts to address growth and land-use problems should have little difficulty withstanding court challenges. Since the 1926 U.S. Supreme Court decision in *Village of Euclid* v. *Ambler Realty Company*,[6] courts have universally held zoning to be a valid exercise of the police power, although the specific applications and provisions of a zoning ordinance remain subject to challenge.

Local development management programs must operate within various parameters. First, a local action may be challenged either if it is unauthorized by a state's statutory delegation of authority (that is, an *ultra vires* challenge) or if it conflicts with a state statute. Second, both the U.S. and state constitutions limit local actions. Invalid land-use regulations are subject to a variety of remedies.

Challenges Based on Inadequate Authority

The question whether a locality has adequate authority to take an action is a threshold issue in any challenge to a local development management program or technique. As discussed in the previous chapter, municipalities have no inherent authority to exercise regulatory authority, to acquire property, to annex territory, to levy taxes, or to make expenditures. Rather, they possess only those powers delegated to them by the state.

In most states, the authority for local governments to engage in zoning is derived from the Standard State Zoning Enabling Act, prepared by the U.S. Department of Commerce in the 1920s and quickly adopted in most states with only minor revisions. Therefore, the basic foundation for controlling land use in most states is quite similar. "Home rule" powers, granted by state constitutions or statutes, are also a source of these powers in some localities.

For a local government to take action of any sort, two elements must be present: the proposed *purpose* must be within the authority granted to the locality by the state, and the specific *technique* or *method* must be within the local government's designated authority. For example, if a municipality wishes to implement a transfer-of-development-rights ordinance to preserve the view from a scenic vista, it must have the authority both to regulate for the purpose of preserving scenic vistas and to use the TDR technique.

Judicial invalidation of a local ordinance for lack of sufficient enabling legislation is rare, but not unheard of. The issue frequently turns on the care with which local ordinances conform to the purposes set forth in the enabling legislation and the powers delegated by that legislation. Invalidation for lack of authority can be remedied by enactment of specific enabling legislation.

Finally, municipal land-use regulations may be invalid when they conflict with state law or frustrate clearly defined state policy. Local regulations that are more restrictive than state regulations, but do not frustrate their purpose, are likely to be upheld if they are based on legitimate local interests. For instance, a local setback requirement from watercourses for on-site septic systems that exceeds minimum state requirements for such systems will likely be upheld. By contrast, a local prohibition of hazardous waste facilities is likely to be struck down if it is contrary to a state statute.

Challenges Based on Constitutional Limitations

The use of the powers delegated to local governments to manage development is subject to several constitutional limits, as well as to statutory and judicially created restraints. Both the U.S. Constitution and state constitutions impose limits on local actions, principally through three types of provisions: due process, the taking of private property without just compensation, and equal protection. State courts often interpret state constitutional provisions to be consistent with the interpretation of similar provisions in the federal constitution. However, this is not always the case, and state courts may find more protection for landowners in state law than is provided in the U.S. Constitution.

Due Process

The U.S. Constitution guarantees all citizens due process of law. The Fifth Amendment applies the due process requirement to federal action, while the Fourteenth Amendment applies the requirement to state and local action. In addition, most state constitutions contain provisions similar to the federal due process clause. Due process requires both that governmental decision making follow fair procedures (procedural due process) and that decisions promote valid public purposes (substantive due process). State courts generally interpret these provisions as having the same effect as the federal due process requirement.

Procedural due process requires that citizens be given adequate notice of a proposed governmental action and a reasonable opportunity to be heard at an impartial hearing when affected by a governmental action. Specific procedural requirements for local decision making are usually set forth in land-use enabling legislation or local ordinances. Courts generally require strict compliance with these statutory procedures. When no statute or ordinance specifies the procedures to be followed in local decision making, courts review the procedures directly under the constitutional requirement to ensure fair notice and the meaningful opportunity to be heard.

A claim based on substantive due process challenges the fundamental reasonableness or fairness of a governmental action. Substantive due process requires that laws and regulations bear a reasonable relationship to (or substantially advance) the accomplishment of a legitimate governmental objective (that is, promoting the public health, safety, and general welfare). A land-use regulation may encounter substantive due process challenges either to its objective or to the means chosen to accomplish the objective.

As noted earlier, since the U.S. Supreme Court's 1926 decision, *Village of Euclid* v. *Ambler Realty Company*, zoning has been universally held to be a valid exercise of the police power, although the specific effects of a zoning ordinance and specific provisions remain subject to challenge.[7]

The *Euclid* decision established the standard of judicial review that is generally applied in land-use challenges: "If the validity of the legislative classification for zoning purposes be fairly debatable, the legitimate judgment must be allowed to control." This standard of review, which grants local ordinances a presumption of validity, remains the standard of review commonly applied in challenges to development management actions. It upholds ordinances unless they are clearly arbitrary and unreasonable. Good faith development management ordinances easily overcome this level of review, which is also followed in most state courts.

Although almost any conceivable public purpose is legitimate, a few are invalid. For example, restrictive or open-space zoning designed to reduce the market value of property or to discourage development to facilitate public acquisition is impermissible. The presence of long-term plans for public acquisition in an area, however, will not in itself undermine the legitimacy of regulations that are based on valid objectives other than reducing the price of land for public acquisition.

The Taking Claim

The most controversial land-use law issue is at what point does regulation of private land become an unconstitutional taking of private property without just compensation. The constitutional limitations on the so-called taking claim are essentially the same as the provisions governing due process. The Fifth Amendment to the U.S. Constitution prohibits the federal government from taking private property without just compensation, while the Fourteenth Amendment extends this prohibition to state and local actions. State constitutions also prohibit the taking of private property without just compensation. State courts frequently, but not always, interpret these prohibitions as having the same force and effect as the federal taking prohibition.

Legal challenges based on these constitutional taking limitations are sometimes viewed as overwhelming impediments to effective local regulation of land development, but they should not be. Often, the specter of a taking challenge is a greater limitation to managing development effectively than is the taking clause itself.

Courts are more likely to invalidate land-use regulations as a taking, as a violation of substantive due process, or on various other grounds if enactment or enforcement of an ordinance has involved procedural irregularities, or *ad hoc* and *post hoc* planning and land regulation, rather than even-handed implementation of comprehensive community planning. As communities prepare development management regulations, they should record and maintain documentation of the adverse effects that their regulations are designed to avoid. Such documentation is necessary for courts to appreciate the importance of community concerns when balanced against the often more direct impact an ordinance may have on an individual landowner.

The taking prohibition clearly prohibits governments from using ordinances or administrative action to physically seize or invade private property for public use. This includes a prohibition on all types of physical invasion without compensation, such as building a road on someone's property or forcing a landowner to allow the public to pass across the land. The severity of the invasion is not important. For example, a city cannot order a landowner to allow a cable television company to place a transformer box on the owner's apartment building against his or her wishes, without paying just compensation for it.[8] The taking clause also has been interpreted to prohibit any regulation of private property in a way that leaves the property with no economically reasonable use. A landowner who wishes to demonstrate in court that a regulation constitutes an invalid taking, must show two things: (a) that the regulation deprives the property of all reasonable economic use and (b) that the decision makers have reached a final, definitive position regarding development of the parcel.

No Reasonable Use. There is no straightforward answer to the question of how far a land-use regulation can go in effectively depriving any economic use of property before it becomes a taking for which compensation is required. In a frequently quoted opinion of Justice Oliver Wendell Holmes, the U.S. Supreme Court held that "The general rule at least is, that while property may be regulated to a certain extent, if regulation goes too far it will be recognized as a taking."[9]

In recent rulings, the U.S. Supreme Court has made it clear that *no* reasonable uses may exist—that is to say, no chance of a viable economic return—before a regulatory taking occurs.[10] In applying these rulings, lower courts use a case-by-case analysis, so that whether a regulation goes "too far" depends on the circumstances of each case. Review by the courts involves two essential inquiries: the character of the government action in question, and the economic impact of the regulation as applied to the specific property. Courts thus balance the public purpose served by the regulation against the severity of the restriction imposed on an individual parcel.

Review of numerous decisions establishes some general rules.

- A diminution in property value, *even a substantial one*, resulting from a regulation or denial of a permit does not in itself constitute a taking. A recent decision upholds regulations that reduce property values by as much as 80 to 90 percent.

- The primary factor is not the difference in the value of the property after the regulation compared to the value before the regulation, but whether the restriction leaves the landowner with some economically reasonable use of the parcel. No recent U.S. Supreme Court decision changes the rule that courts are almost certain to uphold a reasonable land-use regulation when the regulation does not deny a landowner all economically viable use of a parcel.

- Some courts, on occasion, have upheld regulations that deny a landowner the ability to develop a parcel at all. Decisions upholding such regulations have often been based on the doctrine that a landowner has no right to use property in a manner that presents a risk of harm to the public. For this reason, courts are more likely to uphold regulations that prohibit all development of wetlands or floodways (when that development would pose a threat to public safety) than regulations that prohibit all development of other types of property. For example, in an influential wetlands decision, the Wisconsin Supreme Court held that a landowner has no absolute right to "change the essential natural character of his land so as to use it for a purpose for which it was unsuited in its natural state and which injures the rights of others."[11]

In the final analysis, the importance that a court places on the regulatory objective; the reasonableness of the landowner's expectations given the size, location, and character of a parcel; and the perceived fairness of the regulation seem to determine the outcome of the cases.

Final, Definitive Position. The federal courts will not generally address a regulatory taking claim until a landowner has obtained a "final, definitive position" from the local regulators prohibiting any economically reasonable use of the property. State courts generally follow this requirement, but they enforce it with widely varying levels of consistency. Courts impose this requirement because they cannot determine whether a regulation "goes too far" and results in a compensable taking unless they know the precise nature and extent of development that would be permitted on the parcel.[12]

This doctrine typically requires a landowner to attempt all reasonable development options before challenging a regulation or denial as a taking. The rejection of a single site plan or subdivision application typically will not constitute a final, definitive position denying all economically reasonable use of a parcel.

Equal Protection

The Fourteenth Amendment to the U.S. Constitution provides in part that no state shall "deny to any person within its jurisdiction equal protection of the laws." Most state constitutions also guarantee equal protection. In essence, equal protection in the land-use context requires that regulatory distinctions and classifications be made on a rational basis. Any local action that creates a classification—for example, zoning one tract for business and an adjoining tract for residences—potentially raises equal protection questions. Equal protection, however, requires only that a legitimate and rational reason exist for a regulatory classification.

Courts almost always defer to legislative land-use classifications and uphold a classification unless it is completely irrelevant to the stated public objective. For example, courts sustain regulations that apply only to parcels undeveloped at the effective date of the regulation. Likewise, equal protection does not require that all areas subject to a regulatory program come under regulation at the same time. Equal protection only requires some legitimate reason for such distinctions.

The Exaction Doctrine

As noted earlier, an increasing number of municipalities impose land dedication requirements, development exactions, or impact fees as a condition of development approval. These requirements are frequently challenged as takings, violations of substantive due process, and violations of equal protection. Responding to these challenges, courts in most states have formulated a standard requiring that exactions bear a reasonable relationship to the public service needs and impacts created by the new development. Courts vary in the degree to which they insist that the exaction or fee relate to the needs created by the proposal. However, they generally require that the exaction be proportional to the increased demand on public services and facilities resulting from the development. Exactions that go beyond the costs necessary to address the impacts of the development are likely to be struck down.

This area has received increased attention as a result of a June 1987 U.S. Supreme Court decision, *Nollan* v. *California Coastal Commission*,[13] in which the Court held that a condition attached to a building permit requiring dedication of a public access easement constituted an invalid taking. The Court found no reasonable relationship between the required easement and the stated purpose of the easement.

The plaintiffs in the *Nollan* case had an option to purchase an ocean-front bungalow in Ventura County, California. In accordance with California law, the Nollans submitted building plans to the California Coastal Commission to demolish the 500-square-foot bungalow and replace it with a 2,500-square-foot, three-bedroom home. The commission approved the building plans but imposed a condition requiring the Nollans to dedicate a public access easement along the front of their property, between a sea wall and the mean high water line (the point where public ownership begins). Similar restrictions had been imposed on 43 other projects in the same tract to ensure that the public could continue to pass along the beach. The commission concluded that the access easement was necessary, not because the new structure would have an adverse impact on the public's physical access to the beach, but because the Nollans' house would contribute to the creation of a "wall of residential structures" that would prevent the public from enjoying *visual* access to the ocean from behind the house.

The Court deemed that the easement constituted a "permanent physical occupation" of the property, thereby distinguishing the situation from most land-use regulations. Yet the Court also stated that it would apply the same standard in such exaction cases as it applies in regulatory taking cases: A regulation is valid only if it "substantially advances" a "legitimate state interest" and does not deny the landowner the economically viable use of the property.

The Court held that the condition imposed by the California Coastal Commission was invalid because it did not substantially advance the objective of promoting the public's visual access to the beach from behind the house. The Court was not troubled by the commission's goals of increasing public access along the beach and protecting visual and psychological access to the beach. Rather, the Court invalidated the condition for the specific reason that the public access easement bore an insufficient relationship to any problems created by the new larger house. The Court said that it was "impossible to understand" how lateral access along the beach could remedy the commission's concern that the new house would interfere with the public's ability to view the ocean from behind the house.

Although the decision struck down the commission's public access requirement, it confirms the broad scope of governmental authority to impose exactions. The decision also suggested that oceanfront development could be completely denied for blocking public ocean views, interfering with the public's psychological connection to the beach, or for increasing beach congestion (so long as a landowner retains some economically feasible use of the property).

Indeed, the Court even suggested that the commission could condition its approval on dedication of a viewing area on the Nollans' property. A viewing area would be appropriate because it would substantially advance the commission's legitimate interest in preserving the public views and would remedy the house's negative impact on public views. The Court held only that the commission cannot require dedication of a public access easement simply because it is a "good idea," without some reasonable showing that the proposed construction would contribute to the need for increased physical public access to the beach.

The *Nollan* decision provides three important lessons:

- The basic legal rules and standards determining when a taking has occurred and governing land dedications have not changed.
- Local land-use decisions will be scrutinized by the courts to ensure that they do not impose a land dedication requirement or public access condition unless the condition reasonably addresses a public need created by the proposed development.
- Local decision makers should carefully and thoroughly document and articulate the objectives of land-use and exaction programs.

The Vested Rights Doctrine

A legal question that frequently arises whenever a municipality changes its regulations is the point at which a proposed development has the right to go forward without regard to subsequent regulatory changes. An increasing number of state statutes explicitly define this point. In the absence of a specific statute to the contrary, the traditional rule is that the right to complete a project vests when a developer has undertaken substantial construction (for example, poured a foundation) in good faith reliance upon a validly issued building permit. Other states only require the issuance of a building permit. After one has a vested right, government actions to prevent the development will run afoul of various constitutional and statutory provisions.

A Word on Remedies

The traditional remedy for a successful challenge to a land-use regulation is simply to invalidate the offending regulation or the decision based on it. Courts often require a government to revise its ordinances or implementing action. Because of recent judicial developments, damage awards have recently become an important alternative remedy. The possibility of localities having to pay large damage awards has created local concerns and in some cases, reluctance among local officials to go forward with needed growth management strategies.

The 1987 U.S. Supreme Court decision in *First English Evangelical Lutheran Church of Glendale* v. *County of Los Angeles*,[14] did not affect determinations of when, in fact, a government action constitutes a taking. In that decision, however, the Court did establish that the U.S. Constitution requires the payment of damages for any temporary regulatory taking of property in any state. The plaintiff in *First English* was a church that owned 21 acres along a creek that it had developed as a camp for handicapped children. In 1977 a forest fire denuded the upstream watershed. In 1978 a flood destroyed the camp and killed 10 people. Thereafter, the county adopted an interim ordinance (or moratorium) prohibiting reconstruction within the flood-prone area until completion of floodplain mapping.

The church sued the county, alleging, among other claims, that the ordinance constitutes a regulatory taking. The church sought damages to compensate it for the taking, rather than just invalidation of the ordinance. The U.S. Supreme Court accepted the case to rule only on whether the U.S. Constitution prohibits California from limiting the remedies available for a regulatory taking to invalidation or, conversely, whether just compensation is required. In its decision, the Court did not hold or imply that the county's ordinance was invalid; it held only that, assuming a regulation constitutes a taking, the Constitution requires the payment of damages to the landowner.[15] A major unresolved issue is how damages are to be calculated if an ordinance is found to be a taking.

The Civil Rights Act of 1871[16] also authorizes monetary awards and other remedies, including recovery of attorneys' fees, for actions taken "under color of state law" that deprive a citizen of rights protected by the U.S. Constitution or certain federal statutes.

The extraordinary expansion of potential municipal liability for land-use decisions under the Civil Rights Acts is an important recent judicial development. Violations of federally protected rights raise the possibility of a plaintiff recovering damages and attorney's fees from a local government. The Supreme Court has held that good faith municipal action is not immune from damages for interfering with property rights.

CONCLUSION

The 1988 National Park Service Management Policies state that:

> Cooperative regional planning will be undertaken to integrate parks into their regional environments and to address adjacent land use issues that influence park resources. . . . Superintendents will be aware of what uses are planned on adjacent lands. They will seek to encourage compatible adjacent uses and to mitigate potential adverse effects on park values by actively participating in planning and regulatory processes of neighboring jurisdictions.[17]

Park managers can substantially advance these park service policies in many communities by participating effectively in local planning and land-use processes. Effective participation is by no means easy. It requires an understanding of local land-use planning and growth management tools and techniques, sensitivity to the state and federal legal limitations on use of these tools and techniques, appreciation of local political conditions and development practices, and devotion of substantial time and resources to adjacent land-use issues. But, increasingly, it must be done to effectively advance necessary resource management objectives. With diligent and sensitive participation, park managers can become welcome partners in local land-use decision making and, in doing so, can protect park resources and enhance the visitors' experience.

FURTHER INFORMATION

The following references are to relatively widely circulated sources that provide further discussion of local land-use controls and may assist park service personnel to participate more effectively in the development management process.

Multivolume Treatises

Antieau, Chester James. *Local Government Law.* Albany, N.Y.: Matthew Bender.

McQuillin, Eugene. *Treatise on the Law of Municipal Corporations.* Chicago: Callaghan and Company.

Rathkopf, Charles A., and Arden Herman Rathkopf. *Law of Zoning and Planning.* New York: Clark Boardman.

Williams, Norman, Jr., ed. *American Land Planning Law.* Chicago: Callaghan and Company.

Books and Reports

Babcock, Richard F., and Charles L. Siemon. *The Zoning Game Revisited.* Boston: Lincoln Institute of Land Policy, 1985. Updated version of a classic book on zoning and the land-use regulation process. Provides case studies of 11 local and regional land-use programs, their origins, development, legal aspects, and political history.

Bosselman, Fred, David Callies, and John Banta. *The Taking Issue: An Analysis of the Constitutional Limits of Land Use Control.* Washington, D.C.: Council on Environmental Quality, 1973.

Brower, David J., et al. *Managing Development in Small Towns.* Chicago: American Planning Association Press, 1984. Provides a comprehensive overview of the use of growth management measures in small towns, including techniques based on local land acquisition, public spending, taxation, and regulatory powers. Provides tangible guidance in assessing the need for growth management and in implementing specific techniques.

Brown, Warren Lee. *Case Studies in Protecting Parks.* Natural Resources Report 87-2. Denver, Colo.: National Park Service, 1987. This book provides 16 case studies outlining park service accomplishments in protecting parks from the impacts of adjacent land and resource development. It also discusses strategies for effective park protection efforts. Available from National Park Service, c/o Air Quality Division, P.O. Box 25287, Denver, CO 80225-0287.

Chapin, F. Stuart, and Edward J. Kaiser. *Urban Land Use Planning.* 3rd ed. Urbana, Ill.: University of Illinois Press, 1979.

Clark, John. *The Sanibel Report: Formulation of a Comprehensive Plan Based on Natural Systems.* Washington, D.C.: The Conservation Foundation, 1976.

This book explains the process used to create a performance-based planning process and zoning ordinance for Sanibel Island, Florida, which adopted standards for development based on the impacts of the development on vegetation, wildlife, coastal process, geology, or hydrology of the ecological zone in which the development is proposed.

DeGrove, John M. *Land, Growth and Politics.* Chicago: American Planning Association Press, 1984.

In-depth examination of the political and environmental context for the development and implementation of seven state growth management programs—Hawaii, Vermont, Florida, California, Oregon, Colorado, and North Carolina.

Freilich, Robert H., and Eric O. Stuhler. *The Land Use Awakening: Zoning Law in the Seventies.* Chicago: American Bar Association Press, 1981.

Getzels, Judith, and Charles Thurow, eds. *Rural and Small Town Planning.* Chicago: American Planning Association Press, 1980.

Introduces the role of planners in rural towns, natural resource-based planning, small town zoning and development permitting techniques, subdivision regulation, infrastructure planning, and rural transportation and housing services. Includes sample ordinance language.

Godschalk, David R., et al. *Constitutional Issues of Growth Management.* Chicago: American Society of Planning Officials Press, 1979.

Analyzes the legal aspects of growth management. Includes discussion of the rationale for growth management; the constitutional bases of growth management; the variety of types of legal challenges to growth management programs; hypothetical cases illustrating legal issues.

Hagman, Donald G., and Julian Conrad Juergensmeyer. *Urban Planning and Land Development Control Law.* St. Paul, Minn.: West Publishing Company, 1986.

An excellent legal textbook.

Healy, Robert G., and John S. Rosenberg. *Land Use and the States.* Washington, D.C.: Resources for the Future, 1979.

An overview of how several states—Vermont, California, and Florida—have implemented state-level programs to plan for and protect specific land resources. Also discusses issues raised by a greater state role in land-use regulation.

Kusler, Jon A. *Our National Wetlands Heritage: A Protection Guidebook*. Washington, D.C.: Environmental Law Institute, 1983.

_____. *Regulating Sensitive Lands*. Washington, D.C.: Environmental Law Institute, 1980.

This thorough book discusses regulatory programs to protect floodplains, lake and stream shores, coastal zones, wetlands, rivers, areas of scientific interest, and similar sensitive areas. It also discusses state resource protection programs and resource protection legal cases.

Mandelker, Daniel R. *Land Use Law*. Charlottesville, Va.: The Michie Company, 1982.

Provides a thorough and well-organized discussion of land-use law.

Meshenberg, Michael J. *The Administration of Flexible Zoning Techniques*. Planning Advisory Service Report no. 318. Chicago: American Society of Planning Officials, 1976.

Provides an introduction to and analysis of flexible zoning techniques, including PUDs, special permits, floating zones, overlay zoning, tract zoning, incentive zoning, exactions, and TDR.

Natural Resources Defense Council. *Land Use Controls in the United States: A Handbook on the Legal Rights of Citizens*. New York: The Dial Press, 1977.

Patterson, William T. *Land Use Planning Techniques and Implementation*. New York: Van Nostrand Reinhold, 1979.

Sanders, Welford. *The Cluster Subdivision: A Cost-Effective Approach*. Planning Advisory Service Report no. 356. Chicago: American Planning Association, 1980.

Provides detailed guidance on the design of cluster subdivision ordinances. Includes legal guidance and excerpts from several local zoning ordinances.

Scott, Randall W., ed. *Management and Control of Growth: Issues, Techniques, Trends*. Washington, D.C.: Urban Land Institute, 1975.

Siemon, Charles L., Wendy V. Larsen, and Douglas R. Porter. *Vested Rights: Balancing Public and Private Development Expectations*. Washington, D.C.: Urban Land Institute, 1982.

Examines vested rights issue. Looks at the existing legal framework, suggests alternative means by which local governments and developers can avoid vested rights problems.

Smith, Herbert H. *The Citizen's Guide to Planning.* Chicago: American Planning Association, 1979.

A layperson's introduction to planning written by a veteran planner. Provides overviews of the planning process; the role of the local planning commission; the relationship between plans and regulations; and the connection between capital improvements and planning.

_____. *The Citizen's Guide to Zoning.* Chicago: American Planning Association, 1983.

A primer on all aspects of zoning—fundamental principles, developing regulations, the components of a zoning ordinance, zoning variances, the relationship of zoning to other land management techniques, the citizen's role in zoning hearings, and emerging zoning techniques.

Thurow, Charles, William Jones, and Duncan Erley. *Performance Controls for Sensitive Lands: A Practical Guide for Local Administrators.* Planning Advisory Service Report nos. 307, 308. Chicago: American Society of Planning Officials, 1975.

An early, comprehensive discussion of the use of performance standard regulations to protect environmental resources, including streams and lakes, aquifers, wetlands, woodlands, and hillsides. Includes excerpts of illustrative performance control ordinances.

Wright, Robert R., and Susan Webber. *Land Use in a Nutshell.* 2d ed. St. Paul, Minn.: West Publishing Company, 1985.

A concise and readable overview of land-use law.

Yaro, Robert D., et al. *Dealing with Change in the Connecticut River Valley: A Design Manual for Conservation and Development.* Amherst, Mass.: Center for Rural Massachusetts, University of Massachusetts, 1988.

Explains the advantages of clustered development, provides practical standards for preserving distinctive local character while accommodating development, includes sample cluster development ordinance language, and contains excellent aerial graphics showing various landscapes before development, after conventional development, and after creative site-sensitive development.

Articles

Atherton, Judith S. H. "An Assessment of Conservation Easements: One Method of Protecting Utah's Landscape." *Journal of Energy Law and Policy* 6 (1985):55.

Baker, R. Lisle, and Stephen O. Anderson. "Taxing Speculative Land Gains: The Vermont Experience." *Urban Law Annual* 22 (1981):3.

Comment. "Broadway's Newest Hit: Incentive Zoning for Preserving Legitimate Theatres." *Cardozo Arts and Entertainment Law Journal* 3 (1984):377.

Dunford, Richard W. "A Survey of Tax Relief Programs for the Retention of Agricultural and Open Space Lands." *Gonzaga Law Review* 15 (1980):756.

Elrod, Linda. "Vanishing Farmlands and Decaying Downtowns: The Case for Growth Management," *Journal of the Kansas Bar Association* 51 (1982):18.

Fredland, Daniel R. "Environmental Performance Zoning: An Emerging Trend?" *Urban Lawyer* 12 (1980):678.

Geier, Karl E. "Agricultural Districts and Zoning: A State-Local Approach to a National Problem." *Ecology Law Quarterly* 8 (1980):655.

Johnson, Douglas Fifield. "The Future of Farmland and Preservation: Will New Jersey Remain the Garden State?" *Rutgers Law Journal* 12 (1981):713.

Merriam, Dwight H. "Making TDR Work." *North Carolina Law Review* 56 (1978):77.

Myers, David A. "The Legal Aspects of Agricultural Districting." *Indiana Law Journal* 55 (1979):1.

Netherton, Ross D. "Environmental Conservation and Historic Preservation through Recorded Land-Use Agreements." *Real Property, Probate, and Trust Journal* 14 (1979):540.

Robinson, Alan H. "Planning Considerations for Preservation and Use of National Seashores." *Coastal Zone Management Journal* 5 (1979):7.

Sax, Joseph L. "Buying Scenery: Land Acquisitions for the National Park Service." *Duke Law Journal* (1980):709.

_____. "Helpless Giants: The National Parks and the Regulation of Private Lands.'' *Michigan Law Review* 75 (1976):239.

Shepard, Blake. "The Scope of Congress' Constitutional Power under the Property Clause: Regulating Non-Federal Property to Further the Purpose of National Parks and Wilderness Areas.'' *Boston College Environmental Affairs Law Review* 11 (1984):479.

Smith, Clay, III. "Easements to Preserve Open Space Land.'' *Ecology Law Quarterly* 1 (1971):737.

Stone, Carol R. "The Prevention of Urban Sprawl through Utility Extension Control.'' *Urban Lawyer* 14 (1982):357.

Thomas, Charlotte E. "The Cape Cod National Seashore: A Case Study of Federal Administrative Control over Traditionally Local Land Use Decisions.'' *Boston College Environmental Affairs Law Review* 12 (1985):225.

REFERENCES

1. American Planning Association, Planning Policies, APA Action Agenda, APA News (in *Planning* 24B [July 1979]; quoted in Donald G. Hagman and Julian C. Juergensmeyer, *Urban Planning and Land Development Central Law*, 2d ed. (St. Paul, Minn.: West Publishing Co., 1986), p. 25.

2. See John Clark, *The Sanibel Report: Formulation of a Comprehensive Plan Based on Natural Systems* (Washington, D.C.: The Conservation Foundation, 1976).

3. See Robert D. Yaro et al., *Dealing with Change in the Connecticut River Valley: A Design Manual for Conservation and Development* (Amherst, Mass.: University of Massachusetts, Center for Rural Massachusetts, 1988), which provides an excellent demonstration of clustering techniques and shows with aerial graphics how cluster development improves the landscape relative to development under conventional zoning regulations.

4. A growing number of local land conservancies or land trusts—private, nonprofit corporations that acquire and protect sensitive lands—are working in communities around the country to protect natural and cultural resources. Land trusts and the opportunities they offer to assist in protecting park resources are discussed in chapter 12.

5. These decisions, *Nollan* v. *California Coastal Commission* and *First English Evangelical Lutheran Church of Glendale* v. *County of Los Angeles*, are discussed later in this section. These decisions prompted the Reagan administration to issue Executive Order 12630, setting forth guidelines for federal agencies whose activities may affect the use of private property. This executive order applies only to federal actions and not state or local land-use decisions. Regarding involvement of federal park managers in local land-use planning, the order explicitly does not apply to "communications between Federal agencies or departments and State or local land-use planning agencies regarding planned or proposed State or local actions regulating private property.''

6. 272 U.S. 365 (1926).

7. Ibid.

8. See for example, *Loretto* v. *Teleprompter Manhattan CATV Corp.*, 458 U.S. 419 (1982).

9. *Pennsylvania Coal* v. *Mahon*, 260 U.S. 393, 415 (1922).

10. See, for example, *Penn Central Transportation Co.* v. *City of New York*, 438 U.S. 104 (1978); *Agins* v. *City of Tiburon*, 447 U.S. 255 (1980); *San Diego Gas & Electric Co.* v. *City of San Diego*, 450 U.S. 621 (1981); *Williamson County Regional Planning Commission* v. *Hamilton Bank*, 473 U.S. 172 (1985); and *Keystone Bituminous Coal Association* v. *DeBenedictus*, 480 U.S. 470 (1987).

11. *Just* v. *Marinette County*, 56 Wis.2d 7 (1972).

12. See, for example, *MacDonald, Sommer & Frates* v. *Yolo County*, 106 S.Ct 2561 (1986); *Williamson County Regional Planning Commission* v. *Hamilton Bank*, 473 U.S. 172 (1985).

13. 107 S.Ct 3141 (1987).

14. 107 S.Ct 2378 (1987).

15. Indeed, on remand the Appellate Department of the California Superior Court decided the takings issue contrary to the Supreme Court's assumption, holding that the floodplain ordinance at issue did not constitute a taking. *First English Evangelical Lutheran Church* v. *County of Los Angeles*, 258 Cal. Rptr. 893 (1989).

16. This act is often referred to as "Section 1983" because the act is codified at 42 U.S. Code Section 1983.

17. Chapter 2 in U.S. Department of the Interior, National Park Service, *Management Policies* (Washington, D.C.: National Park Service, 1988), pp. 9-10.

Chapter 12

Private Groups and Park Resources

by Philip C. Metzger, Michael A. Mantell, and Christopher J. Duerksen

There are limits to what government agencies and policies—be they federal, state, or local—can do to protect park resources from the harmful effects of development on private lands outside their boundaries. These constraints—political, fiscal, and legal—are not likely to diminish in the next few years. Moreover, governmental initiatives such as regulations, impact statements, and land acquisition will not be sufficient to address all or even many of the resource problems posed by activities on private lands outside park boundaries.

Staff at national parks can help overcome these limitations by strengthening their local constituency building. Private, nonprofit organizations, such as "friends of the parks" groups and land trusts can be particularly effective in protecting valuable resources and assisting parks in ensuring that compatible development takes place outside their boundaries. National Park Service policies require all parks to work more closely with local private organizations to protect park resources. This chapter describes briefly what these groups can do and some of the practical and legal constraints park service staff should be aware of in working with them.

"FRIENDS OF THE PARKS" GROUPS

Volunteers and nonprofit groups have long played an important role in the creation and protection of many National Park System units. Invaluable support has been provided by a whole spectrum of private

211

support groups, including cooperating associations; existing community groups such as Kiwanis, Jaycees, and Garden Clubs; and park-specific "Friends" groups.

Policy statements from the park service director's office in the late 1980s called on the Service to "establish a citizens' friends group for each unit of the National Park System." Noting some of the accomplishments of these groups in the past, official policy states:

> The National Park Service will build on this regard by establishing a citizens' friends group for each unit of the park system. These groups will be informal in nature and will not depend on government funds. Activities that groups could become involved with include assisting with interpretive programs, publicizing critical issues that affect the protection and preservation of park resources, and encouraging private donations to support park programs.[1]

Local citizens' organizations dedicated to safeguarding a particular area can help the park service in a variety of ways:
- by participating in the state and local programs, processes, and development approvals that may affect a park;
- by building local involvement and interest in an area through community celebrations, fund raising, and the like; and
- by helping with resource management activities, such as construction and maintenance of trails, and assisting in monitoring easements, vandalism, and changing resource conditions.

Park superintendents have long been wary of appearing at, for example, local zoning board meetings to voice concerns about the effects of nearby development on park resources, sometimes fearing the political backlash and isolation that such intervention might spur. Supported by an articulate group of respected local individuals, park service officials can present themselves as concerned professionals rather than intrusive outsiders. Fortified by just such local support, for example, park service planners from Santa Monica Mountains were able to present effective testimony in opposition to a proposal in Ventura County to rezone for a development that would have seriously undermined the recreation area's management plan.

"Friends" groups can also be helpful to park system units in building local involvement. When appropriate, ethnic or seasonal community celebrations held in a park can raise the positive visibility of both the group and the park, making the park an active part of local life and generating potential supporters among residents newly introduced to the park and its special resources. Such groups can also assist with fund-raising activities and events, subject to compliance with park service policies.

Finally, "friends" can help with resources management activities, particularly those involving short-term labor for constructing and maintaining trails and certain other visitor-use areas. Of course, this function was the genesis of the Appalachian Trail clubs several decades ago, but the idea has spread far beyond the Appalachian Trail. Sierra Club trail-building trips are increasing in popularity, and some parks near urban areas regularly attract helpers for such projects.

One of the most underused but helpful roles of "friends" is in providing watchful eyes on park resources. Simply in the course of hiking through or driving by a park, interested local residents can help supervise the terms of easements, curb vandalism, and prevent illegal destruction or taking of park resources. And watchful eyes in the community outside a park can become aware of possible development decisions before the park service might learn of them.

It is important that parks enter into specific memorandums of understanding or agreement with these groups to spell out expectations and responsibilities. In doing so, park service staff need to be aware of a few constraints in working with these groups. Park service personnel, for example, can serve in liaison or advising roles, but they cannot be voting board members. Nor can staff engage in fund raising for these groups, particularly on government time. The service, however, can agree to make the parks available for fund-raising projects that are consistent with park purposes and established procedures. (See the model memorandum of agreement prepared by the park service, which appears at the end of this chapter as figure 12.1, for a sample of the type of agreement that is desirable to clarify the expectations and responsibilities of the parties.)

Such groups are not without their costs to park personnel. Helping to form and organize "friends" groups is a major task, requiring considerable amounts of consulting and even hand holding as a group develops and works on various issues. At times, such organizations make demands and take positions with which park personnel disagree, and the organizations frequently demand attention and time that seems to be ill afforded. Nevertheless, the effort spent organizing and working with local allies virtually always pays off in terms of working within the community to protect park resources.

LAND TRUSTS

While "friends" groups work largely in the local political arena and may help parks with such practical tasks as appearing at hearings and helping to maintain park resources, land trusts work in the local real estate market to protect valuable areas from development. More than 750 of these nonprofit, tax-exempt groups operate throughout the United States. Most are quite small and local in nature, though the best-known are national groups such as the Nature Conservancy and the Trust for Public Land. Together, these national and local groups have protected some three million acres.

The *Connecticut Land Trust Handbook* states that:

> A land conservation trust is a private, nonprofit organization devoted to the preservation of locally significant parcels of natural areas and open space. The trust receives its land as gifts from individual landowners (through donations and bequests) and developers, and through purchase. It uses the land for passive purposes which are educational, recreational, and/or scientific in nature. A voluntary board of directors runs the trust, and its membership is open to the general public. In addition, a land trust may provide other educational opportunities and assist its town with acquisition of open space and land use planning.[2]

A local land trust or land conservancy provides an effective method for a group of citizens or a local government to acquire and protect critical natural or recreational lands. Land trusts vary greatly in geographic scope, degree of professionalism, and the types of land resources they seek to preserve. Although not a substitute for governmental land-use controls, a local land trust can be a important complement to governmental action for land and resource conservation. Such land trusts often provide the local leadership, commitment, and flexibility essential to local land protection.

Local land trusts generally serve three important purposes:

- They preserve natural, historic, or other open space lands or provide public recreational access to lands.
- They provide responsible long-term stewardship of important land resources.
- They help public agencies acquire land quickly and efficiently through preacquisition and resale to a public agency.

Many local land trusts maintain the tradition of private land ownership by acquiring easements and other less-than-full-fee property rights that ensure land protection while allowing landowners to continue to live on farms and maintain open land. These less-than-full purchases also enable land to remain on local tax rolls.

Although land or easement acquisition is the conservation technique employed most commonly by local land trusts, many other private land protection tools are available. A common factor in these tools is that they provide land trusts with a means to influence the use of valuable parcels with limited expenditures of money.

Generally operating within relatively small budgets, land trusts protect land through a wide variety of techniques, focusing on the deductibility of federal and state taxes for donations. For example, trusts:

- accept donations of land or of partial interests;
- arrange bargain sales in which a landowner donates part of the land's value and receives cash for the rest;
- acquire interests and resell them to private owners with a reservation of some development or use rights or to government agencies; or
- retain the land or interest and manage the properties or oversee the partial interests acquired.

Working either on their own or in partnership with government entities, these nonprofit organizations have several important strengths:

- Unhindered by statutory requirements to buy only at assessed land value or to purchase by a specified process, trusts can generally purchase land cheaper and quicker than governments can.
- Trusts can work quietly where public disclosure of federal agency activities might cause land values to skyrocket or individuals to protest.
- Trusts are not limited by boundaries, beyond which the park service cannot act without a congressionally authorized change.

Local land trusts may be more adept than state or local recreation departments or environmental protection agencies at acquiring land and easements, negotiating personalized management agreements, and using similar land protection techniques. The board members of a local land trust are usually local landowners or respected members of the community with the ability to influence the owners of key parcels. Public agencies often work with a private land trust as an intermediary for acquiring land because the private land trust can often negotiate and undertake other steps necessary for acquisition faster and with fewer procedural constraints than a public agency can. Government agencies may also be reluctant to acquire easements or enter into other arrangements that may require day-to-day monitoring and a long-term relationship with a landowner.

Trusts may, of course, be useful in acquiring land or development rights from landowners inside park boundaries, but they can be most effective in protecting vulnerable lands and scenic values beyond park boundaries. The Jackson Hole Land Trust has performed this function for several years, protecting traditional ranching land just south of Grand Teton National Park. The capability to devise limited developments can be essential in safeguarding key near-park acreage where land values are especially high. The profits from small-scale development on tracts where the effects on parkland are minimized can often bankroll the purchase of much larger areas of important wildlands.

In a few isolated instances. land trusts have been accused of unreasonable profit taking when selling land back to the government or of forcing changes in acquisition priorities for an agency. Rules have been put into place to help ensure that it is the federal agency, not the trust, which decides what lands need to be purchased and that certain information is disclosed through a letter of intent if the trust seeks prior assurances that the government is interested in the parcel before it seeks to acquire it.[3]

Land trusts have been enormously effective in protecting valuable natural and historic resources, and much of this has benefited the National Park System. With fiscal constraints and reduced land acquisition efforts not likely to diminish in the foreseeable future, these groups promise to become even more important to protecting park resources.

REFERENCES

1. National Park Service, *12-Point Plan: The Challenge, The Action* (Washington, D.C.: U.S. Government Printing Office, 1986), p. 11. As of mid-1989, there were some 80 formally constituted "Friends" groups in existence for the parks. A "Friends" group is generally defined by the Service as a nonprofit organization created primarily to assist a park, several parks, or the system as a whole.

2. Suzanne Wilkins and Roger Koontz, *Connecticut Land Trust Handbook* (Middletown, Conn.: Connecticut Land Trust Service Bureau, 1986), p. I-1.

3. 48 Fed. Reg. 155 (Aug. 10, 1983).

Figure 12.1*

Agreement No. _____

MODEL
MEMORANDUM OF AGREEMENT
BETWEEN THE
NATIONAL PARK SERVICE
AND
[NAME OF COOPERATING ORGANIZATION]

Article I — Background

THIS AGREEMENT is hereby entered into this _____ day of _____, 19____, by and between the [name of cooperating organization], a corporation organized and doing business under the laws of the State of _____, hereinafter referred to as the Corporation, and the National Park Service, U.S. Department of the Interior, covering certain fund raising and philanthropic activities which are intended to benefit the National Park System.

Whereas [name of park], a unit of the National Park System, hereinafter referred to as "the park," would receive [identify benefits to be obtained] through this fund raising effort; and whereas the benefits to the park are consistent with the intent of Congress in authorizing the park as part of the National Park System;

Whereas, the National Park Service through the Secretary of the Interior has authority to accept donations for the purposes embraced by this Memorandum of Agreement (See 41 Stat. 917, 16 U.S.C. 6);

Whereas, nothing in this Agreement shall affect or interfere with fulfillment of the obligations or exercise of the authority of the National Park Service or any other Federal Agency;

Whereas, NPS wishes to recognize and encourage [name of cooperating organization] in conducting its fund raising effort to benefit the park.

Article II — Responsibilities of Parties

NOW THEREFORE the parties agree as follows:

(1) The National Park Service recognizes the Corporation as an organization suited to raise funds for the benefit of the park;

(2) The Corporation intends to donate to the National Park Service funds, materials, or services to [insert a description of the projects and activities to be undertaken] under the following terms and conditions:

The Corporation shall be fully qualified under State and Federal law to engage in fund raising and receive philanthropic contributions for the purposes enumerated herein.

All activities performed under this Agreement will be accomplished in conformance with the formal fund raising policies of the National Park Service which are made a part of this agreement. (See Appendix 1.)

All costs of the fund raising campaign shall be borne by the Corporation.

Funds donated to the National Park Service by the Corporation will be placed in a special donations account and shall be used solely on behalf of and for benefit of the projects and activities set forth above unless otherwise provided by law.

The National Park Service will make available to the Corporation such information and data as may reasonably be required and is generally available to inform potential donors and others about the status of plans for the projects and activities to benefit.

The Corporation is recognized as fund raiser of donations for the purposes and projects enumerated in this Agreement. The National Park Service may choose to enter into similar arrangements with others.

Article III — Term of Agreement

This Memorandum of Agreement shall be effective when signed by both parties and shall remain in effect as needed for up to three years from that date, subject to renewal by mutual agreement for a further period not to exceed three years.

Article IV — Key Officials

Key Officials.

NPS:

Insert: [name of NPS Representative]
           [Mailing address]
           [Telephone number]

[Corporation]:

Insert: [Name of Organization's Representative]
           [Mailing address]
           [Telephone number]

Article V — Property

The Corporation may not construct any structures or buildings on park land or otherwise make any alterations to park land without further written permission from the National Park Service.

Article VI — Prior Approvals

Any materials prepared for public consumption, such as individual promotional activities, brochures, or any other form of publicity will be submitted to the National Park Service for formal review and approval prior to its release. In addition, any agreements the Corporation proposes to enter into with third parties in furtherance of its activities hereunder shall be subject to approval by the National Park Service.

The National Park Service to the extent practicable agrees to arrange for and conduct tours, interpretive events, and inspections for individuals and groups at the request of the Corporation provided that such activities shall not, in the judgement of the National Park Service, unduly infringe upon or detract from normal visitor activities and services of the park. The Corporation shall request such tours and other events through the park Superintendent (hereinafter referred to as "Superintendent") in advance. The Superintendent shall have final decision-making responsibility as to such arrangements, depending upon park workloads and staff availability.

The Corporation shall apply for and abide by terms and conditions of a special events permit for each such event it proposes to conduct. The Superintendent shall have the final authority over the granting of such permits.

Article VII — Reports

Within 60 days of the effective date of this Agreement, the Corporation shall furnish to NPS for approval a plan of operations which will clearly identify the roles of both the National Park Service and the Corporation and will also indicate the overall strategy for fund raising, the specific fund raising techniques to be used, timetables covering the length of time required for the fund raising effort, administrative and support structures, projected costs, and estimated results. Such plan shall be updated as conditions change, and, in any event, on at least an annual basis.

Within 90 days from the execution of this Agreement and quarterly thereafter, the Corporation shall submit status reports to the National Park Service setting forth the progress of the fund raising effort, any present or anticipated problems, and financial projects for remaining work and the progress of the fund raising programs. The report shall also set forth quarterly goals for the fund raising efforts and shall compare the performance during the prior quarter to the goals set forth for that quarter. The reports following the first shall be submitted by the 15th day of the month following the end of each calendar quarter.

Funds received and expended by the Corporation from whatever source and for whatever purposes shall be accounted for under a system of accounts and financial controls meeting accepted professional standards for non-profit charitable organizations; the Corporation shall engage an annual audit by a qualified audit firm, and shall publish an annual report of its activities and finances. All such accounts shall be subject to audit by NPS or its authorized representative.

Article VIII — Termination

The National Park Service or the Corporation may terminate this Agreement by providing sixty days written notice to the other.

Article IX — General

All obligations of the National Park Service hereunder are subject to the availability of funds, and to such direction and instructions as may have been or are hereafter provided by Congress.

During the performance of this agreement, the participants agree to abide by the terms of Executive Order 11246 (Appendix 2) on nondiscrimination and will not discriminate against any person because of race, color, religion, sex, or national origin. The participants will take affirmative action to ensure that applicants are employed without regard to their race, color, religion, sex, or national origin.

No member of or delegate to Congress, or resident commissioner, shall be admitted to any share or part of this agreement, or to any benefit that may arise therefrom; but this provision shall not be construed to extend to this agreement if made with a corporation for its general benefit.

Dated the _____ day of _____, 19____.

AGREED TO BY:

_____

Representative, National Park Service

_____

Representative, [Corporation]

_____

* Prepared by the National Park Service, Special Assistant for Policy Development (October 15, 1986).

Part IV

The Challenges Ahead

Several challenges exist for the national parks—and resource managers in particular—as they seek to grapple with evolving legal concepts, changing environmental conditions, and heightened public awareness. The two remaining chapters look at a few of these key challenges. Chapter 13 discusses courtroom battles involving the parks and how resource managers can best work with attorneys representing the parks. Chapter 14 examines some of the issues confronting the National Park System of the future—liability for injuries caused by natural resource conditions, threats to park resources from activities outside park boundaries, and the appropriate use of resources by visitors—and how our legal and political systems might respond.

Chapter 13

Lawyers, Scientists, and Preparing for Court

by Richard Dawson

Nothing strikes fear or invokes panic as quickly in a National Park Service manager of natural resources as a lawsuit. Some may see it initially as a threat to their integrity as well as to their job security. Moreover, the thought of facing litigation and the incessant badgering by attorneys over minute details and professional opinions that may come with it is rather distasteful, to say the least. The United States is, however, a litigious society in which private citizens and groups sometimes see actions to manage park resources as government attempts to control their rights or as a failure to manage their beloved parks adequately. Therefore, litigation finds its place among the myriad functions that many think to be within the normal business of resource management in the National Park Service.

Resource managers play a major role in lawsuits against the park service (and the Department of the Interior) that challenge, in essence, resource management decisions. Legal battles against the service over commercial fishing in the Everglades and off-road vehicle (ORV) use in Cape Cod, for example, have required resource managers to devote hundreds, if not thousands, of hours to all aspects of the litigation. In fact, conscientious and skillful work by a park's resource manager, combined with solid representation by attorneys in the Interior and Justice departments, can often make the difference in presenting a successful case.

Key to successful participation in litigation by a park service resource manager is developing a sound working relationship with the lead

U.S. attorney handling the case, one based on mutual respect, trust, and understandings of the respective responsibilities involved. The two comprise a team that must work together through difficult issues, seemingly impossible deadlines, and very different disciplines. The resource manager, in particular, has to adapt to a seemingly foreign environment, complete with its own language, rules, and traditions. A strong line of communication between the two is essential. Moreover, to be effective, resource managers need to establish a good line of communications with the lead attorney and be willing to work under his or her direction in carefully researching, documenting, and filing all materials used in arriving at the resource management decision that is being challenged.

The person selected to represent the agency in dealing with the attorneys should be someone who is familiar with the background issues and facts, is not listed by your opponent as a defendant, and has the authority to speak to the policy of the agency. If one is thoroughly prepared, has answered all questions honestly, and has been consistent when responding to his or her opponent, it will be extremely difficult for the opposition to find a weakness to exploit in court. However, if a hidden agenda is pursued or inconsistent responses to challenges occur, a park official's opponent will have enough ammunition to attack his or her position under any one of a variety of rules.

In legal battles, the manner in which resource management decisions were made will most likely be as important as the substance of the decision itself. Attention to documentation, data, plans, notice of hearings, and public comment, therefore, becomes extremely important as the realm of resource management enters the legal arena.

Since most litigation concerning resource management is involved with the decision-making process and the interpretation of available data on which a decision was made, the appropriate venue for the case will be civil court. The standard of review in civil court is one of the preponderance of the evidence or a 51 percent test of the facts. However, usually the way a park official has gone about making a decision comes under attack more than the fitness of his or her data. Therefore, the record of the decision-making process is perused thoroughly not only for completeness but also for procedural compliance. This strategy highlights the importance of consistency in a park official's actions and of thoroughness in answering the opposition's inquiries.

Given this, it is important to understand the role resource managers and scientists play in lawsuits and how one should best go about preparing for that role.

LAWYERS AND RESOURCE MANAGERS: DEVELOPING AN UNDERSTANDING

As a rule, resource managers and scientists are not trained in the law. Therefore, the unknown procedures and protocol of the legal profession, while fascinating, are also intimidating to the scientist or resource manager who is trained to accept certain facts (natural laws) as inviolable (that is, the law of gravity). Attorneys are professionally trained to provide advice on legal matters that often involve the interpretation of human laws that can be violated; they rely somewhat on moral obligation, not necessarily on irrefutable data and peer review, as their guiding tenet. They are in the case to win. However, to be successful in environmental litigation, these two dissimilar professions are forced into an association for their mutual advantage. This relationship is perhaps most aptly termed symbiosis.

There is an understood vulnerability that both parties must accept in this so-called symbiotic relationship. As a consequence, both will ask many questions, which to the respondent may seem very elementary. The adage that no question is a dumb one applies throughout this association.

In this symbiotic relationship the attorney depends on the scientist or resource manager for:
- the interpretation of agency policy or scientific evidence;
- honest and defensible data and arguments with no hidden agendas or political facesaving;
- assistance in framing the issues around good, sound reasoning and data;
- accurate answers to questions of past agency actions; and
- a compilation of past reports, memoranda, and correspondence on which the decision-makers relied for guidance—the so-called administrative record.

An attorney must realize that scientists disdain speculation and deal with probability models and therefore will be hesitant to render an absolute, irrefutable opinion on the potential risk of an action to the environment. In summary, the attorney will depend on the scientist or resource manager to educate him or her as to the data and their interpretations, as well as the policy on which the agency relied in making its decision.

One of the best tools to employ in educating counsel on the issues and their relative importance is to take him or her to the field to tour the resource while discussing the issues, policy, and precedence of your position. This visual briefing can have a tremendous impact in the courtroom. It will enable an attorney to educate the court better on the issues and the park service's position through oral argument, testimony, and cross-examination of witnesses.

On the other hand, a scientist or resource manager depends on the attorney to:

- explain the form and the function of the legal process in which he or she is to participate;
- discuss similar case law and provide copies of relevant cases so as to familiarize the scientist or resource manager with the issues and arguments on which the case may rely for resolution;
- offer an opinion as to their chances in court and the advantages and disadvantages of their position;
- develop a timetable for the litigation since many submissions to the court are under strict deadlines; and
- help in planning for what resources the scientist or resource manager will need to obtain or provide for the litigation.

Additionally, the scientist or resource manager should track the attorney- and court-generated paper trail by maintaining a "pleadings file" with an index so that he or she can refer to past court documents and briefs.

The most likely role for a scientist to play in a case will be as an expert witness. Attorneys' use of a scientist for this purpose can be intimidating. While the Federal Rules of Civil Procedure offer rather wide latitude in expertise to qualify before the court as an expert witness, it is humbling to be interrogated as to one's fitness as a professional in front of a room filled with strangers. Therefore, it is advisable for a scientist to ask his or her attorney if there are similar cases being heard in the area, so that he or she can go to those proceedings prior to the court hearing to get a feel for the atmosphere and protocol. Regardless, it is essential that expert witnesses drill with the park service's counsel prior to an appearance in the courtroom so that the questions do not surprise any park service witness, or, worse, offer some advantage to the service's opponent.

Before going to court, park officials should establish with counsel any other roles they are to play in assisting him or her in the courtroom. This may take the form of anything from sitting in the audience and listening to taking notes on the opposing testimony or arguments and offering suggestions for cross-examination and closing argument. However, the ultimate determination of a park official's courtroom role will depend on his or her familiarity with the record, briefs, and issues weighed against the needs of counsel for expertise in these areas.

While the symbiotic relationship between the attorney and the park scientist relies primarily on trust, it is also borne out of the counsel's need for accurate and defensible technical opinions and knowledge. The consistency of the scientist's position will help defend against any arguments concerning procedural inadequacies. The scientist's interest and depth of understanding of the legal process will assist the attorney in defending the position being challenged by providing him or her with a sounding board for ideas. This is important in framing the issues and arguments in a case.

PRETRIAL PREPARATION

The pretrial preparation by the park service is probably the most important time spent in defending the service's position. This time usually involves a host of responses and fact gathering that can generally be categorized as "discovery." Also, the pretrial period is essential for compiling the complete record of events, reports, memoranda, and other pertinent documents used by the agency in making its decision. This compilation makes up the administrative record (AR) and functions as the bibliography that the attorneys and the court refer to in their arguments and decisions about the issues.

Administrative Record

Ideally, an administrative record should be compiled throughout the decision-making process. It should contain all internal memoranda, correspondence, reports, announcements, meeting minutes, public notices, and so forth—both favorable and unfavorable—that came before the decision makers. It is extremely important to demonstrate through this record that adverse opinion was considered and discussed. This is vital in avoiding a claim that the actions of park officials were "arbitrary and capricious." Above all, the record should clearly display that the agency considered all comments and proposals both before and after its decision. Since the administrative record will be used extensively either to support and defend park service actions or to show error and fault with them, this is by far the most important pretrial effort one can expend. (For a sense of the kinds of documents that comprise such a record, see figure 13.1 at the end of this chapter.)

The court uses the administrative record to define its scope of review and thereby keep the park service's opponent within the bounds of the information and proposals considered by the service prior to its decision. The opposition (that is, the plaintiff) may attempt to go outside this record if it will serve his or her client's claim. Therefore, it is important that park service counsel restrict the court's review to the material included in the AR.

The plaintiff will usually move on the administrative record in one, or a combination, of three ways:

- claim that the action under it violates the U.S. Constitution;
- claim that the action involves arbitrary and capricious behavior; or
- claim that prior, valid promises or rules were legitimately relied on and thus the government is prevented (or estopped in the legal jargon) from changing them in this particular situation.

Constitutional attacks on the AR alleging violations of due process, for example, could center on agency administrative procedures under the National Environmental Policy Act (NEPA), with the plaintiffs asserting that they did not have the opportunity to be heard. To get this claim dismissed, the AR should show a thorough and careful review of *all* comments and alternative proposals as well as a record of procedural steps and public hearings in compliance with agency procedures and NEPA regulations and guidelines.

Another common move that a plaintiff will make against an AR is to claim that the decision was made in an arbitrary and capricious manner. A recent U.S. Supreme Court[1] case sets the applicable standard of review as:

> Normally, an agency rule would be arbitrary and capricious if the agency has relied on factors which Congress has not intended it to consider, entirely failed to consider an important aspect of the problem, offered an explanation for its decision that runs counter to the evidence before the agency, or is so implausible that it could not be ascribed to a difference in view or the product of expertise.

This standard mandates a complete AR showing both favorable and unfavorable comment, interagency review, and consideration of all facts.

Finally, the AR may contain correspondence between individuals of the park service and citizens that may make commitments, elucidate policy, or give promises of certain actions. These alleged promises may be used by the plaintiff to show that, in essence, an implied contract exists between the affected party and the government. This type of action is referred to as estoppel or detrimental reliance. The plaintiff may assert that, based on past promises, the service cannot take a certain action because he or she detrimentally relied on those promises. For example, commercial fishermen in the Everglades claimed they had made large investments and commitments to fish in that park on the basis of past park service policies and correspondence.

As a general rule, courts have held that the government cannot be estopped from the exercise of its sovereign powers. Therefore, including exhibits in the AR that go to this claim (estoppel) should not hurt the case. However, for the overall defense of an estoppel issue, park service officials should be aware that recent court rulings have held that the government can be estopped if the plaintiff can demonstrate that an "affirmative misrepresentation" was made by the service on which the plaintiff had "detrimentally" relied. In these cases, the AR contained subsequent correspondence that was inconsistent with the service's decision.

A properly prepared and complete AR can be extremely useful to the agency in responding to requests by the plaintiff for information during discovery. A well-documented and thoroughly researched AR can also be of assistance to the service's expert witnesses in preparation of testimony or during deposition.

Discovery

Discovery is essentially a method of gathering evidence before trial. It is used by both parties in a lawsuit to prepare for trial. The plaintiff uses discovery to gain access to internal agency documents and studies employed by them in making the litigated decision. Discovery usually occurs before entering court, or in protracted litigation, between appearances. The scope of discovery is determined by the district court based on the completeness and objectivity of the administrative record. If the plaintiffs feel that the AR is incomplete, they will generally file a Motion for Production with the court for additional discovery.

Discovery can take the form of many types of interrogation or testimony. The most common forms of discovery are interrogatories, admissions of facts, depositions, and expert witness testimony.

Interrogatories are a list of questions from one party to which the other party must respond. They are a tool to establish facts and the way certain facts were ascertained or why certain actions were taken. The park service or other responding party is responsible as the signee and the signee then becomes a witness; therefore, the service's counsel cannot answer the interrogatories. All questions in the interrogatory must be answered; however, the service's attorney can object to certain questions. Since these questions are generated by a plaintiff to expose a flaw in the process or lack of adequate facts prior to a decision, a good strategy is to answer all questions stating clearly what normal procedure is rather than admitting that one did not do something.

Admissions of fact are a voluntary acknowledgment of the existence or truth of certain facts. The plaintiff or challenging party generally asks for these stipulations before going to court to save time by mutually agreeing upon facts, and to focus on the real issues under contention. While park service officials answer admissions, they do so under the careful direction of counsel—once a matter is stipulated as fact, it becomes essentially irrefutable.

A deposition is the taking and transcription of sworn testimony of a witness or party. Normally, the government opposes depositions of agency officials, claiming that the administrative record is the controlling evidence. However, if a deposition does take place, the strategy of the plaintiff is to find out everything an official knows about the decision under litigation. Park service counsel should accompany the official to the deposition and can object to questions asked. The counsel, however, cannot instruct the witness not to answer. Once the deposition is taken, the witness has 30 days in which to review the transcript for errors or make changes in a statement, sign it, and return it to the court reporter. If the transcript is not signed within the prescribed period, the court reporter will sign it, and then the document can be submitted as evidence.

THE EXPERT WITNESS

Expert witnesses can be employed by both parties in a lawsuit involving the park service and will generally testify on the environmental effects of the service's action. The service's expert witnesses should thoroughly understand the issues, the process used to make the decision, and the studies, reports, and assessments prepared to assist the decision makers. Expert testimony in federal courts is governed by the Federal Rules of Evidence.

These rules are very liberal and allow testimony by an expert qualified "by knowledge, skill, experience, training, or education" who may testify in the form of an opinion.[2] The rules provide that facts or data "need not be admissible in evidence" if they are "reasonably relied upon by experts in the particular field in forming opinions."[3] In this case, "reasonably" is synonymous with "customarily." This rule allows an expert to testify on evidence that otherwise would be excluded as hearsay because he or she is giving an opinion based on facts or data produced by others. Therefore, the rule allows one expert to testify on what other experts have found. The rules permit testimony on the "ultimate issue to be decided by the trier of fact."

Normally, the expert testimony deals with the "probabilities" of certain effects rather than past occurrences of certain actions causing a certain effect. The park service commonly uses service experts, and the plaintiff generally uses locally and, if he or she can afford it, nationally recognized experts. Testimony usually concentrates on written documents with the purpose of challenging or explaining the conclusions drawn from the data, the consistency with agency policy, and the assessment of the impacts of the agency's action. A common strategy used by those challenging a park service action is to take a deposition of the agency's expert prior to going to court and to use a retained expert in court to refute portions of it.

While the rules qualifying an individual are liberal, they do not necessarily qualify anyone who is remotely conversant with the issue. Those who do not qualify as experts are "lay witnesses" whose testimony is limited to "rationally based perceptions of the witness and opinions or inferences that will be helpful to a clear understanding of one's testimony or the determination of act in issue."[4]

The court allows expert testimony:

- for the resolution of conflicting or opposing scientific views or opinions;
- to determine the impact of its (the court's) decision using the balancing test for preliminary injunction (irreparable injury to plaintiff, injury to plaintiff outweighs threatened harm to defendant, or disservice of the public interest);
- to supplement an inadequately developed administrative record;
- to clarify technical or scientific issues raised in the administrative record; and/or
- to educate the court on complex issues so that it can gain an understanding of the problem.

Generally, the role of the expert is to educate the court on the facts of the litigated issue. Given that an oath is required, the expert needs to be unbiased and truthful. Thorough preparation of experts in environmental cases is essential since the witnesses must be familiar with park service documents on which he or she is to testify. Testimony should be outlined in advance and questions and answers prepared. Since scientific testimony is often complex, it is critical that the attorney order and direct questions so that the answers are short and understandable. The attorney should review the strengths and weaknesses of the expert's testimony and must be confident that the expert will be able to answer convincingly without interruption or additional clarification from counsel. The attorney should not debate the witness on the stand.

The questions asked of the park service and its representatives during discovery and trial are fairly standard. They usually concern themselves with the following topics:

- the park service witness's fitness (educational background, training, prior experience, current duties and responsibilities, and/or duties when he or she made the decision) to give testimony and/or render an opinion;
- methods or data used in making a decision in this case compared with methods accepted in the witness's field of expertise;
- the witness's consideration of opinions and comments of other agencies;
- whether the best available data were used to make decisions and whether they conformed to normally practiced methods in the witness's field;
- how the data were analyzed and the facts were ascertained;
- the data that was rejected;
- the reasons for rejection of data;
- whether the data were weighed equitably or, if not, why;
- whether the basis for weighing of data was arbitrary and capricious or unsupported by normal practices in this field;
- how conclusions were drawn and whether they were supported by the data;
- whether it is possible to reach different conclusions with the same data;
- whether the conclusions reached are consistent with similar studies and data in the witness's field;
- what the park service has done in the past at this location;

- whether past service actions are consistent with what is being done now or, if not, why;
- what statements, correspondence, and representations have been made by the park service to others concerning this issue; and
- whether the park service at all times has been consistent in dealing with public, and, if not, why.

As previously mentioned, it is important that these questions be answered truthfully, thoroughly, and consistently. The chances that a witness will be cross-examined on these facts or on statements made are high, and one inconsistent response can taint an entire testimony.

CONCLUSION

While litigation can be an intimidating experience, a well-prepared park service resource manager can help to make the critical difference between winning and losing. The resource manager or scientist must be *thorough* in his or her examination and recollection of the facts of the case, must be *prepared* to respond to questions concerning those facts or circumstances, and must be *consistent* in replying to challenges from the plaintiff.

It is also vitally important that both the resource manager or scientist and the attorney understand their respective roles in responding to inquiries during discovery, as expert witnesses, and in preparing the administrative record for the case. The resource manager or scientist must develop a rapport and a common set of understandings with the attorney handling the case, so that the best attributes of both professions are marshaled effectively for the legal action ahead.

REFERENCES

1. *Motor Vehicle Manufacturers Association* v. *State Farm Mutual Automobile Insurance Company*, 463 U.S. 29, 43-44, 103 S.Ct. 2856, 2866-67 (1983).
2. Fed. R. Evid. 702.
3. Fed. R. Evid. 703.
4. Fed. R. Evid. 701.

Chapter 14

Frontier Issues

by Michael A. Mantell

Several unresolved issues will greatly influence National Park System resources and National Park Service initiatives in managing those resources in the years ahead. This section looks at a few of the more prominent issues—liability for natural hazards, pressures on resources from activities outside park boundaries, and appropriate use of parks—and suggests ways they might arise and be addressed in the future. As with the evolution of the Organic Act itself, these issues will not be fully resolved soon, if ever, but rather will be refined incrementally as situations and opportunities arise. Moreover, as part of the park service's preservation and use charge, the steps taken toward resolving these issues in specific cases will continue to add to and refine the park ideal.

THE PARK SERVICE, NATURAL HAZARDS, AND LIABILITY

One reads and hears almost daily about the so-called liability insurance crisis. Virtually every sector of society—manufacturers, doctors, consumers, even lawyers—has experienced enormous increases in insurance costs. In some cases, services have been curtailed because of the specter of lawsuits and large damage awards.

The National Park System has not escaped from the current propensity to run to one's lawyer any time injury or death strikes. The park service has been sued by people mauled by grizzly bears, burned by geothermal pools, and paralyzed by falls from trails.[1] Private operators in the parks, especially concessioners and permittees who provide bus tours, river rafting, and horseback trips, have found themselves particularly vulnerable in recent years to these kinds of suits, which sometimes bring the park service into court as well. Will the prospect of these suits and potentially enormous damage awards affect the way parks are managed and the experiences they provide? Could the threat of liability make the parks become more safe and sanitized, almost zoolike, with guardrails and fences more prominent and contact with animals greatly reduced?

These types of suits against the park service, which are called tort actions (claims for injury or death resulting from negligence of others), arise under the Federal Torts Claim Act.[2] In cases involving natural hazards, such as wild animals and maulings, hazardous trees, falling rocks, and flash floods, courts generally have looked at the actions and "reasonable" expectations of the visitor and at the conduct of the park service, focusing on what the service knew or reasonably should have known about the situation and on the actions it did or did not take as a result.

Two issues continually arise in these types of cases:
- What kind of warning or notice is a visitor entitled to concerning a potential natural hazard?
- Was the decision or action that led to the injury or death a discretionary one or one that was taken routinely by the park service?

Warnings

Two cases illustrate the types of concerns that courts typically examine in deciding cases. In a case involving a bear mauling at a Yellowstone campground, the court held that a camper who was given park brochures warning about the dangers of bears assumed the risks of camping in the park and could not recover from the park service.[3] In a case involving a visitor injured by a falling rock in Timpanogos Cave National Monument, the court held that the service was negligent in failing to provide the visitor with adequate warnings of a serious hazard that was known to rangers and that the visitor could not have reasonably discovered herself.[4] The court went on to say, however, that the duty of the government to exercise due care in this situation did not require it to construct protective fences or canopies above the trail leading to the cave.

Several rules of thumb regarding when, where, and how to issue warnings can be discerned from court decisions involving the park service in the natural hazards context:

- No warnings by the park service to visitors are legally required for obvious dangers. Park managers should be slow to assume, however, that dangers are obvious to everyone. Warnings may be advisable. In a case involving a 14-year-old who fell into a thermal pool at Yellowstone, for example, the court said that the park service should have posted warning signs. The injured teenager could not be compensated, however, because he did not exercise due care in avoiding injury.

- Warnings are unnecessary for dangers that are obvious to the expected visitor. Courts have generally found that it is reasonable for visitors to expect that "hidden" hazards have been eliminated or corrected or that warnings are being given of their presence.

- Park personnel are assumed to have knowledge of "hidden" natural hazards and thus should convey the information to visitors. For example, the park service was found liable in a case involving a camper killed by a falling tree in a campground because it had inspected the camp area and should have taken action to remove the hazards presented by a badly decayed tree.

- A warning may be sufficient if it clearly informs individuals of the exact nature of a danger and the visitor then takes the risk with full understanding of the danger. For example, "dangerous undertow" or "uneven bottom" will suffice in many situations instead of "no swimming." Similarly, "area closed" may not be required when signs stating "hazardous trees" or "bubonic plague" are present.

Discretionary Functions

Another major issue in many cases is whether a park service action that led to injury or death was discretionary (that is, subject to policy considerations or not). Because of an exemption under the Federal Torts Claim Act, actions that are found to be discretionary cannot be the basis of a suit against the park service. Thus, for example, a decision by the service to close the garbage dumps for bear feedings in Yellowstone was held to be discretionary and could not be the basis of a suit by an individual who claimed that a bear mauling was the direct result of that action. It is often difficult to determine in advance which actions a court will find to be discretionary; court rulings have varied significantly on this issue.

A recent case illustrating this involved a bus accident along Thoroughfare Pass in Denali National Park. The suit contended that the park service negligently designed, constructed, and maintained the roadway that led to a bus accident resulting in deaths, injuries, and damages. The parties all agreed that the condition of the road was dangerous, so the issue was whether the park service actions concerning it were within the discretionary function exemption.

The park service argued that the road's design and condition were largely a matter of environmental and aesthetic considerations. The court agreed as to the road's design and construction but found that its maintenance was not a discretionary function. Saying there was no link between the roadway policies of the park service and the condition of a road, the court refuted the argument that the existence of a budget for repair work placed the maintenance activity within the protective sphere of the discretionary function exception. It also did not find different policy considerations—a primary indicator of a discretionary function—involved in maintaining the road.[5]

In a case involving the death of three visitors as a result of a broken dam in Rocky Mountain National Park, a court held that the discretionary function exemption also did not apply. The service was found negligent for not having an adequate evacuation plan and, possibly, for not forcibly removing some of the visitors who wished to take pictures of the flood.

Another recent case involved issues of both the discretionary function exception and proper warnings. A plaintiff struck his head on a rock while diving into the Buffalo River. He said that the park service had a duty to warn him about the dangers in the river; the service responded that its actions came under the discretionary function exception. The court ruled that the discretionary function did not apply. It drew a distinction between policy or planning on one hand and operations on the other, with the latter not falling within the exception:

> the negligence was not the decision to institute a policy of warning park users of the hazards of boating and swimming in the Buffalo River, but rather was the failure of Park Service personnel to comply with the previously adopted safety policy.[6]

Because of insufficient warnings, the court went on to find the park service liable for the injuries. In this case, park service brochures on the area warned about the dangers of diving. A park ranger, however, had recommended this particular swimming hole to the plaintiff without giving any warnings. In following the state's law where the suit was brought, the federal court said that once the park service chose to furnish information about the river, it had a duty to do so carefully.[7]

Clearly, determining which decisions or actions can be considered discretionary can be difficult for park managers. Nevertheless, a few pointers should be kept in mind:

- Courts are reluctant to second-guess legislative and administrative decisions based on social, economic, and political policy and thus generally find actions relating to them to be discretionary.
- Courts look at the type of decision involved, rather than the rank of the decision maker, although they recognize that decisions tend to get more discretionary, the higher up in the organization the decision maker is.
- Decisions regarding the expenditures of funds or the execution of a federal project are more likely than other decisions to be considered discretionary.

Liability in the Future

There is growing concern that increases in the number of suits brought for torts related to natural hazards will adversely affect the types of activities national parks provide and the way resources are managed to provide them. Clearly, these suits have affected the types of notices given and signs posted. But beyond that, it remains to be seen whether and how much lawsuits by park visitors for natural hazard situations will cause major changes in natural resources policy or management. While the liability crisis will not be solved in the park context alone, it is troubling to think that it could force major changes in park natural resources management.

Park managers and staff need to be aware of these developments in making decisions and advising visitors. Yet, given the purposes of the parks and the increasing resentment throughout society toward frivolous litigation, one can remain hopeful that these types of suits will have little lasting impact on reducing authenticity or naturalness in the National Park System.

ACTIONS OUTSIDE PARK BOUNDARIES

Two-thirds of reported threats to park resources—for example, water and air pollution, visual and aesthetic intrusions, and inadequate water supplies—originate entirely or largely outside park boundaries.[8] In the future, parks will have increasing difficulty relying on remoteness to protect them from degradation.

Protection of park resources against external pressures requires action outside park boundaries—sometimes miles away, where pollution originates or park wildlife migrates. Yet efforts to assert park values on others' land—even land managed by other federal agencies—can cause the park service to be resented as a bossy neighbor, even if there is clear legal authority to act.

The extent of park service powers regarding activities on lands outside park boundaries that affect park resources has not been fully tested. Although several relevant court decisions have some important language about the need to protect resources, they do not establish how park service powers will be defined judicially in any particular case.

As a practical matter, opportunities to protect against external activities vary, depending on who is responsible for them. In particular, activities located on federal land or dependent on federal funding can be addressed in ways not readily applied to other public and private activities. The most promising long-term initiatives to address this issue may lie less in applying legal requirements than in working cooperatively with local governments and private organizations.

Legal Concepts to Address External Problems

Several legal authorities might be interpreted to allow the park service to protect national parks from activities on lands outside their boundaries. While there are some cases in this area and a few that contain some strong language indicating possible park service power to protect the parks, none of these authorities has been tested definitively.

The Property Clause and the Organic Act

The reach of the Property Clause of the U.S. Constitution to activities on private lands outside park boundaries that pose a threat to park resources is unclear. There is little doubt, however, that the clause, combined with the Commerce Clause, provides authority for Congress to enact legislation giving the park service more authority over activities on adjacent lands that threaten park resources.

At least, two key issues, however, involve the reach of the Constitution:

- How much authority could Congress, by statute, give to the park service to preempt or override state and local land regulation?[9]
- Even without a new statute, do the Constitution and the National Park Service Organic Act authorize or compel the park service to protect park resources from activities on private lands outside park boundaries?

Three key cases show that the Property Clause is a source of potential power.

- In a 1927 case, the U.S. Supreme Court relied on the Property Clause as a basis to uphold the criminal prosecution under a federal statute of an individual who started a fire on private land adjacent to a national forest.[10]
- The Property Clause was also cited as the basis for allowing the secretary of the interior to control hunting on private land adjacent to a wildlife refuge.[11]
- More recently, in a case involving wild burros, the Supreme Court held that "regulations under the property clause may have some effect on private lands not otherwise under federal control." It went on to say that the Property Clause is not limited to regulation required "to protect the public land from damage" but can also be applied to a statute that seeks "to achieve and maintain a thriving natural ecological balance on the public lands."[12]

In addition to the Property Clause, the full reach of the park service statutes—the Organic Act,[13] recent amendments to it,[14] and specific park enabling acts—has not been litigated as to whether these statutes authorize or require the service to address adverse impacts from activities on private lands outside park boundaries. As noted in chapter 2, most of the cases have arisen in the context of activities on private lands within authorized boundaries.

In recent cases of this kind, courts have uniformly concluded that "under this authority to protect public land, Congress' power must extend to regulation of conduct on or off the public land that would threaten the designated purpose of federal lands."[15] This indicates that the park service may have some legal authority to control harmful activities outside the parks. But the extent to which these rulings could be the basis for supporting park service action regarding harmful activities outside park boundaries remains unclear.

The issue of authority over activities on private lands outside park boundaries has been addressed most prominently in the context of Redwood National Park and litigation involving it in the mid-1970s.[16] In these cases, which are discussed in chapter 2, the Sierra Club sued to compel the secretary of the Interior (that is, the park service) to protect the park from the erosional effects of logging on private land upstream, arguing that the secretary had authority to protect the park from outside threats through the enabling legislation and the Organic Act. The suit requested that the secretary seek modification of the park boundary and acquire interests in applicable private lands outside the park or enter into agreements with outside interests to prevent damage to park resources. The court examined whether there was an obligation by the secretary to provide buffer protection for the park and found that, in this context, the statutory scheme imposed "a paramount legal duty" to maintain park resources unimpaired.

While the Redwood cases imposed a duty on the part of the secretary to do all that could be done to protect the park, this duty was limited by the terms of the specific statute involved and the amount of funding Congress was willing to provide. In reaching this result, the court placed substantial reliance on the Redwood enabling statute. To what extent a court might apply this thinking when a park did not have such a specific directive in its enabling legislation is unknown.

In examining the secretary's duties under the Organic Act following the Redwood case, however, the court in *Sierra Club* v. *Andrus*,[17] quoted from the legislative history of the 1978 amendments to the Organic Act:

> The Secretary has an absolute duty, which is not to be compromised, to fulfill the mandate of the 1916 Act to take whatever actions and seek whatever relief as will safeguard the units of the National Park System.

The scope of these duties outside park boundaries, however, remains to be tested and defined judicially. Many observers think that while a court conceivably could find these authorities sufficient to support a park service decision to take action against a threatening or damaging activity on neighboring land, it is unlikely that a court would compel the service to take such action, without a strong and specific enabling law for the particular park affected.

Nuisance

The National Park Service, like any landowner, has common-law rights to be free of nuisance in some situations. Nuisance, in the legal sense, is generally defined as the interference with the use and enjoyment of property. Thus, if odors from a specific source outside a park were interfering with use of the park, an action by the service against the offending landowner to halt the nuisance might be successful. Some have contended that development outside a park that obstructs views from inside the park or impairs important wildlife habitat should also be actionable by the service as a nuisance.

The leading case in this area involved an attempt by the park service to halt construction of high-rise buildings in Arlington, Virginia, claiming such structures would obstruct views and thus be a nuisance to park system monuments across the Potomac River in Washington, D.C. The court in this case did recognize the right of the government to bring such a suit—it had so-called standing—"to protect the rights and properties of the United States."

While the court recognized the right of the government "as a Virginia property owner . . . to question the validity of a nearby zoning that affects his property," it was reluctant to, in effect, give the federal government a right to regulate adjacent land use under the nuisance theory. It noted that "to sustain such an interference with the use of private land without compensation as an exercise of the police power has been farther than the courts have been willing to go."[18]

As a practical matter, judicially accepted constraints on the applications of nuisance theory are likely to limit its value to the park service. One limitation is that nuisance can typically be invoked only after damage is done or appears inevitable. Yet, because such damage is generally provable only after construction has actually begun or after large amounts of money leading up to construction have been spent by the developer, courts find it difficult to intercede and stop it from going further. In other words, the government has to wait to bring the suit so it can show definite interference with its property, but by that time development has proceeded so far that courts are reluctant to halt it—a sort of "Catch-22" dilemma.

Recent decisions also have limited the applicability of nuisance to situations where there are no other remedies under specific federal environmental laws. Thus, for example, since the federal Clean Air and Clean Water acts provide for specific types of standards and for means to enforce those standards, a nuisance action by the federal government against a nearby property owner may not be possible if the claimed interference was due to impacts regulated under those acts.

In theory, nuisance actions might hold promise for protecting parks from harmful activities outside their boundaries, especially if courts recognize the broad purposes and needs of the parks. But current limitations pose some considerable obstacles to using the doctrine. In sum, although nuisance may present some opportunities to protect park resources from the harmful effects of development outside park boundaries, the extent of these opportunities appears to be limited.[19]

Public Trust

The notion that governments hold certain resources in trust for the public and have an affirmative obligation to protect them is called the public trust doctrine. This doctrine, long established for submerged lands under navigable waters, has been expanded by several state courts over the last decade or so to include wetlands, coastal zone areas, and appropriated riparian waters that affect downstream lakes.[20]

In the national park context, it is unclear whether the public trust doctrine imposes any duties on the National Park Service beyond those already contained in the Organic Act. At least two courts have suggested that there are public trust duties, while one has recently held there are not:

> In an 1891 case, the U.S. Supreme Court held that The Secretary [of the Interior] is the guardian of the people of the United States over the public lands. The obligation of his oath of office obliges him to see that the law is carried out, and that none of the public domain is wasted.[21]

In the first Redwood case, the district court said that the discretionary exercise of the secretary's powers to acquire land and enter into contracts with adjacent landowners was "subordinate to his paramount legal duty imposed, not only under his trust obligation but by the statute itself, to protect the park." Thus, the court implied that there might be a trust duty beyond that contained in the Organic and park enabling acts.[22]

Most recently, however, in an action to force the park service to enforce federally reserved water rights to protect park resources, a district court held that "trust duties distinguishable from statutory duties" did not exist.[23]

Given the strong language in the Organic Act and the interpretations given to it, it is not entirely clear that the public trust doctrine, even if made applicable to the parks, would add more strength to park service efforts to address activities on lands outside park boundaries that harm park resources. As discussed in chapter 2, recent judicial interpretations of the Organic Act give the park service strong support when it decides to take action—based on articulated plans, policies, and data—to protect park resources from impairment.

Congressional Initiatives and Partnerships

Several approaches have been suggested to strengthen the power of the National Park Service over threats to the parks that originate on nearby lands. Some are being debated in Congress; others may not need legislative authorization. In examining these approaches, it is useful to distinguish activities on other federal lands, activities receiving federal permits or funds, and other private actions.

Activities on Federal Land[24]

When proposed activities on federal land may harm a park, it has not been enough in most situations simply to require the proposing agency to consult the park service and "consider" its objections. Neither, however, would it be satisfactory to give the park service a veto over the other agency's proposal; other agencies have their own missions to follow and constituencies to consider.

A process is needed that will provide incentives for the park service and its federal neighbors to work out mutually acceptable solutions. The Endangered Species Act has been advanced as an important model for such a process. As discussed in chapter 6, it gives the Fish and Wildlife Service a strong say over federal activities that affect endangered species habitat, but it also sets up a negotiation process that prompts agencies to search for consensus on ways to reduce or avoid adverse impacts. If the parties cannot agree, a special statutory committee can exempt an activity from the requirements of the act. To avoid an all-or-nothing decision by the committee, agencies have a powerful incentive to work out a compromise. A similar provision could be enacted for review of activities that could affect national parks.

Actions by other agencies within the Interior Department could be controlled by a directive from the secretary that requires consultation with the park and moves decisions up to the regional offices of each agency, to the applicable assistant secretaries, and finally to the secretary, if the parties cannot agree.

Rather than waiting until potentially harmful activities are proposed, the park service could also work with other agencies as plans are prepared for land that may affect the parks. To facilitate this cooperation, for example, the service could, with funding from Congress and in consultation with affected agencies, identify "areas of critical park concern" outside park boundaries, lands deemed critical to the future of a park: for example, habitat or migration routes for wildlife, or scenic views. The service could propose development policies, responsive to park needs, to guide federal activities in these areas.

Legislation might require other federal agencies, in preparing their plans and activities for adjacent federal lands, to be as consistent as possible with any specific park service policies established for an area of critical park concern. To handle disagreements, a negotiation process could be established comparable to the consistency negotiation process under the federal Coastal Zone Management Act.

Activities Receiving Federal Funds or Permits

Some activities that affect national parks, although they do not take place on federal land, do receive federal funding or permitting. Legislative proposals have been made to add park protection to the standards for evaluating these projects.

An appropriate model is the Coastal Barrier Resources Act, which bars federal financial assistance or expenditures for projects (such as bridges and sewers) that would affect designated undeveloped coastal barrier areas. Legislation has been proposed to bar federal funding for incompatible projects in areas of critical park concern. If such legislation also followed the model of the Endangered Species Act, it could provide for a reconciliation process to balance park protection and legitimate competing interests.

Activities on Private Land

The need for additional protection against activities on nonfederal lands varies from park to park. So do the local attitudes on land-use controls and participation by federal officials in local and state affairs. In practice, therefore, protective measures need to be highly localized.

The most promising current opportunity to protect the parks against external threats from private lands lies in diverse cooperative mechanisms involving the National Park Service and park neighbors. As discussed in earlier chapters, these partnerships can provide a forum where activities can be discussed, differences thrashed out, consensus developed. Park officials have helped form some local land trusts, for example, and have sometimes advised local coordinating councils and land-use agencies.

In addition, Congress might establish an experimental program in which the park service would take the lead in establishing partnerships at a few specified parks. Part of this program could involve designating formal park protection zones, adjacent to the selected units. Within these zones, special support, such as technical assistance or grants to pay for land-use planning, could be made available to local governments. In addition, the park service could be authorized to accept donations of lands and easements within these zones.

Improving Information and Awareness

If legal doctrines are extended by the courts or new legislative measures are enacted by Congress, they may enhance the National Park Service's capacity to preserve park resources and respond to higher public expectations. Internal and external pressures on park resources seem destined to increase in intensity, however, so even new protective powers may not respond fully to ever-increasing needs.

In the long run, if preservation is to keep pace with intensifying pressures, the political consensus must shift so that protective measures unachievable today—for example, to protect against the impacts of back country users and private landowners—will become achievable tomorrow. Increased understanding of resources can help provide the needed political support. So can enhanced awareness of the pressures on resources and of the measures needed to counteract them.

APPROPRIATE USE OF PARKS: WHEN RESOURCE PROTECTION IS NOT ENOUGH[25]

Preservation initiatives in national parks typically focus on the needs of park resources themselves. But there are situations—and some increasingly important ones—in which the focus is instead on preserving opportunities for visitors' enjoyment of park resources. In those situations, there may be demand for protective measures that go beyond what science or resource management seem to require. If these demands grow, they may increasingly shape not only new laws but the context in which present laws are interpreted.

A recent court case suggests what seems to be happening.[26] As discussed in chapter 2, the case involved a challenge to a park service management plan at Cape Cod National Seashore that permitted (and regulated) the use of off-road vehicles (ORVs) within the park. The park service had commissioned voluminous studies, and the federal district court judge ruled that the park service had adequately considered scientific evidence on the impacts of ORV use on the dunes.

The court found, however, that the service had failed to address another issue mandated by the Seashore Act. That issue was, in the court's words, the "more fundamental, but less scientific, question of whether private and commercial motor vehicle use of the seashore constituted an appropriate recreation use generally." The court returned the case to the park service to decide on the appropriateness of ORV use within the seashore. In response, the service conducted a survey of park users on this issue.

In effect, the court seems to have said, ORVs might be inappropriate for some reason other than their impact on dunes as documented in scientific studies. What is involved in many park management issues, Professor Joseph Sax of The University of California at Berkeley suggests, is not so much protection of resources as protection of a special *visitor experience* of those resources. "A moment's reflection makes it clear that environmental and scientific principles are rarely decisive . . . in settling . . . disputes over protection of . . . parks' natural resources." He also observes:[27]

> [T]he presence of motor boats on the Grand Canyon is not really an ecological issue, though it was regularly put in those terms. Nor is ecological disruption the sole—or even the principal—reason there has been so much objection to snowmobiles or [off-road vehicles.] While one element of preservationist advocacy is scientific and truly based on principles of land management, another . . . is dominated by value judgments. . . . The preservationist constituency [for the parks] is disturbed not only—and not even most importantly—by the physical deterioration of the parks, but by a sense that the style of modern tourism is depriving the parks of their central symbolism, their message about the relationship between man and nature, and man and industrial society.[28]

The preservationist's argument thus can be seen to be based only partly on ecology—essentially using that as far as it takes him or her—but also on a choice among different kinds of visitor experiences.

Ultimately, the conservation community is the guardian of "park values," of a vision of the special experience that the parks can provide. The "scenes of sublimity and beauty" of Frederick Law Olmsted, the "holy temples" of John Muir, and the "wild things" of Aldo Leopold—despite telling differences among the terms—were places protected from the encroachment of civilizing influences. The most frightening vision these writers conjured up was the prospect that, because these special places influence us in ways we don't even fully understand, their disappearance might cause future generations to lose the capacity even to know what they were missing. Parks should be places for "contemplative recreation," Joseph Sax argues, offering relief from the commonplace experiences of urban life and the "artificial recreation" widely available outside the parks.[29]

To those who take this stance, downhill skiing, business conventions, golf courses, supermarkets, beauty parlors, and bars are inappropriate in national parks not necessarily because of their "impacts" on park resources—although some do change the park's natural environment irreversibly and adversely—but because they detract from the quality of the distinctive experiences possible in national parks, experiences that the private market is typically unable to provide.

For many, the vision of unspoiled nature exerts a moral claim that transcends analyses of "user-days" and cost-benefit ratios. For those who have seen this vision, the ultimate test of success of the national parks lies not in their wise use of resources or efficient allocation of benefits but in "identifying what is best in our world and trying to preserve it."[30]

Drawing on this, it seems, are some of the issues that arise over the management of historical and other cultural resources as well. Again, there is an issue over what kind of visitor experience is sought. The way restoration proceeds can affect whether a visitor principally comes to have fun, to understand things intellectually, or to have some sense of awe in perceiving his or her relationship to what has gone before.

Once it is clear that protecting the visitor experience raises issues that go beyond the dictates of science, several issues arise. Three in particular deserve recognition:

Preferring one visitor experience over another. The first of these issues is whether public policy should, as the preservationists claim, favor one vision of the visitor experience over another. Parks should be places for "contemplative recreation," Sax argues, offering relief from the commonplace experiences of urban life and the "artificial recreation" widely available outside the parks.

There are many, of course, who love the parks but do not share this vision. One visitor, for example, may seek the parks less as places of reverence and contemplation than as "pleasuring grounds." He or she may come to the park to go to the beach or to stay at a comfortable lodge in a magnificent setting. This kind of visitor, too, may seek contrast with everyday life but without the physical exertion, adventure, even fear, that the preservationist's vision implies.

Other visitors may seek challenges and the ability to recapture some of the orneriness of the wild frontier. Hiking or mountain climbing may be the goal, but so may parachute jumping, snowmobiling, or speeding up a dune in an off-road vehicle. This visitor seeks a chance to be freer, perhaps rowdier, than is possible back home.

The National Park Service must walk a narrow path as it seeks to serve its diverse constituency. Many within the service share the "park values" that have been an integral part of park tradition since the thoughts and writings of John Muir first received acclaim. As a public agency, however, the park service is pulled by the desire to serve all of its clients—users who have widely different needs and visions of the park experience. Moreover, the service is not entirely free to set its own agenda: its diverse clients also have representatives and senators.

When should visitor-experience arguments be used? This issue, very similar to the first, is really one of tactics: just when should conservationists be up front in arguing for the "elevated" visitor experience, and when should they stick with the tried-and-true resource preservation arguments?

The preservation community has been enormously successful in focusing public attention on the protection of park resources. In part, this success has come about because no one can really oppose resource protection, at least in principle.

By contrast, disputes over park activities—like hang gliding, ORVs, cocktail lounges, and conventions—raise issues where different visions of the visitor's experience may produce different answers. Instead of arguing the motherhood issue of resource preservation, the conservation community may find itself having to admit that it prefers one park vision over the others. Public support is accordingly narrower, and conservationists may even disagree among themselves.

As Joseph Sax has noted, "The preservationist's claim is that he knows something about what other people *ought* to want and how they can go about getting it, and he should not back away from, or conceal, that claim."[31] This is probably right, but in the short run it will not always be easy to follow such advice, for the up front argument based on the preservationist vision may sometimes be less persuasive than the argument based on resource protection. There will have to be some tricky judgment calls as conservationists go beyond resources and find themselves on unfamiliar, shakier ground.

How should the visitor experience be delivered? Finally, there is a continuing, largely hidden issue of *how* the "elevated" visitor experience is to be made accessible. Some conservationists, like the great naturalists who preceded them, have been to the mountaintop and despair of the person who finds sufficient awe in stepping off the tour bus at the scenic overlook.

If they are to broaden the support for their vision of the parks, however, advocates of the preservation message must be sensitive to diverse audiences. They must guard against the reality and appearance of elitism. To sneer (or seem to sneer) at people who enjoy downhill, rather than cross-country skiing, or who prefer motor boats to canoes, or a visit to an amusement park over a hike in the woods, is to miss the point. Americans want—and have—many opportunities to participate in outdoor activities. Forging a new consensus about the "right" uses of our national parks requires a sorting out of activities that belong in national parks and those that belong elsewhere.

If this sorting out is to achieve the results that conservationists want, it is important to enlarge the constituency for their vision of the parks. Important as it is to protect the parks for those already prepared to "take them on their own terms," so is it important to enlarge the number who seek those experiences. Democratic ideals have rightly moved Sax, like Olmsted before him, to argue that parks should help people develop a taste for new recreational experiences—to lift their expectations and satisfactions.

To achieve this, it is important to continue fostering authentic visitor experiences within the parks. Because the National Park System is so large and diverse, there are opportunities to spread awareness of the preservationist vision while competing demands are also being met. To help visitors understand wilderness, for example, and to encourage them to "take the next step," some parks (and areas within them) can provide the initiating experiences, while others remain wilder, riskier, and more solitary.

It follows that the park service's efforts at interpretation, sometimes mistakenly treated as one of its lesser responsibilities, are of central importance to the future of the system. A visitor's appreciation of natural areas will be enhanced when he or she better understands what is being seen: for example, what is "exotic," how the human presence has modified the environment, and how the park service has responded to those changes. Cultural resources, too, can mean more to a visitor who knows why a battle happened in a particular place and what the park service has done to preserve the scene.

Thus, preserving park resources more nearly unimpaired ultimately may depend on more widespread respect, by an increasingly crowded and developed nation, for the visitor experiences that are less and less available outside the national parks. Communicating to a wider audience the experience of awe, solitude, adventure, communion, repose, and reinvigoration to be found in national parks can aid the continuing evolution of the park ideal to help preserve the parks for this and future generations.

REFERENCES

1. Actions by the park service as part of search and rescue operations have also been the subject of much litigation, but since these suits have few implications for resource management, they are not addressed here.

2. 28 U.S.C.A. §1364, 2680 (1988).

3. *Rubenstein v. U.S.*, 338 F. Supp. 654 (N.D. Cal. 1972).

4. *Hulet v. U.S.*, 328 F. Supp. 335 (D. Idaho 1971).

5. *ARA Leisure Services v. U.S.*, 831 F.2d 193 (9th Cir. 1987).

6. *Mandel v. U.S.*, 793 F.2d 964, 967 (8th Cir. 1986).

7. The park service also contended that it was not liable because the accident occurred outside the park. The court said that while there was no general duty to warn of hazards on another person's property, the service was responsible once it undertook to assist in finding a suitable swimming area for the visitor, under the state law being applied in this case.

8. National Park Service, *Natural Resource Assessment and Action Program Report*, March 1988. See also National Park Service, *State of the Parks, 1980* (Washington, D.C.: U.S. Government Printing Office, 1980).

9. See, generally, Joseph I. Sax, "Helpless Giants: The National Parks and the Regulation of Private Lands," *Michigan Law Review* 75 (1976):239.

10. *U.S. v. Alford*, 274 U.S. 264 (1927).

11. *Bailey v. Holland*, 126 F.2d 317 (4th Cir. 1942).

12. *Kleppe v. New Mexico*, 426 U.S. 529 (1976).

13. 16 U.S.C. §1.

14. 16 U.S.C. §1a-1, 1c.

15. *State of Minnesota by Alexander v. Block*, 660 F.2d 1240 (8th Cir. 1981).

16. *Sierra Club v. Department of Interior*, 376 F. Supp. 90 (N.D. Cal. 1974); Ibid., 398 F. Supp. 284 (1975); Ibid., 424 F. Supp. 172 (1976).

17. 487 F. Supp. 443 (D. D.C. 1980).

18. *United States v. County Board of Arlington*, 487 F. Supp. 137 (E.D. Va. 1979).

19. See Comment, "Protecting National Parks from Developments Beyond Their Borders," *University of Pennsylvania Law Review* 132 (1984):1189.

20. See Richard Lazarus, "Changing Conceptions of Property and Sovereignty in Natural Resources: Questioning the Public Trust Doctrine," *Iowa Law Review* 71 (1986):631. For an exploration of its applicability to public lands, see Charles Wilkinson, "The Public Trust Doctrine in Public Land Law," *University of California at Davis Law Review* 14 (1980):269.

21. *Knight v. United Land Association*, 142 U.S. 161 (1891).

22. *Sierra Club v. Department of the Interior*, 376 F. Supp. 90 (N.D. Cal. 1974).

23. *Sierra Club v. Andrus*, 487 F. Supp. 443 (D. D.C. 1980). This opinion was largely relied on by the U.S. General Accounting Office (GAO) to support its conclusion in a recent report that the secretary of the interior does not have "any duties with respect to the parks beyond those created by the applicable statutes." U.S. General Accounting Office, *Threats to the Nation's Parks*, (Washington, D.C.: General Assembly Office, 1987), 51.

24. See, generally, J. L. Sax and R. B. Keiter, "Glacier National Park and its Neighbors: A Study of Federal Interagency Relations," *Ecology Law Quarterly* 14 (1987):207.

25. Much of this section is from a paper prepared by Michael Mantell, John H. Noble, and Phyllis Myers of The Conservation Foundation on "The Limitations of Science in Managing Park Resources: Uncertainty, Politics, and Changing Values," for the Science in Parks Conference, Fort Collins, Colorado, July 1986. It is adapted, in large part, from material contained in The Conservation Foundation's *National Parks for a New Generation: Visions, Realities, Prospects* (Washington, D.C.: The Conservation Foundation, 1985).

26. *Conservation Law Foundation v. Clark*, 590 F. Supp. 1467 (D. Mass. 1984).

27. Joseph L. Sax, "Fashioning a Recreation Policy for Our National Parklands: The Philosophy of Choice and the Choice of Philosophy," *Creighton Law Review* 13, no.4 (1978-79):974.

28. Joseph L. Sax, *Mountains without Handrails: Reflections on the National Parks* (Ann Arbor, Mich.: University of Michigan Press, 1980), pp. 11, 51.

29. Ibid., pp. 42, 45.

30. Mark Sagoff, "We Have Met the Enemy and He Is Us or Conflict and Contradiction in Environmental Law," *Environmental Law* 12 (1982):302.

31. Sax, *Mountains without Handrails*, p. 59.

About the Contributors

Donald J. Barry is general counsel for fisheries and wildlife with the U.S. House of Representatives Committee on Merchant Marine and Fisheries. Upon graduation in 1974 from the University of Wisconsin Law School, he accepted a job in the Honors Program for the Solicitor's Office in the Department of the Interior. He subsequently served as a staff attorney for the U.S. Fish and Wildlife Service from April 1975 until January 1980, at which time he was promoted to the job of assistant solicitor for fish and wildlife, the chief counsel for that agency. He served in that capacity until December 1985, at which time he accepted an offer to assume his current position.

Frank Buono is a park ranger and instructor on natural resource management issues at the Albright Employee Development Center of the National Park Service, a position he has held since 1987. He began work with the National Park Service in 1972 as a seasonal ranger in Dinosaur National Monument (NM). He worked as a seasonal ranger in interpretation, law enforcement, and resource management from 1972 to 1978 at Dinosaur NM, Everglades National Park (NP), Mt. McKinley NP, Carlsbad Caverns NP, Bandelier NM, Olympic NP, and Grand Canyon NP. In 1978, he began his permanent career as a lead park technician at Mount Rainier NP. In January 1981, he transferred to Gateway National Recreation Area in New York City as an assistant district ranger. In 1982, he was selected to participate in the park service's National Resources Specialist Trainee Program, assigned to the Southwest Regional Office and Chaco Culture National Historic Park. In 1984, he transferred to the Energy, Mining, and Minerals Division of the park service's Washington Office.

Richard H. Dawson serves as the resource management specialist in the Southeast Regional Office of the National Park Service. His duties entail resource management planning, barrier islands, fisheries management, minerals management, long-term monitoring, basic resource inventories, biodiversity, and genetic conservation. He served as the resource management specialist for marine resources at Everglades National Park and Fort Jefferson National Monument from 1978 to May 1987. Previous positions include: staff biologist with the South Carolina Coastal Council; marine biologist at the Office of Marine Resource Management, South Carolina Wildlife and Marine Resources Department; and research assistant in biology for St. Francis College in Lorette, Pennsylvania, and Charleston, South Carolina. He has published articles and reports on various aspects of marine resource management.

Christopher J. Duerksen is director of the Office of Airport Gateway Development for the City and County of Denver, where he is responsible for overseeing all aspects of the planning and development of land in the vicinity of the new Denver airport site, which when completed will be the largest in the world. Prior to coming to Denver, Duerksen was director of development and public policy at the Enterprise Foundation, where he was responsible for all aspects of fund raising and also oversaw the foundation's public policy work and publications. Prior to that, he was senior associate at The Conservation Foundation, where he directed the land program. In that position, he authored books on national parks, historic preservation, river conservation, and industrial development. He also served as an elected member of the City Council in Fredericksburg, Virginia, from 1984 to 1987. A 1974 graduate of the University of Chicago Law School, he is former chair of the American Bar Association's Committee on Land Use, Planning, and Zoning and served on the governing council of the Section on Urban, State and Local Government Law. He practiced law in Chicago at Ross and Hardies from 1974 to 1978.

Jacob J. Hoogland is chief of environmental quality within the National Park Service. The Environmental Quality Division is responsible for park service implementation of the National Environmental Policy Act and other environmental mandates as well as related environmental policy matters. Prior to his current appointment, he served for several years at the Denver Service Center in the Legislative Compliance Division and as a planner and specialist in natural and cultural resource compliance on various projects in the Pacific Northwest, Western, and Alaska regions. He has worked as a seasonal and permanent ranger at Mesa Verde National Park and in interpretation at Bighorn Canyon National Recreation Area. He also served an internship as a legislative assistant for former Senator Frank E. Moss. He is a graduate of the University of Utah College of Jaw and Weber State College. He is a member of the Utah Bar Association, Colorado Bar Association, and the American Bar Association section on Natural Resources, Energy, and Environmental Law.

Michael A. Mantell is general counsel of World Wildlife Fund and The Conservation Foundation, where he oversees all legal and congressional matters. He directed and helped create the Successful Communities Program of The Conservation Foundation; directed its Land, Heritage, and Wildlife Program; and managed its State of the Environment and National Parks projects. A principal author of *Creating Successful Communities, National Parks for a New Generation* and *A Handbook on Historic Preservation Law*, he was senior staff member to the National Wetlands Policy Forum, has worked on key legislation affecting national parklands, and directed negotiations to resolve complex environmental policy disputes. Before joining the Foundation in 1979, he was with the city attorney's office in Los Angeles, where he worked on various environmental matters. He is a graduate of the University of California at Berkeley and Lewis and Clark College Law School, is a member of the Bars of California and the District of Columbia, and serves as chairman of an American Bar Association Subcommittee on Federal Land-Use Policy.

Carol McCoy is chief of the Policy and Regulations Section of the Mining and Minerals Branch of the Land Resources Division within the National Park Service. She has a B.A. in Environmental Studies from Brown University and an M.P.P. in Environmental Policy and Management from the University of Michigan–Institute for Public Policy Studies. She is currently working on a law degree at Georgetown University's National Law Center. She has worked for the National Park Service since 1981—first in the Air Quality Division, and then in the Energy, Mining, and Minerals Division (now the Mining and Minerals Branch). She has been extensively involved in the development and implementation of environmental and mineral regulations and policy and has worked closely with other agencies in the Interior Department, particularly the Bureau of Land Management and the Office of Surface Mining Reclamation and Enforcement. Before joining the National Park Service, she worked for the Environmental Protection Agency (EPA), Economic Analysis Division, in Washington, D.C. She also has been employed as a statistical analyst for the University of Michigan and as a program analyst with EPA's Motor Vehicle Emissions Laboratory.

Dwight Merriam is a partner with the law firm of Robinson & Cole in Hartford, Connecticut, and chair of the firm's Land Use Group. He is president of the 7,000-member American Institute of Certified Planners and a director of the 23,000-member American Planning Association. He received his B.A. *cum laude* from the University of Massachusetts, his master's in regional planning from the University of North Carolina, and his J.D. from Yale Law School.

Philip C. Metzger was educated at the University of Michigan, where he received his B.A. in history and political science, an M.S. in Natural Resources Management, and a J.D. in law. He began his career as a policy analyst in the Office of the Secretary of the Interior, where he specialized in land management and water issues. For several years thereafter, he was an associate in the Water Resources Program of

The Conservation Foundation, where he wrote studies on groundwater quality, instream flow, and riparian habitat issues; water problems in Washington, D.C., and Tucson, Arizona; and the social implications of water rights transfer. He was the principal author of the Foundation's publication *America's Water: Current Trends and Emerging Issues*. After serving as counsel to the Senate Judiciary Committee, he took his present position as senior legislative counsel to New York Governor Mario M. Cuomo. In this position, he is a speechwriter and political advisor to the governor and Washington lobbyist for the state of New York on environmental and energy issues.

Luther Propst is the field director for The Conservation Foundation's Successful Communities program, which provides technical assistance through regional offices nationwide in managing growth and protecting distinctive local resources. Before joining The Conservation Foundation, he was an attorney in the Land Use Group with the Hartford, Connecticut, law firm of Robinson & Cole, where he represented local governments, developers, and local environmental organizations in land-use matters. He received his law degree and master's in regional planning from the University of North Carolina at Chapel Hill. He co-authored *Managing Development in Small Towns*, published in 1984 by the American Planning Association, and has taught land-use law as an adjunct professor at the Western New England College of Law.

Molly N. Ross is assistant chief of the Air Quality Division of the National Park Service. She often represents the National Park Service on air quality issues in the Department of the Interior, with other agencies, with Congress, and with the public. Before assuming this position in 1984, she worked primarily on air quality and Alaska issues for six years as an attorney in the Parks and Recreation Branch, Division of Conservation and Wildlife, Department of the Interior. From 1976 to 1978, she was an attorney with the law firm of Morgan, Lewis & Bockius in Washington, D.C., specializing in the area of environmental and energy law. She is a graduate of Harvard College and the University of Chicago Law School.

William E. Shands is a senior associate with The Conservation Foundation, where he specializes in public lands and forest policy. He has directed numerous research projects, including a study of policy for national forests in the eastern United States and work focusing on the implementation of the Forest and Rangeland Renewable Resources Planning Act (RPA) and the National Forest Management Act (NFMA). He has authored, co-authored, or edited numerous books and articles on forestry and forest policy, including *The Lands Nobody Wanted: Policies for National Forests in the Eastern United States*; *National Forest Policy: From Conflict to Consensus*; *A Citizens' Guide to the Forest and Rangeland Renewable Resources Planning Act*; *The Greenhouse Effect: Climate Change and U.S. Forests*; and *Below Cost Timber Sales in the Broad Context of National Forest Management*. On a leave of absence from the Foundation, he served as director of research for the President's Commission on Americans Outdoors and managed the preparation of its 1987 report *Americans Outdoors: The Legacy, the Challenge*. Prior to joining the Foundation, he worked for 11 years on daily newspapers in California and five years in staff positions in the U.S. Senate and House of Representatives. He holds a B.A. in journalism and political science from San Jose State University, California, and a master of planning degree from the University of Virginia.

Barbara West is an operations research analyst within the Policy, Planning and Evaluation Branch of the Water Resources Division of the National Park Service. She holds an A.B. from the University of Chicago and a master's in public affairs from the Lyndon B. Johnson School of Public Affairs at the University of Texas. She has served on the National Commission on Water Quality and was director of research for the Shiprock Research Center, a private environmental organization on the Navajo Reservation. She worked for the Office of Surface Mining Reclamation and Enforcement in the Department of the Interior in several capacities. In 1980, she served as the special assistant for minerals to the assistant secretary for Indian affairs. In 1981, she joined the National Park Service and worked in the Washington Office of the Air Quality Division. In 1983, she transferred to the Energy, Mining, and Minerals Division. Since 1985, she has worked in the Water Resources Division of the park service's Washington Office.

Index

Regular numerals indicate materials in text; italicized numerals indicate figures.